THE DIVINE OFFICE
FOR DODOS*

*(Devout, Obedient Disciples of Our Savior)

A Step-by-Step Guide to
Praying the Liturgy of the Hours

Madeline Pecora Nugent

CATHOLIC BOOK PUBLISHING CORP.
New Jersey

NIHIL OBSTAT: Rev. Msgr. Gerard H. McCarren, S.T.D.
Censor Librorum

IMPRIMATUR: ✠ Most Rev. John J. Myers, J.C.D., D.D.
Archbishop of Newark

(T-416)

ISBN 978-0-89942-482-8

Printed in the U.S.A.

www.catholicbookpublishing.com

Acknowledgments

First of all, I have to thank the Poor Clare nuns of Langhorne, PA, who showed me how to pray the Divine Office. I also thank Msgr. John Darcy, canon lawyer, and Father Peter Damian, FFI, for reading and checking the first draft of this manuscript for accuracy. Father Peter also checked the second draft and made several helpful suggestions. Thanks to Fr. John of the Trinity, Erem. TOCarm, and Father Martin Mary Fonte, FI, both of whom made some helpful suggestions regarding instructions for praying the Office. Thanks, as well, to Connie Kotch, Rosemary Cross, Ellen LeGare, Doris Lucchesi, Jean Munson, Mary J. Sullivan, and Jeanne Tucciaroni for trying to learn to pray the Divine Office using the first manuscript draft. They were "guinea pig dodos" whose comments and frustrations with the first draft enabled me to clarify the confusing sections of this book. Special thanks goes to Louise F. Martin who gave the manuscript to Christine Eiva to critique. Christine had learned how to pray the Divine Office with the Sisters of Divine Providence, and her many valuable tips are included herein. I thank Bruce Fahey for sharing some excellent tips on style for instruction and Mark Gordon who believed enough in this manuscript to have his company publish it initially. Thanks especially to all those people (many of whom I do not know by name) who prayed to have **The Divine Office for Dodos*** reprinted when a company with whom we had contracted went bankrupt. Finally I am grateful to Emilie Cerar of Catholic Book Publishing for her support of **The Divine Office for Dodos*** and her efforts to see the book back in print as quickly as possible.

Table of Contents

"In this section, you'll learn about . . ."

- Introduction to the Divine Office
- Praying the Divine Office as Part of a Rule of Life
- Constructing Bookmarks and Ribbons

BEFORE YOU BEGIN

Introduction

Hi! Let us begin with a secret. You are not a dodo! Not only do you lack a hooked beak and fluffy gray feathers, but you are even fairly smart! I mean, you know how to tie your shoe laces, brush your teeth, and set an alarm clock! Seriously, you do know a good deal about many things, but the Divine Office is not one of them. You might be a bit confused about the Divine Office. Perhaps more than a bit. You probably are frustrated as well. And possibly somewhat angry. You want to become a holier person. Someone told you that praying the Divine Office would nudge you in that direction. Maybe some people tried to help you pray the Office. They also may have given you some instructions to read. But you cannot understand what to do! So you feel like a dodo.

Here is another secret. You have company!

Most people who try to pray the Divine Office experience exactly what you are experiencing. Confusion. Frustration. Anger.

There is hope in these pages! You are going to learn to pray the Divine Office! Honest! Then you will join the ranks of other clergy, religious, and laity, some of whom are non-Catholic, who pray the Divine Office every day.

Did you know that the Divine Office is the official, formal prayer of the Church that was written to pray throughout the day? When you pray the Divine Office, your prayers are united with those of other people who are praying the very same prayers around the world. Great graces come from such communal prayers.

One favor before we begin, please. Would you once in a while remember this book's author in your prayers? Thanks!

Oh, yes. You might be wondering about me. How did I learn to pray the Divine Office? Well, I cheated. I had help you probably do not have. In order to prepare to write a book about St. Clare of Assisi, I stayed for a week in a convent of Poor Clare nuns. Since the nuns prayed all seven offices in the Divine Office, their abbess assigned one of the sisters to help me. With great patience she took this dodo under her wing and showed me where to find each office in the breviary and taught me how to pray it. By the time the week was up, I had practiced fifty offices and knew what I was doing. If you can find a convent of Poor Clare nuns to pray with for a week, then you will not need this book. But, if not, then **The Divine Office for Dodos*** will be your teacher.

Praying the Divine Office as Part of a Rule of Life

Who prays the Divine Office? Clergy and religious do. So do lay people who belong to certain Third Orders and Associations. So do other lay people who want to pray this prayer of the Church daily. It does not matter which category you fall into. This book will help you.

Constructing Bookmarks and Ribbons

In addition to the ribbons that accompany your breviary, this manual uses an additional set of bookmarks and ribbons. You will want to have a set of bookmarks and ribbons before you begin this instruction. You can make your own by following the instructions below. Or you can save yourself the trouble by ordering a ribbon and bookmark set from the Confraternity of Penitents, a lay association whose members pray the Divine Office as part of a Rule of Life lived in their own homes. This sturdy set of bookmarks and ribbons is available for $9.95 post paid from the Confraternity of Penitents Holy Angels Gift Shop, 520 Oliphant Lane, Middletown RI 02842-4600 USA or online at http://penitents.org/giftshopdodos.html. The sixteen bookmarks are preprinted on thin, flexible plastic and the eight ribbons are attached to a cardboard insert that will slip into the spine of your breviary. If you have more than one breviary, obtain or make a set of bookmarks and ribbons for each one.

To mark certain places in your breviary (the book that contains the Divine Office), you will need eight thin ribbons in the following colors:

| White | Green | Red | Silver |
| Orange | Black | Blue | Purple |

You can use the ribbons that come with the breviary if they are in some of these colors. For those ribbons that are not in these colors, you can make a ribbon set by gluing one end of each new, appropriately-colored ribbon to a short length of cardboard that will fit into the spine of your breviary. The ribbons should be long enough to dangle out of your breviary. When the glue is dry, insert the ribbon set into your breviary's spine. Do not worry about how to use the ribbons. This manual will teach you.

This manual also uses a set of 16 different bookmarks. To make yours, cut 16 bookmarks from strips of cardboard. Make them long enough so that they protrude from the top of your breviary and wide enough to write on (ours measure $1^1/_2$" wide and $8^1/_2$" long). On the upper part of each bookmark, write the following terms so that you can read them when the breviary is closed. Write one of the 16 terms on both sides of one of the bookmarks, at the top.

Hymns
Hymn Index
Proper of Seasons
Daytime Prayer Hymns
Psalter
Night Prayer
Complementary Psalmody
Proper of Saints
Common: Primary Office
Common: Secondary Office
Office of Readings: Biblical
Office of Readings: Non-Biblical
Office of Readings: Psalter
Daytime (Midmorning) Prayer
Daytime (Midday) Prayer
Daytime (Midafternoon) Prayer

Keep the bookmarks in the back of your breviary until you learn how to use them.

SECTION ONE
Getting Familiar With the Breviary

"In this section, you'll learn about . . ."

- How to Use This Book
- The Liturgy of the Hours
- The Divine Office
- Times of Prayer
- The Breviary
- Your Breviary's Table of Contents
- Exploring the Breviary

SECTION ONE: GETTING FAMILIAR WITH THE BREVIARY

Lesson 1: How to Use This Book

So you want to learn to pray the Divine Office? Great!

Do you think you can spend some time to do so? Wonderful!

But you are a dodo at this, you say. You cannot seem to learn new things quickly.

The Divine Office for Dodos is for dodos just like you!

The lessons work for everyone!

If you are a fast-learning dodo, speed up the lessons!

If you are a slow-learning dodo, slow them down.

But please do not be an erratic dodo and skip around. Be an orderly dodo, taking the lessons in order, just as they are written, and learning the material in each before waddling on.

You might be a confused dodo who has noticed that different religious communities pray the Divine Office a bit differently. Who is right? Probably they all are! One community is using one option and another community is using a different one. *The Divine Office for Dodos* teaches the most basic and complete way of praying the Divine Office. At the end of the book, it tells you about the options.

You might be a frustrated dodo who has tried to pray the Divine Office and stomped on your breviary in disgust. Can you learn to pray this? Of course! But go easy on yourself. You have much new material to learn. *The Divine Office for Dodos* will teach it to you, step by simple step. Bye, bye frustration.

Ready to begin? Wonderful.

Start by paging through the manual.

Notice that the book is divided into SECTIONS. Each section focuses on one major portion of the Office.

Hey, the sections are divided into LESSONS! How long do these take? For most dodos, no lesson will take more than thirty minutes and most will take considerably less time. Whew! Now for a secret. To get the maximum benefit from the lessons, follow these tips.

14

- Do the lessons in order no matter how much experience you have in praying the Divine Office or how much you already know.
- Do each lesson's activities and answer the questions correctly before proceeding. Yes, you may look back in the lesson to find the answers!
- Repeat any lesson until you master it before moving on.
- If you have forgotten a technique, do not despair! Refer back to already discussed material, using the Table of Contents to help you find what you need.
- Take as long as you need to complete one lesson. Fully understand it before moving on.

Now, before we begin, here is some information about type styles. The typefaces in this book have a meaning.

- Whenever a term is INTRODUCED, it is printed in CAPITAL LETTERS.
- **Rules for understanding and praying the Divine Office are printed in bold type.**
- Underlining emphasizes certain key points.
- *Italics is used to print instructions that apply only to a four-volume breviary. So if you are using a four-volume breviary, you have more work. You ought to complete all the instructions in this book. But if you are using a one-volume breviary, you can skip the instructions written in italics. Lucky you!*

Oh, yes. Every section of *The Divine Office for Dodos* contains a Dodo Self-Check. You can skip this, but you will probably learn how to pray the Divine Office a lot faster and a lot smoother if you answer the questions. You decide! No one is checking on you but you!

DODO
SELF CHECK #1

1. What are the five secrets for successfully using this manual?

2. When you see a word written in all CAPITALS, what does that mean?

3. **What will it mean when you see something in bold type?**

4. How is underlining used in this book?

5. *When are italics used?*

6. How long might one lesson take to complete?

Did you answer the questions correctly? Good for you!

Ready for Lesson 2? Wonderful! However, before we move on, you will need a book that contains the Divine Office! This book is called a BREVIARY. If you do not have a breviary, fast forward to Lesson 5, read all about breviaries, and get one! Then come back and do lessons 2, 3, and 4.

Once you have a breviary, can you dive right into Lesson 2? Not so fast! Before you begin this instruction, you will need a set of bookmarks and ribbons which you will learn how to use later. Instructions on making or obtaining these are in the BEFORE YOU BEGIN section of this manual. Keep the ribbons and bookmarks in the back of your breviary so that you will be able to find them when you need them!

Lesson 2: The Liturgy of the Hours

It is good to begin any spiritual work with the Bible. Have a look at Mark 15:25-34 and note the hours. You will notice that Jesus was crucified at the third hour and that darkness fell over the land from the sixth to the ninth hour. What times do those correspond with today? Well, Jesus was crucified at 9 a.m. and darkness covered the land from noon until 3 p.m.

In Bible times, people told time using the word "hours" instead of "o'clock." **THE LITURGY OF THE HOURS is a liturgy, meaning a formal rite for public worship that is prayed at certain hours of a twenty-four hour day.** In modern usage, a store or restaurant that is open for twenty-four hours a day is said to be open "around the clock." **The "Liturgy of the Hours" means "Praying Formal Prayers around the Clock."**

Traditionally, religious prayed the Liturgy of the Hours seven times daily. Some clergy, religious, and laity still do! Others pray the Liturgy of the Hours two or three times daily. How often will you pray? That will depend on your likes, your time, and your obligations.

How do we get seven hours? They originated from careful reading of Scripture and from tradition. Psalm 119 (verse 164) states "Seven times a day I will praise you." The Bible enumerates six of these times.

- People in Biblical times prayed together at the last hour of the day when lamps were lit and at the first hour of the dawn. That is similar to us modern believers praying when we awaken and then again before we go to sleep. All right, that is two times a day. But the Jews prayed more often than that.

- In the Acts of the Apostles, the disciples came together for prayer at the third hour (9 a.m.) See Acts 1:14 coupled with Acts 2: 1-15. Taken together, these two passages indicate that the believers were gathered together in prayer on Pentecost.

> **DODO**
> **SELF CHECK #2**
>
> 1. What is the Liturgy of the Hours? What does the word "hour" mean? How did it come to mean this? What would be a modern translation of the term "Liturgy of the Hours"?
>
> 2. Traditionally, how many times daily did people pray the Liturgy of the Hours? How is it prayed differently today?
>
> 3. How did the seven traditional hours of prayer come about? Give the Biblical history in general terms.
>
> 4. What is the "opus Dei?"

- Peter went to the housetop to pray about the sixth hour (Noon). See Acts 10:9.

- Peter and John were going up to the temple for prayer at the ninth hour (3 p.m.). See Acts 3:1.

- Late at night, Paul and Silas were praying (about midnight). See Acts 16:25.

- Sometime between 3 and 6 a.m. Jesus ended His prayer time to walk across the Sea of Galilee and approach his disciples who were battling a storm.

Add up those times. Seven hours total.

Saint Benedict, the great monastic founder, wanted his monks to pray seven hours daily, to correspond with Scripture. He called the seven hours of prayer the "opus Dei," the work of God. Christians began to formally pray at these hours, thus developing the Liturgy of the Hours.

That was not too difficult, was it? Ready for Lesson 3? Here we go!

Lesson 3: The Divine Office

Just what is the Divine Office? And how does it differ from the Liturgy of the Hours? Read on and find out!

To pray the Liturgy of the Hours, certain prayers were composed to pray "around the clock." These formal prayers are called OFFICES. Many different Offices exist such as the Little Office of the Blessed Virgin and Offices written by various saints. But there is only one "official Office" written by the Church. **The "official Office" written by the Church is called the DIVINE OFFICE.** The other Offices are good. The Divine Office is the best, so good, in fact, that it is called "Divine"!

Each Office has certain parts to it. One part is prayed at one hour (a certain time) and another part at another hour (a different time) and so on. Now read the next line carefully! **Each part of an Office is also called an office.** Here is an easy way to understand this: Hint: Look at the capital and lower case letters. Do you notice that one Office begins with a capital and the other office does not? Here is a familiar parallel: Scripture and scripture. If someone is reading Scripture (capitalized), they mean the entire Bible. If they are quoting a scripture (lower case), they mean a Bible verse. The capitalized word is the whole, the lower case a part. Same with Office (the whole) and office (a part).

Today we hear the terms "Liturgy of the Hours" and "Divine Office" used interchangeably. That is common practice, but, for the record, **Liturgy of the Hours means <u>any</u> formal prayers said at specific times around the clock while the Divine Office was the term traditionally applied to the <u>official</u> prayer composed by the Church to pray around the clock.**

Want to become an even smarter dodo? Then do not use the word "hour" when you mean to refer to an office. People do not pray the "hour of Evening Prayer"—they pray the office of prayer that is said at approximately 6 p.m. Moreover, an "hour," as in Liturgy of the Hours, does not mean sixty minutes of prayer. No office takes sixty minutes, to pray. You might be glad to know that!

The Divine Office is nearly as old as the Church itself. It was meant to be prayed with others, but that does not happen too often today outside of religious communities. Today most parish priests and laity pray the Divine Office alone, although more and more priests are initiating times to pray the Divine Office with parishioners. What a wonderful trend!

The Divine Office contains seven daily offices that correspond to the seven traditional hours of prayer in the Liturgy of the Hours. The modern names of these offices are THE OFFICE OF READINGS, THE OFFICE OF MORNING PRAYER, THE OFFICE OF MIDMORNING PRAYER, THE OFFICE OF MID-DAY PRAYER, THE OFFICE OF MIDAFTERNOON PRAYER, THE OFFICE OF EVENING PRAYER, and THE OFFICE OF NIGHT PRAYER. I bet if you read those over a few times, you will have them memorized.

Where do you find the Divine Office? **The DIVINE OFFICE has been printed in a special book called a BREVIARY.** Now hold on because there is more than one kind of breviary. Here are the variations:

DODO SELF CHECK #3

1. What is an Office? An office?

2. Why were Offices written?

3. How are the Liturgy of the Hours and the Divine Office different?

4. How many daily offices are there? What are their names?

5. What is the general name of the book that contains the Divine Office? Describe the three types of breviaries.

6. How was the Divine Office meant to be prayed? May one pray the Divine Office alone?

- Breviary Biggie Size: Four fat volumes. Contains every single prayer and reading of the Divine Office (some publishers title this *Liturgy of the Hours*).
- Breviary Basic: One fat volume. For those who wish to pray only some of the offices (some publishers title this *Christian Prayer*).
- Breviary Mini: One thin volume. An abbreviated form of the Divine Office that many people take along while traveling (some publishers title this *Shorter Christian Prayer*).

Which edition works with *The Divine Office for Dodos?* All of them!

Lesson 4: Times of Prayer

Dodos are creatures of habit. They tend to do certain things at the same time of day. People have a similar tendency. Religious in monasteries and cathedrals set specific times for praying the Divine Office. Here is a nifty chart. The traditional seven hours of prayer and the traditional times prayed are charted here along with the modern name for the office and the current time to pray it. Also listed are the accepted abbreviation and approximate length of time to pray that office.

Current Name of Office	Traditional Name of Office	Abbreviation and Number Minutes to Pray	Current Time of Prayer	Traditional Time
Office of Readings	Vigils or Matins	OOR (15-20 Minutes)	Anytime during the day	Midnight
Morning Prayer	Lauds	MP (10- 14 minutes)	Between 6 and 11 a.m.	Dawn
————	Prime	————	No longer prayed	6 a.m.
Midmorning Prayer	Terce	(5 minutes)	About 9 a.m.	9 a.m.
Midday Prayer	Sext	(5 minutes)	About noon	Noon
Midafternoon Prayer	None	(5 minutes)	About 3 p.m.	3 p.m.
Evening Prayer	Vespers	EP (10-14 minutes)	Between 4 and 11 p.m.	3 to 6 p.m.
Night Prayer	Compline	NP (7-10 minutes)	Before bedtime	Before bedtime

In the above chart, there are eight hours, not seven. Why? Because in medieval times, people prayed an eighth office called Prime. Prime was generally prayed about the same time as Lauds. Today the office of Prime has been suppressed. That means, we do not pray it any longer.

So, what offices do people pray?

Most people pray at least Morning and Evening Prayer. Many pray Night Prayer as well. Those in religious orders pray whatever offices are required by their Order.

What offices will you be praying? That is up to you!

Lesson 5: The Breviary

> **DODO**
> **SELF CHECK #4**
>
> 1. How many offices were traditionally prayed?
> 2. Which office is no longer prayed?
> 3. What is the current name of each office, its abbreviation, the length of time it takes to pray each office, and the time the office is currently prayed? You can peek at the chart while you answer.
> 4. Which office can be prayed at any time during the day?
> 5. Which offices do most people pray?

A breviary is not very brief. It is actually quite bulky. **A BREVIARY is a prayer book that contains the Divine Office so you are going to need a breviary.** Which of the three types should you get?

A. Breviary Biggie Size: **The complete breviary is printed in four volumes, one volume for Lent and the Easter Season, one volume for Advent and the Christmas Season, and two volumes for Ordinary Time.** This is the most expensive breviary because it fills four volumes. Four volumes? Why? Because most people do not want to carry around an eight- or ten-pound book, which is how much the breviary would weigh if all the offices were printed in one volume.

The four-volume breviary contains the complete Divine Office for all seven hours of the day, offering different Readings for the Office of Readings for every day of the year. It also has all year's

MEMORIALS, FEASTS, AND SOLEMNITIES. Later we will discuss these terms in detail.

If you wish to pray all seven hours, you will need a four-volume breviary. Maybe a few caring friends or relatives can each give you a volume for your birthday. Be sure they coordinate their gifts so that you receive one of each volume and not four of the same one.

B. Breviary Basic: **The most widely used breviary is a one-volume breviary.** It contains complete Morning, Evening, and Night Prayer for the entire year as well as the most important prayers and Readings for the Memorials, Feasts, and Solemnities of the year. The Readings for the Office of Readings are a selection of those available in the four-volume breviary. Some publishers include the complete Daytime Prayer Psalter while others include only a selection of the Daytime Prayer Psalms or none at all.

If you want to pray only Morning, Evening, and Night Prayer, save yourself some money and purchase the one-volume breviary. It costs about a quarter of the price of the Biggie.

C. Breviary Mini: **The travelers' breviary, also called SHORTER CHRISTIAN PRAYER, is a slender volume designed to fit into a brief-case or purse.** Its Morning, Evening, and Night Prayers are complete, but it has only the barest minimum of prayers for the Feasts and Solemnities and none for the Memorials. It does not contain the Office of Readings or Midmorning, Midday, and Midafternoon prayer. Use the travelers' breviary when traveling, and either the Basic or Biggie the rest of the time.

DODO
SELF CHECK #5

1. Compare the four-volume, one-volume, and travelers' breviaries. How many volumes does each contain? What offices does each contain? Which is most expensive? Why would someone purchase the four-volume breviary? The one-volume breviary? The travelers' breviary?

2. What offices do you wish to pray?

3. Which breviary should you obtain? How can you obtain it?

4. What cautions should you observe in purchasing a breviary?

When you go to order a breviary, what do you ask for? You are not going to ask for Breviary Biggie, Basic, or Mini! You should not even give a title for the breviary because **different publishers have different titles. Tell the bookstore clerk, "I would like to purchase a breviary that will enable me to observe the Liturgy of the Hours by praying the Divine Office of the Catholic Church." Add whether you want a one- or four-volume breviary.**

A note of caution: Some companies have published Books of Prayer based on the Divine Office and following the Liturgy of the Hours. These have adaptations and modifications so they are NOT the official prayers of the Church. If you want the official prayers of the Church and are considering a book that appears to be a breviary but that is not published by the companies mentioned below, do a little sleuthing before using or purchasing. A priest or religious should be able to tell you if what you are considering is, in fact, the Divine Office as composed by the Church rather than something that has been adapted by an individual or group.

Two companies that currently publish real, genuine breviaries are:

Catholic Book Publishing (77 West End Road, Totowa, NJ, 07512; phone: 973-890-2400, www.catholicbookpublishing.com): four-volume, one-volume, and travelers' breviaries. Catholic Book Publishing also publishes a *Daytime Prayer* supplementary breviary which includes the complete Daytime Prayer offices for the entire year. This is meant to accompany some one-volume breviaries whose Daytime Prayer offices are incomplete. It is also useful for praying Daytime Prayer while at work.

Pauline Books and Media (50 St. Paul's Avenue, Boston, MA 02130; phone 800-876-4463, www.pauline.org): one-volume breviary which includes the complete Daytime Prayer offices.

Note: You will need a breviary to continue with these instructions.

Lesson 6: Getting to Know Your Breviary's Table of Contents

In this lesson, you get to be a Breviary Doctor. You are going to examine your breviary to see what it is all about.

If you have a four-volume breviary, select one of the volumes for ORDINARY TIME for these instructions.

Start by poking around in a breviary. If you have a new breviary, first look in your breviary or its package for any loose inserts. Place these special prayers inside the front or back cover of the breviary and remember that you have them. We will discuss them later.

Now look at the title page. What can you learn from it?

Turn to the Table of Contents which will follow the title page. This is a critical part of your breviary, somewhat like the brain in a human body. Find the following sections in the Table of Contents and then see if you can find them in the breviary. Check off the terms as you find them:

Proper of Seasons
The Ordinary
Psalter
Proper of Saints
Commons
Office for the Dead

Now go back and read the subheadings under each of these. Which sections are divided into months?

What can you learn by reading the subheadings under Commons?

Find Night Prayer.

Find the Complementary Psalmody (not in the travelers' breviary).

What appendices does your breviary have? What can you learn from these headings?

What indices does your breviary have? What can you learn from these?

Whew! That was some looking! Ready to nose around some more?

Why not start with the seasons of the Church year? No, they are not summer, fall, winter, and spring. **There are three seasons of the church year—Lent, Advent, and Ordinary Time. A breviary is arranged around these seasons.**

> **DODO**
> **SELF CHECK #6**
>
> 1. What words best describe your first contact with the breviary? Hopeful? Anxious? Eager? Frustrated? Confused? Delighted? Any of these reactions is normal for a person who is paging through a breviary for the first time.

In the four-volume breviary, there is one volume for Lent and Easter Seasons, one for Advent and Christmas Seasons, and two for Ordinary Time. All of these seasons are contained in some manner in the one-volume and travelers' breviaries.

Leaf through your breviary. Can you find sections for Lent, Advent, and Ordinary Time? Are they in more than one place?

Lesson 7: Exploring the Breviary

Why not start off in a simple way? Open your breviary to the Table of Contents in the front section.

Can you find the heading marked Psalter? Look at the subheadings. Find Week I, Week II, Week III, and Week IV. **The Psalter is used every day throughout the year in a four-week repeating cycle. These weeks are Week I, Week II, Week III, and Week IV.** After Week IV is completed, return to Week I. Using the four-week Psalter is somewhat like running laps around a track. Around and around and around. More about this later.

Time for a little "exploratory surgery." Time to look more deeply into the breviary. Open your breviary to the first page of Week I. What day of the week is this? Page through this section. Look for the following headings and check them off in this book as you find them:

Evening Prayer I
Invitatory
Office of Readings
Morning Prayer
Daytime Prayer
Evening Prayer II

Now go back to the first page of Week I. Page forward again, looking for the following headings. Check them off in this book as you find them:

Hymn
Psalmody
Antiphon
Psalm
Psalm-Prayer

Keep paging through until you reach Monday.

What have you noticed about the frequency of the above headings? Have you noticed other headings not yet discussed? Are you feeling pretty dodo-y, not knowing what all these mean? Not to worry!

Soon you will learn! A breviary is like the human body, many different parts that all work together. It takes time to learn all the parts! If you want to learn about the human body, you first become familiar with the general characteristics of the body, and then you start looking at the details. That is what we are doing here.

DODO
SELF CHECK #7

1. List all the new terms you found in the breviary.

2. What have you noticed about the repetition of these terms?

3. What is the Psalter? How many weeks does it contain? What happens when you finish praying Week IV?

SECTION TWO
General Instructions

"In this section, you'll learn about . . ."

- **Bookmarks and Ribbons**
- **Hymns**
- **Praying Aloud**
- **Beginning and Ending the Divine Office**
- **Psalms and Canticles**
- **The Responsory**
- **Evening Prayers I and II**

SECTION TWO: GENERAL INSTRUCTIONS

If you have a four-volume breviary, use one of the volumes for Ordinary Time for this section.

Lesson 8: Bookmarks and Ribbons

This instructional manual uses a system of ribbons and bookmarks to help you find your place in the breviary. You have either made a set or ordered one.

Now, let me make one thing perfectly clear. You may not use every ribbon and bookmark. What you use will depend on your breviary, its publisher, and the offices that you wish to pray. So what do you do with the extra ones? Good question. Maybe you have a creative answer!

Even though you do not know where to put the ribbons and bookmarks right now, you can learn these two rules about them.

The "restful ribbons" mark prayers that are repeated frequently. Once you put a ribbon into its proper place, hands off! It rests in that place forever.

The bouncing bookmarks bounce along as you pray the offices.

Please keep the bookmarks and ribbons in the back of your breviary until you need them. Very soon you will be using them.

If you are using a four-volume breviary, you may wish to make or order a set of bookmarks and ribbons for each volume so that you do not have to move them from volume to volume. If you make or order three additional sets now, you will have them on hand when you need them in this instruction. Refer back to the **Constructing Bookmarks and Ribbons** *section in the Introduction to this manual.*

**DODO
SELF CHECK #8**

1. How will the "restful ribbons" be used?
2. How will the "bouncing bookmarks" be used?

Lesson 9: Hymns

A dodo did not have the voice of a nightingale. If you are like me, you do not have the voice of a nightingale either. But whether or not you can carry a tune, you can "make a joyful noise to the Lord." This lesson will be about the "joyful noises" in the Divine Office. The joyful noises are called HYMNS, and some people can actually sing them.

Every office uses a Hymn shortly after its beginning _**whether or not a Hymn is printed or referred to in your breviary.**_

The Hymn may be sung, but, if you do not know the tune, make one up or use a tune you do know.

A Hymn may be chanted. You can create a simple chant by singing the same note for every syllable. If you want to get fancy, other more complicated chants exist. Usually a convent can teach you some chants if you want to learn them.

If you cannot sing or chant, just recite the Hymn. Recitation is OK, too.

Can you eliminate the Hymn? No. Each office is to begin with "a joyful noise to the Lord."

How do you find the Hymns? Look in your breviary's Table of Contents. Some breviaries have a special Hymn section.

Next look at the Psalter. Some breviaries have a Hymn printed at the beginning of each office. Sometimes more than one Hymn is printed, but **you will use only one Hymn at the beginning of each office, even though several may be printed.**

Does your breviary have a Hymn number or page to which you should refer for that office? Some breviaries do.

Do the Hymns in your breviary have only words or do they contain the notes as well?

Do Hymns without notes have a notation at the bottom listing the melody to be sung? If so, page through the breviary and see if you recognize any of those melodies.

DODO
SELF CHECK #9

1. How are Hymns arranged in your breviary?

2. Would you prefer to sing, chant, or recite the Hymns?

3. How will you find a Hymn when you need one?

4. How many Hymns do you use at the beginning of each office?

Now we get to do something fun. We get to use our first bookmark! **If you have a Hymn section, insert the Hymn bookmark into that section now.** If you do not have a Hymn section, do not fret. You will get to use another bookmark soon.

Turn to the indices of your breviary. Does your breviary have an index of Hymns and pages on which they are found? Study the indices carefully. How are the Hymns arranged? To what seasons do they refer?

If your breviary has an index of Hymns, telling you which Hymns to use on certain days, insert the Hymn Index bookmark into the breviary at the beginning of the Index of Hymns.

Lesson 10: Praying Aloud

Here is something many people do not know. **The Divine Office is intended to be prayed out loud.** Some people read aloud, sing, or chant the Divine Office to help them pray better. If you cannot or do not want to do that, you can at least move your lips when you pray. Moving your lips keeps you in line with tradition and reminds you that other people elsewhere are praying the Divine Office together and out loud.

Here is another thing many people do not know. The HEADINGS, SUBHEADINGS, and INTRODUCTIONS are not prayed out loud. You can read them silently if you wish.

How can you distinguish the Office from the headings, subheadings, and introductions? Read on!

Take your breviary. Turn to the Psalter **and put the Psalter bookmark in place somewhere in the Psalter.** Now page through the Psalter. You will notice many, many headings. Find Wednesday, Week IV. Look for the following headings.

Invitatory
Morning Prayer
Ant. 1
Psalm 108
Ant. 2
Canticle

Page through all of the offices for Wednesday, Week IV, moving the bookmark along as you go. What other headings do you notice?

Now use that bright dodo eye of yours. How did the publisher of your breviary distinguish the headings from the prayers? Often the headings are printed in a different color or type style (bolder, lighter, larger, smaller, italics) than the Office itself.

Now look at Morning Prayer for Wednesday, Week IV. Find Psalm 108. Under the heading "Psalm 108" will be a subheading and an introduction. These read "Praise of God and a plea for help" and "Since the Son of God has been exalted above the heavens, his glory is proclaimed through all the earth (Arnobius)." Arnobius is the ancient writer who wrote this reflection. I bet you knew that already!

> **DODO**
> **SELF CHECK #10**
> 1. Is the Divine Office meant to be prayed silently or aloud?
> 2. Is the Divine Office sometimes sung or chanted?
> 3. What parts in the Office do you read silently? How can you distinguish these from the Office itself?
> 4. What does "R" mean when printed in the breviary? For now, how should you treat this instruction?

How does the publisher of your breviary distinguish the subheading and introduction from Psalm 108? Most publishers use a different color or style of type (bolder, lighter, smaller, larger, italics) to distinguish subheadings and introductions from the Office.

Page through the remainder of the Psalter, looking for headings, subheadings, and introductions in the offices for all of Wednesday,

Thursday, and Friday of Week IV. Move the Psalter bookmark along as you go. Were you able to find more examples of each of these?

When praying the Divine Office, silently read the headings, sub-headings, and introductions but do not say them out loud.

Look in the Psalter for Sunday Evening Prayer, Week IV. Page through until you come to the Canticle of Revelation 19:1-7. Look for a capital letter "R" written here and there throughout the Canticle. **The "R" written before some lines in the breviary means "Response."** It is used as an instruction when groups are praying the office together. Right now, pay no attention to any "R's" in the breviary. Much later we will learn how to pray with them.

Lesson 11: Beginning and Ending the Office and the Glory Be

Feeling brave today? I hope so because today you are going to begin to actually pray an office. I say "begin" because you will have quite a few other lessons before you will be praying a complete office. Today is just a beginning.

If you have a four-volume breviary, use the two volumes for Ordinary Time until instructed to do otherwise.

Ready? Go!

First off, there are certain things that are always done, but the breviary does not tell you to do them. Why not? Because you are supposed to know. Since you do not know, let me tell you.

First thing you are supposed to know. **Every office begins and ends with the SIGN OF THE CROSS, prayed silently, even though it is not printed in the breviary.** To make the Sign of the

DODO
SELF CHECK #11

1. How does every office begin and end?

2. How is the "Glory Be" prayed in the Divine Office. Try to memorize this form.

3. When is the "Glory Be" prayed in the Divine Office? Are there exceptions to this?

4. If your breviary does not tell you to pray the "Glory Be" after every Psalm and Canticle, does this mean that you can skip praying it?

Cross, bless yourself and think, "In the name of the Father and of the Son and of the Holy Spirit. Amen."

Second thing you are supposed to know: **The GLORY BE is prayed after every single Psalm and Canticle, or section thereof, in the Divine Office with one exception which you will learn later. It is prayed even though the breviary does not tell you to pray it.**

Third thing you are supposed to know: The Glory Be in the Divine Office is prayed with a special ending, like this: **Glory to the Father, and to the Son, and to the Holy Spirit, as it was in the beginning is now and will be forever. Amen.** Write this ending on your Hymn bookmark to help you remember. This is already printed on the preprinted bookmarks.

In order to show reverence, every time you pray the Glory Be, you may wish to bow while praying the words "Glory to the Father, and to the Son, and to the Holy Spirit." You may straighten for the remainder of the prayer.

Lesson 12: Psalms and Canticles in the Psalmody

How about nosing around a bit more in the breviary? Page through the Psalter (Weeks I, II, III, and IV). Look for the section marked PSALMODY. **The PSALMODY is a section at the beginning of each office.** It follows the Hymn.

Look at the Psalmody in several offices. Can you find PSALMS? CANTICLES? ANTIPHONS (abbreviated ANT.)? PSALM-PRAYERS? Go on. Find a lot of each of these. The more you find, the easier the rest of this lesson will be.

PSALMS and CANTICLES are poetic prayers found in the Bible. They were often sung. You can sing them if you wish, but you can also recite them.

ANTIPHONS, often abbreviated Ant., are short, repeated prayers that accompany the Psalms and Canticles. **Antiphons are**

prayed before each Psalm and Canticle. Here is an insider secret. The Antiphons are generally prayed after each Psalm and Canticle, too. But your breviary may not print them after, only before.

PSALM-PRAYERS are short reflections that follow some of the Psalms and Canticles. **You may pray or skip the Psalm Prayers.** We will pray them in this instruction, but you may do as you wish.

Look in your breviary for Evening Prayer for Friday, Week III. Find the Psalmody. You will notice that it begins with an Antiphon called ANTIPHON 1 or ANT. 1. Antiphon 1 reads, "Great is the Lord, our God, transcending all other gods." Boy, is that the truth!

In the one-volume breviary and the travelers' breviary, you will see two other Antiphons printed in smaller type following Antiphon 1. One smaller Antiphon is marked "December 17-23" and the other is marked "Easter." I bet you know what seasons those are for! For now, we will ignore those seasonal Antiphons, even if we are in those seasons!

Do you notice that Psalm 135 has a subheading? It reads, "Praise for the wonderful things God does for us."

Psalm 135 also has an introduction that reads, "He has won us for himself . . . and you must proclaim what he has done for you. He has called you out of darkness into his own wonderful light (see 1 Peter 2:9)."

When you pray the Divine Office, will you pray aloud this heading, subheading, and introduction? Did you answer no? If so, you are correct!

Psalm 135 begins with the words, "Praise the name of the Lord." In just a

---

DODO SELF CHECK #12

1. What are Psalms? Antiphons? Psalm-Prayers? Canticles?

2. In praying the Divine Office, what prayer is said following each Psalm or Canticle or portion thereof?

3. Where do you pray the Antiphon for the Psalms and Canticles? If the Antiphon is not reprinted after the Psalm or Canticle, are you to pray it anyway?

4. Do you pray the Psalm-Prayer aloud?

moment, you will be praying this Psalm all the way down to the words, "on his people his land he bestowed." Some breviaries have the word "Glory . . . " after this. Others do not. Can you guess what the "Glory" means? Yes! It is a hint to pray the Glory Be here. Do you pray the Glory Be even if your breviary does not print the word "Glory"? You bet you do!

> **TECHNIQUE**
>
> **The procedure for praying the Psalms and Canticles in the Psalmody is as follows:**
>
> **Pray Antiphon 1.**
> **Pray the first Psalm or Canticle.**
> **Say the full Glory Be.**
> **Pray or skip any Psalm-Prayer that may follow.**
> **Repeat Antiphon 1.**
>
> **Pause briefly for silent reflection.**
>
> **Pray Antiphon 2.**
> **Pray the second Psalm or Canticle.**
> **Say the full Glory-Be.**
> **Pray or skip any Psalm-Prayer that may follow.**
> **Repeat Antiphon 2.**
>
> **Pause briefly for silent reflection.**
>
> **Pray Antiphon 3.**
> **Pray the third Psalm or Canticle.**
> **Say the full Glory Be.**
> **Pray or skip any Psalm-Prayer that may follow.**
> **Repeat Antiphon 3.**

Some breviaries reprint Antiphon 1 following Psalm 135; others do not. In either case, Antiphon 1 is often prayed following the first Psalm. As noted earlier, we will pray it both before and after in this instruction. **After praying the Antiphon at the end of the Psalm, pause briefly for silent reflection on the Psalm itself.**

Now you are ready. Take a deep breath and pray Psalm 135, with its Antiphon and Glory Be. All done? You did it! You just prayed a Psalm from the Divine Office. Want to try another one?

Find Antiphon 2. It reads, "House of Israel, bless the Lord! Sing Psalms to him, for he is merciful." Both the one-volume breviary and travelers' breviary again record the December and Easter Antiphons. Ignore these for now.

Look at the Psalm. It is marked "II." Does that seem odd? **A Psalm with the heading "II" is the second part of the preceding Psalm.** The section that begins "Lord, your name stands for ever," and that ends, "he who dwells in Jerusalem," is the second half of Psalm 135.

In some breviaries, the word "Glory . . . " is again printed after the last line of the Psalm. Whether it is printed or not, you know what to do, you smartie. Pray the "Glory Be" after the Psalm.

Then you will notice a Psalm-Prayer that begins, "Father, your name and your memory last for ever" and that ends "on us in our lowliness." In some breviaries, Antiphon 2 is reprinted following the Psalm-Prayer. In this instruction, whether or not Antiphon 2 is reprinted, we will pray Antiphon 2 again, then pause briefly for reflection before continuing.

Look for Antiphon 3. What does it read? Does it precede another Psalm or a Canticle? How would you pray this?

— · — · — · — · — · — · —

PRACTICE: Following this outline, pray the Psalmody for Friday Evening Prayer, Week III. Check how you did by referring to Appendix A.

EXTRA PRACTICE: Turn to Week II. Pray the Morning and Evening Prayer Psalmody for Monday, Tuesday, Wednesday, and Thursday. Use the outline on page 35 to help you.

Lesson 13: The Responsory

I bet you can figure out what a RESPONSORY is. Something you respond to, right? A RESPONSORY follows the Scripture Reading in every office.

The simplest Responsories are those for Midmorning, Midday, and Midafternoon prayer. They are only two lines long. A typical Responsory for these three little offices is:

We do well to praise the Lord.
    To sing to you, our God most high.

To pray the Responsory if praying alone, pray the first line and then the second. What could be simpler?

The Responsories for Morning, Evening, and Night Prayer and the Office of Readings are longer. They also have some lines that end with a series of three dots (. . .). Most dodos know that three dots mean that something is continuing. What is it? The previous Responsory line! **The Responsory line with three dots is to be read in full just the way it appears previously in the Responsory.**

For example, one Responsory for the Office of Readings for the Twenty-Second Sunday in Ordinary Time is printed like this in a four-volume breviary:

> I will give thanks to you, O Lord my God, with all my heart,
>   for great is your mercy toward me.
>
> You are my God, I give you thanks; my God, I give praise to you.
>   For great is . . .

The three dots mean that the fourth line is to be read in full as it appears previously. When you pray this Responsory, you will say it as follows:

> I will give thanks to you, O Lord my God, with all my heart,
>   for great is your mercy toward me.
> You are my God, I give you thanks; my God, I give praise to you.
>   For great is your mercy toward me.

The Responsories for Morning, Evening, and Night Prayer add a portion of the Glory Be to the Responsory. This is written as "Glory be to the Father . . . " Here is another secret most people do not know. In the Responsory, only the first line of the Glory Be is prayed—"Glory to the Father and to the Son and to the Holy Spirit." The second line of the Glory Be is not prayed in the Responsory. Why not? Because in early times, the complete prayer was "Glory to the Father and to the Son and to the Holy Spirit." The whole prayer was prayed in the Responsory back when the Divine Office was first being prayed. The words "as it was in the beginning, is now, and will be forever. Amen." were added to the Glory Be at a later date to combat Arianism, a heresy that denied that God the Father and God the Son existed together from all eternity. However, the Responsory never added the addition!

In the breviary, the Responsory for Tuesday Morning Prayer, Week I, is written as follows:

My God stands by me, all my trust is in him.
  My God stands by me, all my trust is in him.

I find refuge in him, and I am truly free;
  all my trust is in him.

Glory to the Father . . .
  My God stands . . .

Following the guidelines earlier in this lesson, can you figure out how to pray this Responsory? Did you think it would be something like this:

My God stands by me, all my trust is in him.
  My God stands by me, all my trust is in him.

I find refuge in him, and I am truly free;
  all my trust is in him.

Glory to the Father and to the Son and to the Holy Spirit.
  My God stands by me, all my trust is in him.

Are you getting it? I bet you are! Go ahead and feel smart. You have a right to.

After praying the complete Responsory, it is good to pause for silent reflection before continuing to pray the office.

— · — · — · — · — · — · —

PRACTICE: In your breviary, find a Responsory for Morning, Evening, or Night Prayer. Using the above format as an outline, pray this Responsory.

EXTRA PRACTICE: Find ten more Responsories in your breviary. Pray them, using the above instruction as a guide.

Lesson 14: Evening Prayers I and II

Evening Prayers I and II? Does this mean you have to pray two Evening Prayers? Only if you are talking about praying on two evenings.

Find your breviary's Psalter and page through it. Look for Saturday prayers. Keep going until you find an office marked "Saturday, Evening Prayer."

Could you find it? Do not feel dodo-y if "Saturday Evening Prayer" eluded you. Why? Because you will not find any "Saturday Evening Prayer" unless you are using a bogus breviary.

Oh, so we do not pray Saturday Evening Prayer? Wrong! **The office prayed on Saturday evening is called SUNDAY, EVENING PRAYER I.**

Now why in the world . . . ? The designations, Evening Prayer I and Evening Prayer II, did not develop to confuse people. When they developed in medieval times, everyone knew exactly what those terms meant. When knights were riding about in shining armor and rescuing fair damsels in distress, people considered Sunday as beginning at sundown on Saturday evening. So the office for Saturday evening would naturally be called Sunday, Evening Prayer I. And the office for Sunday evening would naturally be called Sunday, Evening Prayer II. If you start to think like a knight or a damsel, you will grasp the distinction which the Psalter has kept.

Look for Sunday, Evening Prayer I in the Psalter. Can you find one of these offices?

Now page forward and look for Sunday, Evening Prayer II. Did you find it?

Great! Before long, you will be an expert in understanding these two offices.

DODO SELF CHECK #14

1. What is the name of the office that is prayed on Saturday evening?
2. What is the name of the office that is prayed on Sunday evening?
3. Why are these designations in the Psalter?

SECTION THREE
Praying Night Prayer

"In this section, you'll learn about . . ."

- **Introduction to Night Prayer**
- **Beginning the Divine Office**
- **Concluding the Divine Office**
- **Praying the Office of Night Prayer**
- **Praying Night Prayer Every Night**

SECTION THREE: PRAYING NIGHT PRAYER

Lesson 15: Introduction to Night Prayer

"Now I lay me down to sleep . . ." That is a night prayer, all right, but not the one in the Divine Office. Night Prayer is a very important office. Here is something really great about it. It is one of the easiest offices to learn! Yipee! Want to get started?

How does your breviary arrange Night Prayer?

Some breviaries begin Night Prayer with Night Prayer after Evening Prayer I on Sundays and Solemnities (this is prayed Saturday night, remember, oh you brave knight or fair damsel!) Other breviaries begin the Night Prayer section with Sunday Night Prayer. How about your breviary? Go look!

Flip through the Night Prayer section. Check off the following terms as you fly by them:

Hymn

Psalmody (Psalm)

Reading

Responsory

Gospel Canticle (also called the Canticle of Simeon or the Nunc Dimittis)

Prayer

Conclusion that reads, "May the all-powerful Lord grant us a restful night and a peaceful death" (hint: this will be either at the end of each Night Prayer or else right after Friday Night Prayer)

Antiphons in honor of the Blessed Virgin (hint: these may be at the very end of the Night Prayer section)

Night Prayer after Evening Prayer I on Sundays

Night Prayer after Evening Prayer II on Sundays

Night Prayer for Monday, Tuesday, and other weekdays to Friday

Were you able to find all these terms? If not, keep looking until you do.

TECHNIQUE

Every office, other than the first office, begins with these four steps:

a. The Sign of the Cross made silently. The rest of the office prayed aloud.

b. The introduction, "God, come to my assistance. Lord, make haste to help me."

c. The Glory Be as learned in Lesson 11 and printed on the Hymn bookmark.

d. "Alleluia" prayed after the "Glory Be" except during Lent.

Lesson 16: Beginning the Divine Office

Guess what? Every office has certain prayers that are always prayed with that particular office. That simplifies things a bit, right? Well, not really. Because these prayers are repeated in every office, many breviaries do not print them. You see, if these prayers were printed in every single office, your breviary would be a lot thicker and a lot more expensive. Your breviary publisher saved you some money by not printing out all the repetitive prayers.

No despairing, now. The following lessons will teach you these repetitive prayers. These prayers are prayed whether or not they are printed in the proper place in the breviary.

Let us begin with a repetitive word. When you hear the word "Alleluia," do you think of Christmas? Or Easter? **"Alleluia" is a cry of joy. It is often used in the Divine Office. During Lent the Church keeps a somber attitude and does not pray the "Alleluia."** This is reflected in how the Divine Office begins.

First a word about the first office of the day. The first office of the day begins in a special way. Later you will

**DODO
SELF CHECK #16**

1. How does every office except the first office of the day begin?

2. How is the Glory Be prayed at the beginning of these offices?

3. What exclamation of praise follows the Glory Be at the beginning of the offices? When is this exclamation not prayed? Why is it not prayed then?

4. Is "Alleluia" prayed after the Glory Be which follows the Psalms and Canticles in the Psalmody?

learn how to begin the very first office of the day. But now we are talking about the last office of the day: Night Prayer.

"Alleluia" is prayed after the Glory Be only at the beginning of the office. "Alleluia" is not prayed after the Glory Be when the Glory Be follows the Psalms and Canticles in the Psalmody.

On the Psalter bookmark print the procedure for beginning the Divine Office. It is already printed on the preprinted bookmarks. Consult the bookmark if you forget how to begin!

Lesson 17: Concluding the Divine Office

We are going to make a Night Prayer "sandwich." We just began our "sandwich" with the "top slice of bread," the beginning of the office. Now for the "bottom slice of bread," the end of the office.

Every office of the Divine Office ends with a Concluding Prayer. It is called a Concluding Prayer because it concludes the office. Duh. Even a dodo can understand that! In some breviaries, this Concluding Prayer is written out in full. In others, it is not. If it is not written out in your breviary, how do you know what to pray?

Here is the process. **First ask, "Who is the Concluding Prayer addressing?"** God the Father? God the Son? God the Holy Spirit?

If the Concluding Prayer begins by addressing God the Father or God the Holy Spirit, its ending is either "We ask this . . . " or "Grant this . . . " followed by "through our Lord Jesus Christ, your Son, who lives and reigns with you and the Holy Spirit, one God, forever and ever. Amen." See, the Son is mentioned in the conclusion.

If the Concluding Prayer begins by addressing God the Son, it concludes with "You live and reign with the Father and the Holy Spirit, one God, for ever and ever. Amen." See, the Father and Spirit are mentioned in the conclusion.

DODO SELF CHECK #17

1. If a Concluding Prayer is not written out in full, how do you determine its ending?
2. Where can you find the endings to the Concluding Prayers?

You do not have to remember these. If you ordered bookmarks, these endings are printed on the Psalter bookmark. If you made your own bookmarks, copy these endings and keep them on a small card inside the front cover of your breviary.

Lesson 18: Praying Night Prayer (Part One)

Review time! What have you already learned? You have learned how to begin and end an office, how to pray the Glory Be, and what many of the terms and parts of the Divine Office are. You have also learned some background on the Divine Office including why the offices are named as they are and how the hours came to be designated. Do you feel as dodo-y as you used to feel? I hope not!

Now we are really going to pray a full office. Honest! But first we get to use another bookmark. Can you guess which one?

Did you guess Night Prayer? Oh, you are smart! **Insert the Night Prayer bookmark in your breviary at Night Prayer after Evening Prayer I on Sundays. Hint: See Lesson 14 if you do not remember when this prayer is prayed.**

What is at the beginning of the Night Prayer office that is not at the beginning of any other office? An Examination of Conscience and Prayer of Forgiveness! To help you remember, write these two phrases on the Night Prayer bookmark. They are already printed on the preprinted bookmark.

Why do we have an examination of conscience and a prayer of forgiveness in Night Prayer? Because we want to go to bed with a clean conscience and a forgiving heart, just in case we wake up at the Pearly Gates.

Night Prayer is the only office that contains an Examination of Conscience. The examination is made silently. Thankfully, especially if you are praying this office in the presence of others!

You probably have your own method of making an Examination of Conscience. If not, silently ask God to help you recall your behavior, speech, thoughts, omissions, and attitudes during the day. Examine these for any sin or failing. Ask God's forgiveness. Resolve to go to confession as soon as possible for any major sins. Ask God's grace to help you to do better tomorrow.

Follow the Examination of Conscience with a short Prayer of Forgiveness. Use a formal Act of Contrition or ask for forgiveness in your own words. You might get to use the first ribbon of the "resting ribbon" set right here. Check your breviary to see if it prints some Prayers of Forgiveness in a certain section (not all breviaries do). **If yours does, draw the black (for sorrow for sin) ribbon down through the breviary to mark the Prayers of Forgiveness section.**

Then sing a Hymn, if you like to sing, that is. If you prefer to chant or recite the Hymn, that is fine, too. **Some breviaries print a Hymn at the beginning of each Night Prayer office. Others refer you to certain Hymns in the Hymn section which you have already bookmarked. Some breviaries have a separate section for Night Prayer Hymns alone. If yours does, draw the orange (for sunset) ribbon down through the Night Prayer Hymn section of your breviary.**

You have learned how to begin Night Prayer. How do you conclude it? Night Prayer ends with the conclusion "May the all-powerful Lord grant us a restful night and a peaceful death. Amen." followed by the Sign of the Cross and an ANTIPHON IN HONOR OF THE BLESSED VIRGIN. Write this conclusion on your Night Prayer bookmark. It is already printed on the preprinted bookmark.

**DODO
SELF CHECK #18**

1. Could you find every section listed above? Be sure to locate them before proceeding,

2. What bookmark marks Night Prayer? What is printed on that bookmark?

3. What color ribbon marks the Night Prayer Hymns?

4. What color ribbon marks the Antiphons in Honor of the Blessed Virgin?

5. What color ribbon marks the Prayers of Forgiveness?

What is that ANTIPHON IN HONOR OF THE BLESSED VIRGIN? Where is it?

The Antiphons in Honor of the Blessed Virgin are really prayers or Hymns to Our Lady. You know some of them. "The Hail Mary." "Hail, Holy Queen."

Flip through the Night Prayer section of your breviary. Is an Antiphon to the Blessed Virgin written after each Night Prayer office? Or is there an Antiphon Section, usually at the end of the Night Prayer section? **If your breviary has an Antiphon Section for Antiphons in honor of the Blessed Mother, draw the purple (for queenliness) ribbon from your ribbon set down through that section to mark it.**

You have just completed the "upper slice of bread" and the "lower slice of bread" in the Night Prayer sandwich. First a Dodo Self Check and then we will add the "filling."

Lesson 19: Praying Night Prayer (Part Two)

How about starting this lesson with some pretending? **No matter what day of the week it is when you do this lesson or what time of day, pretend it is Friday evening. Move your Night Prayer bookmark to Friday Night Prayer.** Now remember, we are just pretending. You may still have to set your alarm, get up early, and go to work tomorrow.

Page through Friday Night Prayer, looking at its various parts.

Where are the Night Prayer Hymns? The Prayers of Forgiveness? The Antiphons in Honor of the Blessed Mother? What color ribbon marks each of these?

The "filling" for the Night Prayer "sandwich" consists of Psalms, Antiphons, Responsory, and Canticle. You have already practiced praying those in Lessons 12 and 13. So you are ready to put it all together. Now we will see what this "bedtime bite to eat" looks like. We are ready to pray!

The Night Prayer, Friday, "Sandwich"

Look at the front of your Night Prayer bookmark.

Make the Sign of the Cross.

Pray, "God, come to my assistance. Lord, make haste to help me."

Pray the Glory Be as learned in Lesson 11 and printed on the Hymn bookmark.

Say, "Alleluia." (Omit during Lent.)

Silently make an Examination of Conscience.

End with a Prayer of Forgiveness.

Sing, chant, or recite an appropriate Hymn.

Say the Antiphon. (In one-volume breviaries, ignore for now the Antiphon marked "Easter" and pray the other Antiphon that begins "Day and night . . . ")

Read Psalm 88. End the Psalm with the Glory Be as printed on the Hymn bookmark. Say the Antiphon (not the one marked Easter but the "Day and night" one) again.

Pause briefly to think about Psalm 88.

Read the Reading.

Read the Responsory as described in Lesson 13 (In one-volume breviaries, ignore for now the Responsory marked Easter).

Pause briefly.

Say the Antiphon that begins "Protect us, Lord." (In one-volume breviaries, ignore for now the Alleluia written in parentheses after this Antiphon.)

At the first line of the Gospel Canticle from Luke 2, the line that reads, "Lord, now you let your servant go in peace," make the Sign of the Cross silently.

Read the Gospel Canticle.

Pray the Glory Be.

Say the Antiphon again (do not say the Alleluia in parentheses).

Pause briefly.

Say, "Let us pray."

Read the prayer.

Look at the back of your Night Prayer bookmark. Read "May

the all powerful Lord grant us a restful night and a peaceful death.
Amen."

Make the Sign of the Cross.

Pray ONE of the Antiphons in honor of the Blessed Virgin.

Can you believe it? You have just prayed an entire office! Was it
easier than you thought?

This entire Office, as it would be prayed, is written out in full in
Appendix B. Compare how you did with how it is written there.

— · — · — · — · — · — · — · —

EXTRA PRACTICE: Spend a few days praying only this particular office—Night Prayer for Friday—until you are familiar with its
sections and how to use your bookmark and ribbons. Use your breviary, not Appendix B, to pray this Night Prayer. Check with this
instruction or with Appendix B only to see if you are praying correctly. In learning to pray the Divine Office, a wise dodo will pray
Night Prayer at least three to five times before proceeding with this
instruction.

Lesson 20: Praying Night Prayer Every Night

Now you are really getting good. How would you like to pray
Night Prayer every night?

A quickie review here. Find the Night Prayer section of your
breviary. On what night will you pray Night Prayer After Evening
Prayer I on Sundays? Refer back to Lesson 14 if you are not sure.

A few little details here and a bit more pretending. No matter
what season of the year it is, pretend that it is plain, old Ordinary
time, like the middle of July.

Now find Night Prayer after Evening Prayer I (in some breviaries marked "Saturday") and after Evening Prayer II on Sundays
(in some breviaries marked "Sunday"). Look at the Concluding
Prayers to these two offices. Eeeks! Two prayers! Which one do you

use? Remember, we are pretending it is the middle of July. So for now, in Night Prayer after Evening Prayer I and II on Sundays, use the first Concluding Prayer and ignore the second. We are also going to ignore any instructions that refer to any season other than Ordinary Time. Christmas and Easter seasons do not fall in July! When you get really smart, later on, you will learn how to pray Night Prayer during these other seasons.

OK. Time to get started. Set up your breviary to pray Night Prayer tonight, on this day of the week in the middle of July.

First, find the Night Prayer that is appropriate for today. Place the "Night Prayer" bookmark at that spot.

Next select a Hymn if one is not given. What color ribbon marks the Night Prayer hymns? (Hint: color of sunset).

> **DODO**
> **SELF CHECK #20**
>
> 1. Be a smart dodo. Before proceeding to the next section, be comfortable with praying Night Prayer. You can check to see if you are praying correctly by referring back to Lessons 9 through 19 and to Appendix B. Move the bouncing Night Prayer bookmark ahead as you pray but keep the resting ribbons in place.

Select the Prayer of Forgiveness that you wish to use. What color ribbon marks the Prayers of Forgiveness? (Hint: color of sorrow for sin).

If your breviary has a section of Antiphons in Honor of the Blessed Virgin, select the Antiphon that you wish to use. What color ribbon marks the Antiphons in honor of the Blessed Virgin? (Hint: queenly color).

- - - - - - - - - -

PRACTICE: From now on, you might want to pray Night Prayer every night.

Night Prayer is prayed right before going to bed, no matter if that is early in the evening or after midnight. You might want to arrange your schedule so that you are able to pray Night Prayer.

SECTION FOUR

Praying Morning and Evening Prayer on Weekdays During Ordinary Time

"In this section, you'll learn about . . ."

- Growing Familiar with the Psalter
- Morning and Evening Prayer Canticles
- Invitatory
- Intercessions
- Concluding Morning and Evening Prayer
- Praying Morning and Evening Prayer
- Two- and Three-Part Psalms

SECTION FOUR: PRAYING MORNING AND EVENING PRAYER ON WEEKDAYS DURING ORDINARY TIME

If you have a four-volume breviary, continue to use the volumes for Ordinary Time for these instructions.

Lesson 21: Growing Familiar with the Psalter

Oh, the Psalter. Does the Psalter seem somewhat scary? Soon it will be an old friend.

You have already inserted the Psalter bookmark someplace in the Psalter. Flip through the Psalter, looking for the headings "Week I," "II", "III", and "IV." Now that you know where they are, move the Psalter bookmark to Monday, Week I. Find the INVITATORY for this day. It should be listed first, right under the title of the day and the week.

Put on your thinking cap. An Invitatory is a prayer that i_____ you to begin to pray. Did you fill in the word "invites?" Good for you! More about the Invitatory later.

Page through the Psalter for Monday, Week I, bouncing the bookmark along and answering the following questions as you go.

What office is listed right under the Invitatory? The Office of Readings? Morning Prayer?

On a piece of paper, write the offices in order as you come to them. You might want to read these out loud a few times, just to set the order of them in your brain.

You should now be at the beginning of the office for Tuesday, Week I. Page through the offices for Tuesday, Wednesday, Thursday, and Friday, Week I. Compare them with each other and with what you have written on your paper. Do you see a pattern? Patterns make things easier!

Right here, we are going to skip a lot of stuff. In some breviaries, the Office of Readings will precede Morning Prayer, and Daytime

Prayer offices will follow Morning Prayer. We are going to skip the Office of Readings and Daytime Prayer for now. Oh, we will get to them later, all right, but right now we are concentrating on praying Morning and Evening Prayer.

Do not stop now. Keep paging through the Psalter, all the way to Saturday Morning Prayer for Week IV. Keep paging. Can you find Sunday prayers for Week V? No? Good for you! Why? Because **there is no Week V in the Psalter. The Psalter covers only four weeks. Think of the Psalter as a wheel. When you finish praying the offices under Week IV of the Psalter, you return to Week I of the Psalter.** Around and around and around, Weeks I, II, III, IV, all year through. That was easy! Do you agree?

Here are some examples. Suppose that on Saturday, June 5, you are praying the offices for Saturday, Week IV. When you complete these, you continue the Divine Office by returning to Week I of the Psalter. Where will you find the offices for Monday, June 7? In Monday, Week I of the Psalter.

**DODO
SELF CHECK #21**

1. What are the parts of the offices in order? You can peek when you answer.

2. How many weeks are in the Psalter? I hope you do not have to peek for this one.

3. What do you do when you complete the offices for Saturday, Week IV? Hint. Think of a circle.

So how do you pray, using the Psalter? You use it day after day, in order, until you reach the Saturday offices of Week IV. When you complete these, you go back to Week I of the Psalter and begin all over again.

Lesson 22: Morning and Evening Prayer Canticles (Part One)

Do you think "Canticle" is a beautiful word? Sounds like a song! And that is just what a Canticle is. In Morning, Evening, and Night Prayer, there is always a Canticle to sing God's praises. You are already familiar with **the Night Prayer Canticle, the CANTI-CLE OF SIMEON. ("Lord, now you let your servant go in peace . . . "). This was the song of praise sung by Simeon when he held the Infant Christ in the Temple (Luke 2:29-32).** What are the other two?

The other two main Canticles prayed in the Divine Office are taken from St. Luke's Gospel. You have heard them read at Sunday Mass. **THE CANTICLE OF ZECHARIAH, which is the Morning Prayer Canticle, is Zechariah's song of praise upon the birth of John the Baptist (Luke 1:68-79). THE CANTI-CLE OF MARY, which is the Evening Prayer Canticle, is Mary's Magnificat, sung upon visiting her cousin Elizabeth shortly after Mary conceived Our Lord (Luke 1:46-55).**

So if you look in the Morning and Evening Prayer Offices, you will find the two Canticles, right? Wrong!

Well, why not?

Because the Canticles are more of those repeated prayers that, if printed every time you prayed them, would make your breviary very, very large and expensive.

All right. You can understand that. But where are the Canticles? Do you have to go to the Gospel of Luke every time to pray them?

Not at all. The breviary makes things easier than that! Honest!

Do you recall the cards or printed prayers that come with some breviaries? You may have placed these inside either the front or back cover of your breviary. The Canticle of Zechariah and the Canticle of Mary may be printed on those cards, perhaps marked as Gospel Canticle under Morning Prayer and Evening Prayer. Check and see.

If your pet goat ate the cards, or you do not have them for any other reason, then look in your breviary's Table of Contents in the front of the book and find the page for the Ordinary of the Divine Office. Flip through the Ordinary until you find the instructions for Morning Prayer. Then flip through Morning Prayer instructions, until you find the Canticle of Zechariah (Gospel Canticle).

Double check by seeing if the Bible reference on the right side above it reads Luke 1:68-79. **Draw the silver ribbon (for the silver notes of morning that greet the rising sun) from the ribbon set down through the breviary to mark the Canticle of Zechariah.**

Now that you are all geared up, how about finding the Evening Prayer Canticle? If you suspect that it is in the Ordinary, you are quite an intuitive dodo. Flip through the Ordinary until you come to Evening Prayer. Page ahead in Evening Prayer, looking for the Canticle of Mary, which may also be called the Gospel Canticle. When the Bible reference at the top right of this Canticle reads Luke 1:46-55 you have found it! **Draw the blue ribbon (blue is the color traditionally associated with Our Lady) down through the breviary to mark the Canticle of Mary.**

If you are a super intellectual dodo, you might want to compare the translations of the two Canticles in your breviary with the translations of the same Canticles in your Bible.

Now that you have marked the Canticles, how do you pray them?

We will look at Morning Prayer first because, well, morning comes first in the day. Turn to Monday, Week I in your breviary. Find Morning Prayer and page through it until you find the Canticle of Zechariah (in some breviaries called the Benedictus or Old Testament Canticle) and mark it with the Psalter bookmark.

But, hey, in most breviaries, it is not the whole Canticle. It is only an Antiphon. The silver ribbon marks the whole Canticle.

So what do you do?

You flip from Antiphon to Canticle to Antiphon again.

DODO SELF CHECK #22

1. What is the Canticle of Zechariah?

2. What is the Canticle of Mary?

3. Where are these in your breviary?

4. What color ribbons mark each?

5. What is printed in the Morning and Evening Offices, where these Canticles are to be prayed?

Here are the details. To pray the Morning Prayer Canticle, first pray the Antiphon marked by the Psalter bookmark, then flip to the Canticle marked by the silver ribbon, then a Glory Be as prayed in the Office, and then flip back to the Antiphon again. Easy as breathing, right?

Now try Evening Prayer. Oh, slow down! You are moving fast! That is right, keep flipping through the office for Monday, Week I, until you get to Evening Prayer. Look for the Canticle of Mary (in some breviaries called the Magnificat or New Testament Canticle). Bet you knew it was only an Antiphon!

Bet you know how to pray this, too. Antiphon marked by Psalter bookmark, Canticle marked by blue ribbon, Glory Be as prayed in the Office, Antiphon.

You are doing great, you know!

TECHNIQUE

To pray the Canticle of Zechariah, follow this procedure:

Say the Antiphon as printed in the Psalter.

Use the silver ribbon to turn to the Canticle of Zechariah (Luke 1:68-79).

Make the Sign of the Cross.

Read the whole Canticle through prayerfully.

At the end of the Canticle say the Glory Be in full as printed on the Hymn bookmark.

Pray the Antiphon again as written in the Psalter.

Lesson 23: Morning and Evening Prayer Canticles (Part Two)

I bet you noticed that we talked about praying the Morning and Evening Prayer Canticles in the last lesson, but we did not pray them. In this lesson, you will learn the fine points of praying these beautiful songs.

First go back to where we were in the last chapter. Turn to the Psalter and find Week I, Monday, Morning Prayer. Flip ahead to the Canticle of Zechariah's Antiphon that reads, "Blessed be the Lord our God." **Place the Psalter bookmark at this spot for now.**

Before we pray, we are going on an Antiphon treasure hunt. Each Anti-

**DODO
SELF CHECK #23**

1. Are the Antiphons for the Canticles of Zechariah and Mary the same every day or do they change with the day?

2. How will you know which Antiphon to pray for the Canticles?

3. Is the Antiphon prayed between the verses of the Canticles?

4. What prayer is said at the end of each Canticle? (Hint: It is printed on the Hymn bookmark.)

5. During which office is the Canticle of Zechariah always prayed?

6. During which office is the Canticle of Mary always prayed?

phon is like a little nugget of gold. How many can you find? Page ahead to Tuesday, Morning Prayer, Week I. **The guide words at the top of the pages will help you locate offices in the Psalter.** What is the Antiphon written under the Canticle of Zechariah for Tuesday, Morning Prayer, Week I?

Page ahead and look at the Antiphons for the Canticle of Zechariah on Wednesday, Thursday, and Friday Morning Prayer, Week I. Are they the same or different?

Go back to the Canticle of Zechariah for Monday, Week I, marked with the Psalter bookmark. Now you know that "Blessed be the Lord our God" is not the Canticle but only the Antiphon for the Canticle. You know, too, that the silver ribbon marks the actual Canticle.

Memory jog here. Do you recall that the Glory Be is prayed after every Psalm and Canticle in the Psalter with one exception which you will learn later? How do you pray the Glory Be in the Divine Office? Hint: Consult the Hymn bookmark.

Follow the technique and pray the Canticle of Zechariah for Monday, Week I. When you are done, give yourself a pat on the back, if you can reach around that far. If you cannot, let your spouse or friend do it for you. Double check to see if you prayed this correctly by checking Appendix C.

Do you remember how to pray the Canticle of Mary? The same way!

Flip ahead in Monday, Week I, to Evening Prayer. Page through this until you find the Canticle of Mary. The Antiphon for the

Canticle will read, "My soul proclaims the greatness of the Lord, for he has looked with favor on his lowly servant." **Move the Psalter bookmark to this spot.**

Now we are going on another treasure hunt, looking for Evening Prayer Antiphons. Page ahead in the Psalter. Find the Canticle of Mary for Tuesday, Wednesday, Thursday, and Friday of Week I. Read these Antiphons. Are they the same or different?

See how much you are learning!

In praying the Divine Office, the Canticle of Zechariah is said during every single Morning Prayer. The Canticle of Mary is said during every single Evening Prayer. The Antiphons change, but the Canticles are always the same.

> **TECHNIQUE**
>
> To pray the Canticle of Mary, follow this procedure:
>
> Say the Antiphon as printed in the Psalter.
>
> Use the blue ribbon to turn to the Canticle of Mary (Luke 1:46-55).
>
> Make the Sign of the Cross.
>
> Read the whole Canticle through prayerfully.
>
> At the end of the Canticle say the Glory Be in full as written on the Hymn bookmark.
>
> Pray the Antiphon again as written in the Psalter.

Go back to Monday, Evening Prayer, Week I and find the Canticle of Mary. Well, the Antiphon for the Canticle. Where is the actual Canticle? Yes, the blue ribbon tells you.

Now pray the Canticle of Mary for Monday, Week I. How did you do? Great? Congratulations! Check Appendix C to double check if you prayed this Office correctly.

Lesson 24: Invitatory

Here is an invitation to pray the Invitatory. Do you accept?

The INVITATORY is an invitation to praise God. It is the very first prayer of the day when praying the Divine Office.

Do you remember which two offices may be prayed first in the day?

The first office of the day may be either the Office of Readings or Morning Prayer. Whatever office you choose to pray first, you will begin it with the **INVITATORY**.

Psalm 95 is usually said as the Invitatory Psalm.

Psalm 95 is in your breviary. I bet you know that it is not printed at the beginning of every Office of Readings or every Morning Prayer. Bet you know why, too.

I also bet that you have an inkling of where to find the Invitatory. Either on those prayer cards that came with your breviary or in the Ordinary. Remember how to find the Ordinary? Look up the page number in the Table of Contents.

Oh, there it is, at the beginning of the Ordinary. Invitatory Psalm, Psalm 95.

DODO SELF CHECK #24

1. What is the Invitatory? When is it said?
2. Which two offices may be said first in the day?
3. How do you begin the very first office that you pray?
4. How does one pray the Antiphon in the Invitatory? How does this differ from the way one prays it in the other Psalms and Canticles of the Divine Office?
5. What prayer ends the Invitatory?

Draw the white ribbon (white for the white dawn rising) down through the breviary to mark Psalm 95, the Invitatory Psalm. Now examine Psalm 95. Notice how the verses are separated. Your breviary may have the words "Antiphon" or "Antiphon repeated" between each verse. **Although you may omit it when praying alone, it is customary to repeat the Antiphon after first praying it and to pray the Antiphon between each verse. This is <u>not</u> the procedure for any other Psalm or Canticle. In all the other Psalms and Canticles of the Divine Office, the Antiphon is said only before and after the Psalms and Canticles and NOT between the verses.**

Read Psalm 95. Find the third verse that begins "Come, then, let us bow down and worship, bending the knee before the Lord, our maker." **For the third verse of the Invitatory, if you want to, you may either bow or kneel while praying, then rise for**

TECHNIQUE

To pray the Invitatory, follow this procedure:

Make the Sign of the Cross silently on your lips.

Say, "Lord, open my lips."

Respond with, "And my mouth will proclaim your praise."

Pray the Antiphon as written in the breviary and marked by the Psalter bookmark.

Pray the verses of the Invitatory Psalm, as marked by the white ribbon, repeating the Antiphon after each one. You may wish to bow or kneel while praying verse 3.

End the Invitatory Psalm with the "Glory Be" as printed on the Hymn bookmark.

Repeat the Antiphon.

---

the fourth verse. If you want to make one of these acts of reverence, you can write "Bow" or "Kneel" next to this verse as a reminder. No one is going to scold you for writing in your own breviary.

Exactly where do we pray the Invitatory? Turn to Week I, Monday, of the Psalter. Your Psalter bookmark is probably still in Monday, Week 1, so finding this spot will be a breeze. Go to the very first page of these Monday offices. Almost the very first thing written will be the word "Invitatory." Under this will be a short phrase ("Lord, open my lips") and an Antiphon. Did you guess that this is the Invitatory Antiphon for Monday, Week 1? You bet it is! Put the Psalter bookmark here.

Before going further, we are going to have an Invitatory Antiphon treasure hunt. Page ahead in your breviary to Tuesday, Week I. Read the Antiphon for the Invitatory. Is it the same as Monday's? Look at the Invitatory Antiphons for Wednesday, Thursday, and Friday? Are they all the same or do they differ from each other?

Flip back to the Invitatory for Monday, Week I. **The Invitatory always begins with the Sign of the Cross on your lips while praying the words, "Lord, open my lips. And my mouth shall proclaim your praise." This may not be written out in full in your breviary. The Invitatory always ends with the full Glory Be even though this may not be written out in your breviary. You may wish to print this procedure on the**

Psalter bookmark. It is already printed on the preprinted bookmark.

Using the technique on page 60, pray the Invitatory for Monday, Week I. Not too difficult, was it? Check with Appendix D to see if you have prayed this properly.

Lesson 25: Intercessions and Concluding Morning and Evening Prayer

You know what Intercessions are from attending Sunday Mass. **INTERCESSIONS are prayers of petition. In the Divine Office, they are prayed during Morning and Evening Prayer.**

Turn to Monday, Week I in the breviary. Yes, we will pray from some other days in the Psalter, eventually. Honest! Right now, you are becoming an expert about Monday, Week I! Page along until you come to Morning Prayer for Monday, Week I. Now page through until you come to the Intercessions which follow the Canticle of Zechariah. Mark this spot with the Psalter bookmark and move on!

Keep paging until you come to Evening Prayer for Monday, Week I. Page through this until you come to the Intercessions. Did you guess that they follow the Canticle of Mary? Pretty clever, you.

Keep your finger here and turn back to the Morning Prayer Intercessions. What is similar about the two sets of Intercessions? What is different? Do you

> **DODO SELF CHECK #25**
>
> 1. What are the Intercessions?
>
> 2. May you add some Intercessions of your own?
>
> 3. What is the Refrain? How is it printed in your breviary? When do you pray the Refrain?
>
> 4. Following the Intercessions, what familiar prayer do you pray in full?
>
> 5. When do you say "Amen"?
>
> 6. What dismissal do you pray even though it is not written in the breviary?
>
> 7. How do you end Morning and Evening Prayer?

TECHNIQUE

How to pray the Intercessions for Morning and Evening Prayer and how to end both offices:

Pray the first Intercessions straight through, reading one line after the next exactly as it is written. Pray the Refrain exactly where it is written and nowhere else.

If you wish, you <u>may</u> add Intercessions of your own at the end before the words "Our Father." <u>If you add Intercessions, pray the Refrain after each of your own added Intercessions.</u>

Following the Intercessions, pray the <u>entire</u> Lord's Prayer that begins "Our Father who art in heaven, hallowed be thy name . . . " <u>Pray this whole prayer through to the end even though only the first words are written in your breviary.</u>

Do <u>not</u> say "Amen" at the end of the Lord's Prayer.

Read the prayer that follows in the breviary, using the ending printed on the Psalter bookmark or which you have copied and placed in the front of your breviary.

At the end of that prayer, add the dismissal words "May the Lord bless us, protect us from all evil and bring us to everlasting life. Amen." <u>Pray this dismissal even though it is not written in your breviary.</u>

Make the Sign of the Cross silently <u>even though this is not written in your breviary.</u> This Sign of the Cross ends Morning and Evening Prayer.

notice the words "Our Father . . . " following the Intercessions? If you think it means that you will pray the "Our Father" here, you are right!

Do you like Christmas songs? Many Christmas songs have a refrain, a verse that is repeated at intervals through the song. A familiar refrain comes at the end of each verse of "Silent Night." "Sleep in heavenly peace. Sleep in heavenly peace." Another Christmas song with a refrain is "Deck the Halls." The refrain is "Fa la la la la, la la la la."

No fa la la la's in the Divine Office. But there are refrains. Want to look for them?

Return to the Intercessions for Monday Morning Prayer, Week I. You will notice that, **following the introduction to the Intercessions, there is a line printed in a different type. This may be in darker, lighter, smaller, larger, or italicized type. This is called the REFRAIN.** For Monday Morning Prayer, Week I, the Refrain reads, *Give us your Spirit, Lord.* This means it is repeated between the intercessions, under certain conditions (we will tell you which in a bit).

Time for an Intercession and Refrain treasure hunt. Look ahead in your breviary to Morning Prayer and Evening Prayer for Tuesday, Wednesday, Thursday, and Friday of Week I. Are the Intercessions the same for each day or do they change? Is the Refrain the same or does it change?

Now all we have to do is find the Conclusion to the Morning and Evening Offices and we are ready to pray again. If you have preprinted bookmarks, look on the back of the Psalter bookmark. The Conclusion of the Divine Office is printed there. If you made your own bookmarks, you have copied these conclusions on a card which you placed in the front of your breviary (see Lesson 17).

— · — · — · — · — · — · —

PRACTICE: Using these guidelines and your breviary, pray the Intercessions and Concluding Prayers for Monday Morning Prayer, Week I. Check how you did by comparing your praying with the Intercessions and Conclusion as written out in full in Appendix E.

EXTRA PRACTICE: Page through your breviary to Monday Evening Prayer, Week I. The very same format listed above is used to pray the Intercessions for Evening Prayer as for Morning Prayer. Pray Monday Evening Prayer, Week I, following the guidelines on page 62. Check how you did by comparing your prayer with that in Appendix F.

Lesson 26: Praying Morning Prayer

Are you ready, really ready? Because you are going to begin to pray Morning Prayer for Ordinary Time. When? Right now!

Guess which office we will use? If you guessed the ever-friendly office, Monday Morning Prayer, Week I, you guessed right. Let us pretend that this will be the first prayer of your day. If you have not already done so, **move the Psalter bookmark to this Monday Morning Prayer, Week 1.**

Now a little comparison work and maybe a "gotcha." If you have not been praying Night Prayer regularly, then we "gotcha." Why? Because it is time to compare Morning Prayer with Night Prayer. Page through the Morning and Night Prayer offices. Quick now. What parts of Morning Prayer are not in Night Prayer?

Did you answer Psalm-Prayers, the Canticle of Zechariah, Intercessions, and the Our Father? And maybe the Invitatory? Good for you!

We have not discussed Psalm-Prayers very much yet. **PSALM-PRAYERS follow many of the Psalms and Canticles in Morning and Evening Prayer. They are prayerful reflections on the preceding Psalm or Canticle. You may read these or skip them. In this instruction, we will consistently read them. The full GLORY BE is prayed <u>after</u> the Psalm or Canticle but <u>before</u> the Psalm-Prayer.**

Can you believe it? You are almost ready to pray Morning Prayer! First, you have to choose a Hymn. Some breviaries have a Hymn with the Morning Prayer. Others have a section of Hymns with indices. You have already bookmarked the Hymn Index so look there for Hymns for Morning Prayer, Ordinary Time.

Only one Hymn is sung for Morning Prayer. Choose one suggested or a different one.

Use the "Hymn" bookmark to mark the Hymn that you have chosen.

Now, to be really ready to pray, you might want to review all the following lessons:

Lesson 9 (Hymns)

Lesson 10 (Praying Aloud)

Lesson 11 (How to Begin and End the Office and How to Pray the Glory Be)

Lessons 22 and 23 (Praying the Morning and Evening Prayer Canticles) What color ribbon marks the Canticle of Zechariah? What color ribbon marks the Canticle of Mary?

Lesson 24 (Praying the Invitatory) What color ribbon marks the Invitatory?

Lesson 25 (Praying the Intercessions and Concluding Morning and Evening Prayer)

Reminders on how to begin and end Morning and Evening Prayer are printed on the preprinted "Psalter" bookmark or on your handmade Psalter bookmark, as well as on the card you have placed in the front of your breviary.

— · — · — · — · — · — · — · —

PRACTICE: Now you are ready to pray Morning Prayer for Monday, Week I, Ordinary Time. As you pray, move the bookmark along as you turn the pages.

TECHNIQUE
for praying Morning Prayer, Ordinary Time,
as the first prayer of the day

Look at the front of the Psalter bookmark. Follow the procedure for beginning Morning Prayer.
Make the Sign of the Cross.
Say, "Lord, open my lips."
Respond, "And my mouth will proclaim your praise."

Pray the Antiphon for the Invitatory.
Pray the Invitatory as taught in Lesson 24.
End the Invitatory with the "Glory Be" prayed in full.

Sing, chant, or recite the Hymn you have chosen.

Pray Antiphon 1 written in your breviary's Psalter.
Pray the first Psalm (Psalm 5: 2-10, 12-13) to the end.
Pray the "Glory Be."   *continued on next page . . .*

continued from previous page . . .
Say the Psalm-Prayer.
Repeat Antiphon 1.

Pause briefly for silent reflection.

Pray Antiphon 2.
Pray the Canticle (1 Chronicles 29:10–13) to the end.
Say the "Glory Be."
Repeat Antiphon 2.

Pause briefly for silent reflection.

Say Antiphon 3.
Pray the Psalm (Psalm 29) all the way through to the end.
Pray the "Glory Be."
Pray the Psalm-Prayer.
Repeat Antiphon 3.

Pause briefly for silent reflection.

Read the Reading.
Read the Responsory, following the guidelines in Lesson 13.

Pause briefly for silent reflection.

Pray the Antiphon for the Canticle of Zechariah.
Pray the Canticle of Zechariah as taught in Lesson 23 all the way
    through.
Pray the full "Glory Be."
Repeat the Antiphon for the Canticle of Zechariah.

Pause briefly for silent reflection.

Pray the Intercessions.

Recite the Our Father.

Pray the Concluding Prayer.

Look at the back of your Psalter bookmark for the conclusion to the
office.
Pray, "May the Lord bless us, protect us from all evil, and bring us
to everlasting life. Amen."
End with the Sign of the Cross.

Lesson 27: Beginning All the Offices Except the First Office of the Day and Praying Evening Prayer

You are moving right along so this lesson will be a snap. Ready? Go!

You already know how to pray Morning Prayer. You just prayed it! Praying Evening Prayer is very similar to praying Morning Prayer. There are only two differences. One you already know. The Canticle of Mary, not the Canticle of Zechariah, is prayed during Evening Prayer.

The other difference has to do with how to begin the office of Evening Prayer. **Only the FIRST office of the day begins with the Invitatory. All the other offices except the first begin by making the Sign of the Cross while saying, "God, come to my assistance. Lord, make haste to help me." Then the full "Glory Be" is prayed. Pray "Alleluia" after the "Glory Be" unless it is Lent.** Ever hear this beginning before? Right you are! Night Prayer begins just like this. You will find this introduction printed on the preprinted Psalter bookmark. Hand-print it on your homemade Psalter bookmark.

Let us get ready to pray Evening Prayer. Back to your user-friendly Monday Week I. **Page through this office until you come to Evening Prayer for Monday, Week I and move the Psalter bookmark to this spot.**

Select an Evening Prayer Hymn, as you did for Morning Prayer. Move the Hymn bookmark to this spot.

DODO SELF CHECK #27

1. What is similar between the office of Evening Prayer and the office of Morning Prayer? What is different?

2. How does one begin the first office of the day? How does one begin all the other offices of the day?

3. Where is "Alleluia" said? During which season of the year is it omitted? Why is it omitted then?

TECHNIQUE
for Praying Evening Prayer, Monday, Week I, Ordinary Time.

Look at the Psalter bookmark.
Make the Sign of the Cross.
Say, "God, come to my assistance."
Respond, "Lord, make haste to help me."
Pray the "Glory Be" all the way through to the end.
Say "Alleluia." (Omit the "Alleluia" during Lent.)

Sing, chant, or recite the Hymn you have chosen.

Pray Antiphon I as written in your breviary's Psalter.
Pray the first Psalm (Psalm 11) to the end.
Pray the "Glory Be."
Say the Psalm-Prayer.
Repeat Antiphon 1.

Pause briefly for silent reflection.

Pray Antiphon 2.
Pray the second Psalm (Psalm 15) to the end.
Say the "Glory Be."
Say the Psalm-Prayer.
Repeat Antiphon 2.

Pause briefly for silent reflection.

Pray Antiphon 3.
Pray the Canticle (Ephesians 1: 3-10) all the way through to the end.
Pray the "Glory Be."
Repeat Antiphon 3.

Pause briefly for silent reflection.

Read the Reading.
Read the Responsory, following the guidelines in Lesson 13.

Pause briefly for silent reflection.

Pray the Antiphon for the Canticle of Mary.
Pray the Canticle of Mary as taught in Lesson 23 all the way through.
Say the full "Glory Be."
Repeat the Antiphon for the Canticle of Mary.

Pause briefly for silent reflection.

continued from previous page . . .
Pray the Intercessions.
Recite the Our Father.
Pray the Concluding Prayer.
Look at the back of the Psalter bookmark. Or check your home-made bookmark and also refer to the card you have placed in the front of your breviary.
Pray, "May the Lord bless us, protect us from all evil, and bring us to everlasting life. Amen."
End with the Sign of the Cross.
Congratulations! You have just prayed Evening Prayer!

Now, if you want a good review, check back with the following lessons:

Lesson 9 (Hymns)

Lesson 10 (Praying Aloud)

Lesson 11 (How to Begin and End the Office and How to Pray the Glory Be)

Lessons 22 and 23 (Praying the Morning and Evening Prayer Canticles)

Lesson 25 (Praying the Intercessions and Concluding Morning and Evening Prayer)

Lessons 18 and 19 (Praying Night Prayer)

You are all set to pray Evening Prayer!

Time for some comparisons. Compare Evening Prayer for Monday, Week I, with some other Evening Prayers in the Psalter. What is the same in these offices? What is different?

Lesson 28: Two- and Three-Part Psalms

Here is another easy lesson. Did you ever think that praying the Divine Office would be a breeze?

Have you ever read the whole Book of Psalms in the Bible? If you have, you know that some Psalms are short, some are long, some are very long. and some are in between. The long and very long Psalms are broken up into sections in the breviary's Psalter. Can you find an example of this in your breviary? Check out the Psalmody for Evening Prayer, Wednesday, Week I. Did you find the first Psalm, Psalm 27? Do you see Roman Numeral I over this Psalm?

Now page ahead to the second Psalm. Do you notice that this Psalm has Roman Numeral II written over it? This means that Psalm 27, which is a long Psalm, has been broken into two parts (Part I and Part II) for the Office.

Page through the Psalter right now, looking for other offices in which a Psalm or Canticle is split into one (I), two (II), and sometimes even three (III) sections. If you find ten or more other examples, go reward yourself with a milk shake and then come back to finish the lesson!

> **DODO**
> **SELF CHECK #28**
>
> 1. When the Psalter breaks up a Psalm or Canticle into sections, how are the sections prayed?

How do you pray these split Psalms or Canticles? Just as if each section was an individual Psalm or Canticle. **When you pray an office in which a Psalm or Canticle is split, many people treat each section as if it was a complete Psalm or Canticle. Pray the Antiphons as you have learned to do <u>before and after each section</u>. The Glory Be is prayed after <u>each section</u> of the Psalm or Canticle.** There is an alternate technique which you will learn later.

PRACTICE: Here is an example. Go back to Wednesday Evening Prayer, Week I. Look at the first Psalm, Psalm 27. To pray Psalm 27 in this office, follow this procedure:

Pray Antiphon 1.

Pray Psalm 27 from the first line ("The Lord is my light and my help") all the way through to the last line of the first section ("I will sing and make music for the Lord").

Pray the Glory Be.

Repeat Antiphon I.

Pause briefly.

Pray Antiphon 2.

Pray the second section of Psalm 27 straight through beginning with "O Lord, hear my voice when I call" and ending with "Hope in the Lord!"

Pray the Glory Be.

Read the Psalm-Prayer.

Repeat Antiphon 2 and continue with the office as you have learned.

Lesson 29: Praying Morning Prayer and Evening Prayer Every Weekday

PRACTICE: From now on, try to pray Morning Prayer and Evening Prayer every weekday. For now, do not worry about using the proper season of the year or about special Church celebrations. Do not pray Morning and Evening prayer on weekends just yet. Soon, you will learn how to use your breviary to pray at all these times. For right now, however, pray Morning and Evening Prayer for Monday, Tuesday, Wednesday, Thursday, and Friday, using only the Psalter.

Page through the Psalter. Look for the headings that say Week I, Week II, Week III, and Week IV. How will you know which week you are in?

Make a phone call to a priest, religious, or religious community. Tell them that you are going to be praying the Divine Office. Ask them what week we are currently in (Week I, II, III, or IV). Turn to that week in the Psalter. Find today's day of the week. **Look for Morning Prayer for today. Put your Psalter bookmark at that spot.**

If it is still morning when you do this, pray Morning Prayer for today. **If it is evening, move your Psalter bookmark ahead to Evening Prayer** for today and pray Evening Prayer. And if it is in between, choose one or the other office to pray!

GENERAL TECHNIQUE
for Praying Morning and Evening Prayer

Make the Sign of the Cross.

Beginning of Office of Morning Prayer

Say, "Lord, open my lips."
Respond, "And my mouth will proclaim your praise."
Pray the Antiphon for the Invitatory.
Pray the Invitatory as taught in Lesson 24.
End the Invitatory with the "Glory Be" prayed in full.

Beginning of Office of Evening Prayer

Say, "God, come to my assistance."
Respond, "Lord, make haste to help me."
Pray the "Glory Be" all the way through to the end.
Say "Alleluia." (Omit "Alleluia" during Lent.)

Both Offices Continue As Follows:

Sing, chant, or recite the Hymn you have chosen.

Pray Antiphon I.
Pray the first Psalm or Canticle (or section thereof).
Pray the "Glory Be"
Say the Psalm-Prayer if one follows.
Repeat Antiphon 1.

Pause briefly for silent reflection.

Pray Antiphon 2.
Pray the second Psalm or Canticle (or section thereof).

Say the "Glory Be."
Say the Psalm-Prayer if one follows.
Repeat Antiphon 2.

Pause briefly for silent reflection.

Say Antiphon 3.
Pray the third Psalm or Canticle (or section thereof).
Pray the "Glory Be."
Pray the Psalm-Prayer if one follows.
Repeat Antiphon 3.

Pause briefly for silent reflection.

continued from previous page . . .

Read the Reading.

Read the Responsory, following the guidelines in Lesson 13.

Pause briefly for silent reflection.

Pray the Antiphon for the Canticle of Zechariah (Morning Prayer) or the Canticle of Mary (Evening Prayer).

Pray the Canticle all the way through as taught in Lessons 22 and 23.

Pray the full "Glory Be."

Repeat the Antiphon for the Canticle of Zechariah (Morning Prayer) or the Canticle of Mary (Evening Prayer).

Pause briefly for silent reflection.

Pray the Intercessions.

Recite the Our Father.

Pray the Concluding Prayer.

End with the Dismissal as written on the Psalter bookmark, ending with the Sign of the Cross.

EXTRA PRACTICE FOR WISE DODOS: Before moving on in this instruction, you might want to take two full weeks of practice to pray Morning and Evening Prayer for Monday, Tuesday, Wednesday, Thursday, and Friday, using the offices from the Psalter for Ordinary Time. Ignore the Saturday and Sunday offices for now. If you complete Week IV of the Psalter, you know what to do. Go back to Week I.

And remember to continue to pray Night Prayer every night.

When you are comfortable praying Morning, Evening, and Night Prayer, as instructed so far, then be my guest and proceed with these instructions.

SECTION FIVE

Praying Morning and Evening Prayer on Saturdays and Sundays During Ordinary Time

"In this section, you'll learn about . . ."

- **Saturday Morning and Evening Prayer**
- **The Proper of Seasons**
- **Sunday Offices in Ordinary Time**
- **Strophes and Singing**
- **The Canticle of Daniel**

SECTION FIVE: PRAYING MORNING AND EVENING PRAYER ON SATURDAYS AND SUNDAYS DURING ORDINARY TIME

Lesson 30: Saturday Morning Prayer and Saturday Evening Prayer (Sunday, Evening Prayer I)

If you have a four-volume breviary, use all four-volumes for these instructions.

Get those dodo dancing feet ready. Why? Because we are going to learn some fancy footwork here.

Open your breviary to Saturday Morning Prayer, Week I and examine it closely. Does it look like the same format for Monday, Tuesday, Wednesday, Thursday, and Friday Morning Prayer?

Now look at Saturday Morning Prayer for Weeks II, III, and IV. Do these look like the same formats for the Morning Prayers of the week?

That was just a warm up jig because Saturday Morning Prayer is prayed in exactly the same manner as Morning Prayer on the weekdays.

We are getting ready for some new side steps here. Look for Saturday Evening Prayer, Week I. Cannot find it? Remember why not? Good for you! You cannot find Saturday Evening prayer because **Saturday Evening Prayer is marked Sunday, Evening Prayer I.**

Look in your breviary for Week I, Sunday, Evening Prayer I. Look carefully at the order of the office. What do you notice about the Canticle of Mary? What do you notice about the prayer following the Our Father?

> **DODO
> SELF CHECK #30**
>
> 1. Compare praying Saturday Morning Prayer with praying Morning Prayer on the weekdays. How are they similar?
>
> 2. What parts of the office are not printed in the Psalter for Sunday Evening Prayer I, Sunday Morning Prayer, and Sunday Evening Prayer II? Where are these parts located?

You will notice that these spots refer you to a section of the breviary called "THE PROPER OF SEASONS." Oh, no! What is that? Where is that? We will dance over there in a bit, but we are not ready to leave this part of the ballroom yet. Keep dancing along through the Week I offices to Sunday Morning Prayer and Sunday Evening Prayer II. What do these say at the Canticle of Mary, the Canticle of Zechariah, and the Prayer following the Our Father?

Move ahead through your breviary to Weeks II, III, and IV, looking at Sunday Evening Prayer I, Sunday Morning Prayer, and Sunday Evening Prayer II. What is similar about all of them? What is different?

Lesson 31: The Proper of Seasons

Are you anxious to know what the Proper of Seasons is? It has the word "seasons" in it. Is that a clue?

THE PROPER OF SEASONS is the section of the Psalter that contains various parts of offices that change with the week and season of the year. Makes sense, right?

So where is the Proper of Seasons?

Turn to the ever popular Table of Contents in the front of your breviary. Look for the Proper of Seasons. Read all the subheadings below it. What do you notice? Keep track of them. Why? Hint: See Question 2 of the Dodo Self Check.

Now turn to the Proper of Seasons in the breviary and page through it. What do you notice? **Place the Proper of Seasons bookmark anywhere in the Proper of Seasons.**

DODO SELF CHECK #31

1. What is the Proper of Seasons? Where is it in your breviary?

2. List five things you notice about the Proper of Seasons.

3. What is your first reaction upon studying this section of the breviary? Most people feel like they have been tossed into the middle of a Hollywood musical and they do not have the foggiest idea about the choreography. Not to worry. Pretty soon you will be high stepping with the best of them.

If you have a four-volume breviary, page through the Proper of Seasons in all four-volumes of your breviary. What season does Volume I cover? Volume II? Volume III? Volume IV?

Still dancing? Good for you!

Lesson 32: Sunday Offices in Ordinary Time

If you have a four-volume breviary, use the two volumes for Ordinary Time for this instruction.

Find the Proper of Seasons in your breviary's Table of Contents. Look under the Proper of Seasons to find the section(s) marked Ordinary Time. Turn to the section(s). Page through them, looking at the numbers of the weeks. **The guide words at the tops of the pages will help you find your place in the Proper of Seasons.** How many weeks are there in Ordinary Time? Thirty-four, right? Numbered in order from 1 to 34. That was fairly easy!

What is Ordinary Time? **Ordinary Time is the season of the Church Year that is not a Lenten/Easter or Advent/Christmas season. Ordinary Time begins following the end of the Christmas season and is interrupted by Lent/Easter, resuming again following Pentecost.**

Use the Table of Contents to look for the First Sunday of Ordinary Time in the Proper of Seasons. Can you find it? No? Did your breviary publisher inadvertently leave it out? Do you have a defective breviary?

No, all is well. You will not find the First Sunday of Ordinary Time because the Baptism of the Lord takes place on the First Sunday of Ordinary Time. How about that?

So where is the Baptism of the Lord? It is the very last day of celebration for the Christmas Season.

Here is where we diverge a bit. Depending on your breviary, complete the following:

One-volume Breviary Instruction

In one-volume breviaries, you will notice a prayer under the title "First Week of Ordinary Time" that follows the Baptism of the Lord. The prayer reads,

"Father of love,
hear our prayers.
Help us to know your will
and to do it with courage and faith.
Grant this through our Lord Jesus Christ, you Son,
who lives and reigns with you and the Holy Spirit,
one God, for ever and ever."

This prayer is all that you will see under the heading "First Week of Ordinary Time." The next heading will be "Second Sunday in Ordinary Time."

Why is this prayer here? This prayer is the Concluding Prayer for the Office of Readings for the First Week in Ordinary Time. We will discuss how to pray the Office of Readings later in this manual. Since we are not praying the Office of Readings now, you can ignore this prayer for the time being.

Now look for the Second Sunday of Ordinary Time. It will be right after the Baptism of the Lord. What do you notice about this Sunday? Look at the Third, Fourth, Fifth, and Sixth Sundays of Ordinary Time. How are these similar to the Second Sunday? How are they different?

Four-volume Breviary Instruction

If you have a four-volume breviary, take Volume III for the first seventeen weeks of Ordinary Time and page through the Proper of Seasons. Look for the First Week of Ordinary Time. You will see a title for each day of the week and below that the words "Office of Readings." Under the "Office of Readings," you will find a First Reading followed by a Responsory and then a Second Reading followed by another Responsory and then a Prayer.

Look at the Office of Readings for Monday through Saturday of the First Week of Ordinary Time. Find the Concluding Prayer for the Office

of Readings for each day of the First Week of Ordinary Time. You will see that it is the very same prayer printed above under the instruction for one-volume breviaries.

Now look ahead to the Second Sunday in Ordinary Time. Do you see the heading Evening Prayer I with the Canticle of Mary and Prayer printed beneath it? Now page through the Office of Readings for the Second Sunday in Ordinary Time until you come to the heading Morning Prayer. What do you see under this heading? Now page ahead and look for Evening Prayer II. What do you see under this heading?

Page through the Proper of Seasons looking at the Second Week of Ordinary Time. Compare the offices for the days of the week with the offices for the Third Sunday of Ordinary Time. Now look quickly through the Proper of Seasons in all four-volumes of your breviary. What do you see?

You will see that, in the four-volume breviary, every single day has two long Readings for the Office of Readings. The Readings for the Office of Readings are printed first in each office in the Proper of Seasons. You will learn how to pray the Office of Readings later in this manual. For right now, skip all the Offices of Readings that are printed in the Proper of Seasons.

Now we wish to focus on the Sunday offices of Evening Prayer I, Morning Prayer, and Evening Prayer II. Find these offices for the Fourth, Fifth, and Sixth Sundays of Ordinary Time.

Instruction for All Breviaries (One- or Four-volume)

OK. All breviary users are back together again in one disco. Before joining this dance, you might want to polka back to review Lesson 30. Here is what you will find there:

DODO
SELF CHECK #32

1. What is the season of Ordinary Time? When does it begin? How many weeks are in Ordinary Time? What breaks up Ordinary Time? When does it resume?

2. What is the First Sunday of Ordinary Time?

3. What parts of the Sunday Offices are in the Proper of Seasons?

4. How does one pray the Alternative Prayer?

For the Sundays of Ordinary Time (Sunday Evening Prayer I, Sunday Morning Prayer I, and Sunday Evening Prayer II), the Antiphons for the Canticle of Mary and the Canticle of Zechariah and the Concluding Prayer of the Sunday offices are printed in the Proper of Seasons.

You have the Proper of Seasons marked with a bookmark. Look again for the Second Sunday in Ordinary Time. Some (not all) breviaries print both a prayer and an ALTERNATIVE PRAYER. **When praying the offices for Sunday, you may choose as a Concluding Prayer either the Prayer, which is the prayer usually said, or the ALTERNATIVE PRAYER. Only one of these prayers is prayed in each office.**

Lesson 33: Strophes and Singing

A what-phe? Dodos were curious birds. So be curious about stophes and keep dancing. You are going to learn some tunes to dance to!

Find the Sunday offices for Week II in the Psalter. Turn to Evening Prayer for Sunday, Week II. There are, as always, three Psalms and/or Canticles. Turn to the third which is a Canticle from the Book of Revelation, Chapter 19, verses 1 to 7. Look over this Canticle. Do you see "Alleluia" sometimes written in parentheses, perhaps with a capital "R" before it? What do you think that means?

Most breviaries contain some instruction right before the Canticle begins. If yours does, read the instruction. It probably says, "The following Canticle is said with the Alleluia when Evening Prayer is sung; when the office is recited, the Alleluia may be said at the beginning and end of each strophe."

There is that word again. What is a strophe (pronounced "stro-fee")? **A STROPHE is one section of the Psalm or Canticle. You would probably call it a verse. A space separates one strophe from the next.**

Look again at the Canticle from Revelation 19:1-7. The first strophe, as printed in your breviary, is

> Alleluia.
> Salvation, glory, and power to our God:
> (R. Alleluia)
> his judgments are honest and true.
> R. Alleluia (Alleluia).

A space separates this strophe from the second strophe. How many strophes are there in this Canticle? Yes, four.

All Psalms and Canticles are divided into strophes. Look at the first Psalm for Sunday Evening Prayer II, Week II. It is Psalm 110:1-5, 7. How many strophes in that Psalm? Right-o. Six.

Now look at the second Psalm, Psalm 115. How many strophes does it have? Nine-o, baby!

Well, how about that? You have been praying strophes right along and did not know it! How about that!

Now read again the instruction that precedes the Canticle from Revelation. The instruction tells you that, if you sing the Evening Prayer, you are to sing all the Alleluias. If you recite the office, you are to skip those Alleluias that are in paren-

> **DODO**
> **SELF CHECK #33**
> 1. What is a strophe? How can you tell how many strophes are in a Psalm or Canticle?
> 2. How would you pray the Canticle from Revelation 19:1-7?

theses. If it is OK with you, since we have been reciting the office, we will skip the Alleluias that are in parentheses. And if it is not OK and you want to sing, you go right ahead.

PRACTICE: Pray this Canticle through as if you were <u>reciting</u> it. Therefore, skip all the Alleluias in parentheses, unless you really want to sing. In which case, be my guest.

Lesson 34: Praying the Sunday Offices for the Second Week in Ordinary Time (Part One)

Still dancing? Good for you!

Turn to the Proper of Seasons. **Move the Proper of Seasons bookmark to mark the spot for the Second Sunday in Ordinary Time.** Right under the words "Second Sunday in Ordinary Time," your breviary has printed the words, "Psalter, Week II." This means that the Sunday offices for the Second Sunday in Ordinary Time are the Sunday offices for Week II of the Psalter. Pretty clever way to clue you in, right?

Look in the Psalter for Week II, Sunday Evening Prayer I. This will be the very first office for Week II. **Move the Psalter bookmark to this spot.** Time for a memory check. Is this office prayed on Saturday or on Sunday evening?

Sunday Evening Prayer I is prayed on Saturday evening. Did you remember that?

Page through Sunday Evening Prayer I for Week II. If you have a one-volume breviary, you will notice that the Psalms have a variety of Antiphons listed for Advent, certain Sundays in Lent, and Easter.

If you are using a four-volume breviary, you are using Volume III (Ordinary Time) and you will not see these Antiphons. That is because, in the four-volume breviary, these Antiphons are in the appropriate Lent/Easter and Advent/Christmas volumes.

Time for some pretending if today happens to fall in the Advent/Christmas or Lent/Easter season. Since we are going to practice praying Sunday offices for Ordinary Time, we are going to pretend it is Ordinary Time even if it is not. Therefore, we will ignore all seasonal Antiphons for now. Later on you will get to pretend it is Lent/Easter or Advent/Christmas even if it is not.

Keep paging through Sunday Evening Prayer I for Week II until you come to the Antiphon for the Canticle of Mary. Whoops! No Antiphon. Remember why? That's right, the Antiphon is in the Proper of Seasons.

Your Proper of Seasons bookmark should mark the Second Sunday in Ordinary Time in the Proper of Seasons. Good for you if it is still there. Turn there now. Do you see the Antiphon for the Canticle of Mary under Evening Prayer I?

Now use your Psalter bookmark to turn back to the Psalter. Look for the Concluding Prayer for Sunday Evening Prayer I, Week II. Oh, no. Not there. Where does the breviary refer you?

Flip back to the Proper of Seasons bookmark. In a one-volume breviary, you will not see a prayer after Evening Prayer I *(it is written there in the four-volume breviary)*. In a one-volume breviary, only one prayer (and possibly an alternative prayer) is written. It is placed after the Morning Prayer heading. *In a four-volume breviary, there is also only one prayer printed after the Morning Prayer heading. If you have a four-volume breviary, page ahead to the Morning Prayer heading for the Second Sunday in Ordinary Time.* **The prayer written after the Morning Prayer heading in the Proper of Seasons is the same prayer said for Evening Prayer I, Morning Prayer, and Evening Prayer II for that day.** The prayer is not written again to avoid repetition and to save paper. But, then, you already knew that!

The conclusion of these concluding office prayers is printed on the preprinted Proper of Seasons bookmark. Add it to your home-made bookmark by writing "Grant this (We ask this) through our Lord Jesus Christ, your Son, who lives and reigns with you and the Holy Spirit, one God, for ever and ever. May the Lord bless us, protect us from all evil, and bring us to everlasting life. Amen. (Sign of the Cross prayed silently)."

Look in the Psalter for Sunday Morning Prayer Week II. Where is the Antiphon for the Canticle of Zechariah? Yes. Proper of Seasons. Can you find it under the Second Sunday of Ordinary Time?

Return to the Psalter. Where is the prayer that you will say to conclude Morning Prayer? Page ahead in the Psalter to Sunday Evening Prayer II for Week II. Where is the Antiphon for the Canticle of Mary? Where is the Concluding Prayer?

Do you get the hang of this two-step rumba? Proper of Seasons to Psalter to Proper of Seasons to Psalter.

In order to pray Sunday Evening Prayer I, Sunday Morning Prayer, and Sunday Evening Prayer II, you must go to the Proper of Seasons for the Antiphons for the Canticles of Mary and Zechariah and for the Concluding Prayer. Use the bookmarks to help you rumba along through the breviary.

Lesson 35: Praying the Sunday Offices for the Second Week in Ordinary Time (Part Two)

Have you, like a wise dodo, been praying the weekday offices for Monday, Tuesday, Wednesday, Thursday, and Friday as suggested in Lesson 29? I hope so. Because if you have, you are familiar with the order of these offices and how to pray the Invitatory, the Canticle of Zechariah, and the Canticle of Mary. The Sunday offices are prayed in exactly the same manner except that you must refer to the Proper of Seasons for the Antiphons for the Canticles of Mary and Zechariah and for the Concluding Prayer.

━ ━·━·━·━·━·━·━

PRACTICE: No matter what season of the year it is, practice praying the three Sunday offices for Ordinary Time. For the best chance of success, we suggest this schedule:

Move the Hymn bookmark to an appropriate Hymn.

Move the Psalter bookmark to Sunday Evening Prayer I, Week II in the Psalter.

Move the Proper of Seasons bookmark to the Second Sunday of Ordinary Time in the Proper of Seasons.

Day One: Pray Sunday Evening Prayer I for the Second Sunday of Ordinary Time.

Day Two: Pray Sunday Morning Prayer for the Second Sunday of Ordinary Time.

Day Three: Pray Sunday Evening Prayer II for the Second Sunday of Ordinary Time.

TECHNIQUE
for praying the Sunday Offices (Sunday Evening Prayer I,
Sunday Morning Prayer, and Sunday Evening Prayer II):

Put the Psalter bookmark in the correct place in the Psalter.

Put the Proper of Seasons bookmark in the correct place in the Proper of Seasons.

Choose a Hymn for the office that you will be saying and mark it with the Hymn bookmark.

The ribbons should be in place in the breviary (silver—Canticle of Zechariah; white—Invitatory; blue—Canticle of Mary)

Turn to the Psalter.

Begin the office following the format that you have written on the front of the Psalter bookmark.

For Morning Prayer, follow the format that you learned in Lesson 26.

For Evening Prayer, follow the format that you learned in Lesson 27.

When you get to the Antiphons for the Canticle of Mary and the Canticle of Zechariah, refer to the Proper of Seasons. Use the ribbons to locate the Canticles.

Continue with the offices as written in the Psalter.

Conclude with the Concluding Prayer written in the Proper of Seasons.

End the office as written on the Proper of Seasons bookmark.

Now move the Psalter bookmark to Sunday Evening Prayer I, Week IV in the Psalter.

Move the Proper of Seasons bookmark to the Fourth Sunday of Ordinary Time in the Proper of Seasons.

Move the Hymn bookmark to an appropriate Hymn.

Day Four: Pray Sunday Evening Prayer I for the Fourth Sunday of Ordinary Time.

Day Five: Pray Sunday Morning Prayer for the Fourth Sunday of Ordinary Time.

Day Six: Pray Sunday Evening Prayer II for the Fourth Sunday of Ordinary Time.

Here is a word to the wise dodos among you. Be very comfortable praying all three Sunday offices before proceeding with these instructions. Check back with, or repeat, some or all of Lessons 30 through 35 if you wish. If you want to learn to pray the Divine Office successfully, then before you continue with these instructions, you must be able to pray with relative ease all of the offices learned so far.

Lesson 36: The Canticle of Daniel 3:57-88, 56

Time for a memory jog. As you have learned, **all the Psalms and Canticles in the Psalter, with one exception, end with the prayer "Glory Be." The "Glory Be" is prayed at the end of the Psalms and Canticles even though it is not written in the breviary.**

> **TECHNIQUE**
> To pray the Canticle of Daniel 3:57-88, 56, first pray the Antiphon for the Canticle. Then pray the Canticle all the way through, but do not pray the Glory Be. Pray the Antiphon again.

Did you wonder about that exception? Now it is time to learn about it.

Look in the Psalter for Sunday Morning Prayer, Week I. Find the Canticle of Daniel 3:57-88, 56. Read this through to the end.

Does your breviary end this Canticle with a note saying that the "Glory Be to the Father" is not said at the Canticle's end?

Go to the Table of Contents. Find the section marked Psalter. Turn to the page marked Week III. Page forward until you reach Sunday Morning Prayer for Week III. Look under Sunday Morning Prayer, Week III, for the Canticle of Daniel. Yes. That is the same Canticle as in Sunday Morning Prayer Week I. And the breviary has the same ending note to the Canticle, too.

> **DODO**
> **SELF CHECK #36**
>
> 1. When is the Glory Be prayed in the Psalter?
>
> 2. After which Canticle is the Glory Be not prayed? Where can you find this Canticle in the Psalter?
>
> 3. The Psalter contains two other Canticles from the Book of Daniel. Is the Glory Be prayed after these?

The **CANTICLE OF DANIEL 3:57-88, 56 is the only Canticle in the Psalter after which the "Glory Be" is not prayed.** Why not? Because the Canticle ends with a Hymn of high praise to God that is similar to the "Glory Be." Admittedly, the text "Let us bless the Father, and the Son, and the Holy Spirit" is not in the Canticle of Daniel in Scripture. No one in Daniel's time even suspected that the Son and the Holy Spirit existed! The Church inserted this phrase in praise of the Trinity into the text of the Canticle for the Divine Office. And rightly so! The Canticle praises God's creation, so it is only right that we praise God in all Three Persons of the Trinity!

The Psalter contains two other Canticles from the Biblical Book of Daniel, Daniel 3:52-57 and Daniel 3: 26, 27, 29, and 34-41. The "Glory Be" is prayed after these other Canticles of Daniel.

— · — · — · — · — · — · —

PRACTICE: Turn to Sunday Morning Prayer Week I in the Psalter and pray the Canticle of Daniel with its Antiphons.

SECTION SIX
Praying Morning, Evening, and Night Prayer throughout the Seasons of the Church Year

"In this section, you'll learn about . . ."

- The Seasons of the Church Year
- Navigating the Seasons in the Breviary
- Invitatory Antiphons for Lent/Easter
- Invitatory Antiphons for Advent/Christmas
- Hymns for Lent/Easter
- Hymns for Advent/Christmas
- Using the Proper of Seasons

SECTION SIX: PRAYING MORNING, EVENING, AND NIGHT PRAYER THROUGHOUT THE SEASONS OF THE CHURCH YEAR

If you have a four-volume breviary, you will need all four-volumes to complete these lessons.

Lesson 37: The Four-volume Breviary (Part One)

This instruction is only for those who have a four-volume breviary. If you have a one-volume breviary, you may skip this section and proceed to Lesson 40. If you have a four-volume breviary, complete this lesson and the two following before proceeding to Lesson 40. They are not difficult lessons, but they are important.

The four-volume breviary is actually one massive breviary that is printed in four volumes *because it would be too large and cumbersome to be in one volume. You already knew that, right? In the instructions that follow, when you are told to "page through your breviary," you must take this to mean that you must "page through all four-volumes of your breviary" until you find the section that is being discussed in the lesson. If the lesson says to "page through Ordinary Time until you come to Lent" or to another season of the Church year, then you will need to find the volume that has that season in it.*

In order to do this, you will have to know which volume of your breviary covers which season of the year. Makes sense, right?

Some breviaries print the season of the year on the front outside cover of each volume, either on the front cover or on the spine of the book. If yours does, one outside cover will be marked "Lent/Easter," another "Christmas/Advent," one "Ordinary Time/Weeks 1-17" and another "Ordinary Time/Weeks 18-34." The volume number should also be printed on the cover. You are lucky and do not have to do one thing more here to distinguish your breviaries.

Some four-volume breviaries are color coded for different seasons of the year. If your breviary is color coded, what colors are each of the seasons?

Can you think of any way to associate the color with its corresponding season so that you will remember which season is in which color volume?

Some four-volume breviaries, however, are not color coded nor do they have the titles printed on the volume covers. If your breviary is like this, do not fret. We can mark the breviaries so you can easily distinguish one from the other.

Take all four volumes and open each to the title page right in the front of the book. Your breviary may have two title pages, one with just "The Liturgy of the Hours" or the words "The Divine Office" written on it and a following page that has the same title but more information including the publisher at the bottom of the page. It is this more extensive title page that you must find.

Look at all four title pages. The seasons of the year are written on each title page. What season does Volume I cover? Volume II? Volume III? Volume IV?

You might want to use a permanent marking pen to write the season and volume number on the front outside cover of the breviary. On the cover of the Lent/Easter breviary you might write, "Lent/Easter" and put the volume number. On the cover of the Christmas/Advent breviary, you might write, "Christmas/Advent" and the volume number. You might mark the covers of the Ordinary Time breviaries with the words "Ordinary Time/Weeks 1-17" and "Ordinary Time/Weeks 18-34" and the volume numbers. Or you

DODO SELF CHECK #37

1. Is the four-volume breviary "four different breviaries" or is it really "one breviary in four volumes?" If this manual asks you to "page through your breviary," will you page through one volume or through all four volumes?

2. How can you tell which of the four volumes to use by looking at your breviary's cover?

3. If one of the following instructions tells you to "page through the Ordinary Time offices of your breviary until you come to Lent," are you going to find Lent in the volume with Ordinary Time? Where are the Lenten offices?

4. If one of the following instructions tells you to "page through the offices of Ordinary Time until you come to Advent," will you find the Advent offices in the volume with Ordinary Time? Where are the Advent offices?

might prefer to write the season on a piece of paper and tape it to your breviary's outside cover. Being able to distinguish the breviaries will help you to find quickly the breviary that you need for this instruction.

Lesson 38: The Four-volume Breviary (Part Two)

In order to proceed with the instruction in this book, it is best to have each volume of the four-volume breviary marked with ribbons and bookmarks. Refer to the Introduction to order or to make three more sets. When you have four sets of ribbons and bookmarks, you can complete this lesson.

First we will work with the ribbons.

Take each of the volumes of your breviary. Look in the Table of Contents for the Ordinary. In the Ordinary of each volume:

a. Find the Invitatory Psalm. Mark it with a white ribbon.

b. Find the Canticle of Zechariah. Mark it with a silver ribbon.

c. Find the Canticle of Mary. Mark it with a blue ribbon.

d. Find the Antiphons in honor of the Blessed Mother, following the Night Prayer offices. Mark these with a purple ribbon.

e. Find the Night Prayer hymns. Mark these with an orange ribbon.

f. The four-volume breviary does not have Prayers of Forgiveness. It does, however, have a Poetry Section in the back of each volume. If you like, you can use a black ribbon to mark the Poetry Section.

Now we will work with the bookmarks.

Bookmark Night Prayer in each volume.

Bookmark the Hymn Index in each volume.

Bookmark the Hymns. In Ordinary Time, the Hymns are printed in the Psalter on each day. However, in Advent/Christmas (Volume I) and Lent/Easter (Volume II), the Hymns are printed all together in the Proper of Seasons (not in the Psalter). Place the Hymn bookmarks in Volumes I and II. You will find the Hymns at the very beginning of the Proper of Seasons in these volumes. You only need one Hymn bookmark for each

*volume even though the Lenten and Advent Hymns are in a different spot
from the Easter and Christmas Hymns. This is because you will be singing
these Hymns at the appropriate seasons, and you can move your bookmark as needed.*

Bookmark the Psalter in each volume.

Bookmark the Proper of Seasons in each volume.

*From now on, whenever you are told to mark a section of the breviary
with a ribbon or a bookmark, mark <u>all four volumes</u> of your breviary.*

Whew! That is done! Give yourself a well-deserved pat on the back.

Lesson 39: The Four-volume Breviary (Part Three)

*You are moving right along and doing a great job! It is time to com-
pare the Psalters of each volume. In <u>each</u> of the four volumes, find the
Psalter. In each volume, find Tuesday Evening Prayer, Week III. Move the
Psalter bookmark in <u>each</u> volume to Tuesday Evening Prayer, Week III.
First compare the office in the two volumes for Ordinary Time. What is
the same about the Tuesday Evening Prayer Office for Week III in both
volumes of Ordinary Time? What is different? Everything is the same.
Nothing is different. It is the <u>same</u> office.*

*Now compare Tuesday Evening Prayer, Week III, in the Ordinary
Time volumes with Tuesday Evening Prayer, Week III, in the Lent/Easter
and Christmas/Advent volumes. Compare the Hymn, Antiphons, Psalms,
Psalm-Prayers, Canticles. Do you see that, in certain seasons, the
Antiphons differ from those during Ordinary Time?*

*Now do not start giving up here because you feel a little confused.
Confusion is normal for dodos at this stage of the game. You are just
exploring what is in the Psalter. You do not have to memorize anything.*

*Now in each volume page through Tuesday Evening Prayer, Week III,
until you reach the end of the Canticle of Revelation and its ending
Antiphon. In the volumes for Ordinary Time, what parts of the office follow this Antiphon? Do these same parts of the office follow the Antiphon
in the Lent/Easter and Advent/Christmas volumes?*

In the Advent/Christmas volume, you are referred to the Proper of Seasons for the rest of the office. In the Lent/Easter volume, you are referred to the "Office of the day" for the remainder of the office. The "Office of the day" is in the Proper of Seasons as well.

Now compare, in all four volumes, these offices:
Friday, Morning Prayer, Week I
Thursday, Evening Prayer, Week II
Wednesday, Morning Prayer, Week IV
What is the same about each office in each volume? What differs?

By this comparison, you should realize that <u>when you are in a particular season of the year, every part of the Divine Office that you will need will be in the volume for that season. You will NOT EVER use TWO OR MORE volumes at once. You will only have to flip to different parts of one volume in order to pray the Divine Office for that season of the Church year</u>. How convenient!

Lesson 40: Seasons of the Church Year

Remember when we talked about the Seasons of the Church year? They are not summer, fall, winter, spring! The Church year is divided into special seasons of worship. So the Church year does not begin on January 1 like a secular year does. **The Church Year begins with the first Sunday of Advent. The seasons of the Church year are, in order:**

> **DODO**
> **SELF CHECK #40**
>
> 1. When does the Church year begin? How does this differ from what we usually think of as a year?
>
> 2. What are the seasons of the Church year? How do these differ from what we usually think of as seasons?

Advent
Christmas ending with the Baptism of the Lord
Ordinary Time
Lent
Easter ending with Pentecost
Continuation of Ordinary Time until first Sunday of Advent.

The Divine Office follows this cycle.

Lesson 41: The Divine Office during the Seasons of the Church Year

You will be happy to know that praying the Divine Office during the various seasons of the Church year is somewhat like praying the Sunday Offices during Ordinary Time.

Do you recall how, when praying the Sunday Offices (Sunday Evening Prayer I, Sunday Morning Prayer, and Sunday Evening Prayer II), you did the two-step rumba by flipping back and forth from the Psalter to the Proper of Seasons to find the Antiphons for the Canticles of Zechariah and Mary and also to find the Concluding Prayer? When praying the Office during Lent/Easter and Advent/Christmas you will be doing the two-step rumba every day. You will have to flip to the Proper of Seasons to find certain parts of some of the offices.

Let us see how this works. **During Ordinary Time, use the Psalter first. Refer to the Proper of Seasons only when told to go there.** So, in the Psalter, look up Wednesday Morning Prayer, Week II. Pretend that it is Ordinary Time. Page through this office. Is there any place in this office that refers you to the Proper of Seasons for Ordinary Time? There is no place. To pray Wednesday Morning Prayer, Week II, for Ordinary Time, the Psalter is sufficient. **Place the Psalter bookmark at Wednesday Morning Prayer, Week II.**

> **TECHNIQUE**
> **On how to treat the Proper of Seasons in praying the Divine Office:**
>
> **During Ordinary Time,** use the Psalter first. Refer to the Proper of Seasons only when told to go there.
>
> **During Lent/Easter and Advent/Christmas,** use the Proper of Seasons first. For the parts not in the Proper of Seasons, refer to the Psalter unless directed by the breviary to refer elsewhere.
>
> A convenient reminder regarding this technique is printed on the pre-printed Proper of Seasons bookmark. Print it on your homemade bookmark to remind you.

Now hang on because things are going to get a little complicated. But you can learn the technique if you can remember one word. REPLACE. Let us say it again. REPLACE. Got it?

REPLACE.

Let us go on. Wednesday Morning Prayer, Week II, is also the office prayed on Wednesday Morning during Holy Week. Holy Week, you will recall, is the last week of Lent, immediately preceding Easter. **During Lent/Easter and Advent/Christmas, use the Proper of Seasons first. For the parts <u>not</u> in the Proper of Seasons, refer to the Psalter unless directed by the breviary to refer elsewhere.**

How does this work? Remember that key word? REPLACE. First find Wednesday Morning Prayer of Holy Week in the Proper of Seasons. *In the four-volume breviary, Holy Week is in the Lent/Easter Volume.*

Use the Table of Contents to locate the Lenten and Holy Week offices in the Proper of Seasons. Page through this section until you find Wednesday Morning Prayer of Holy Week. **The guide words at the top of the pages will help you find your place in the Proper of Seasons. Move the Proper of Seasons bookmark to Wednesday Morning Prayer of Holy Week.** Look through this office in the Proper of Seasons. Now say that key word three times: REPLACE. REPLACE. REPLACE. <u>Every single part of the office that is written here, in the Proper of Seasons, will REPLACE those same parts in the Psalter. If a part is not</u>

**DODO
SELF CHECK #41**

1. How does one use the Proper of Seasons and the Psalter during Ordinary Time?

2. How does one use the Proper of Seasons and Psalter during Lent/Easter and Advent/Christmas?

3. How can you use the guidewords in the Proper of Seasons?

4. In your breviary, what parts of the office for Wednesday Morning of Holy Week are written in the Proper of Seasons and which are written in the Psalter?

5. What is the key word to remember in praying the offices during certain seasons of the Church year? Why is that word key?

written here, in the Proper of Seasons, refer to the Psalter.

Compare the Psalter for Wednesday Morning Prayer, Week II, with Wednesday Morning Prayer of Holy Week. Some one-volume breviaries have certain parts of the Wednesday Morning Prayer for Holy Week written in the Psalter but in a different type and so marked as being for Holy Week. Other one-volume breviaries and most four-volume breviaries have all the parts for Wednesday of Holy Week written in the Proper of Seasons. What is the format of your breviary?

And what is that key word again?

Lesson 42: Invitatory Antiphons during Lent/ Easter and Advent/Christmas

You know the key word. REPLACE. We are going to start talking about some of the times we will be REPLACING one part of the office with another. Ready to dive in?

One REPLACEMENT is the Invitatory Antiphons. **Lent/Easter and Advent/Christmas use special Antiphons for the Invitatory Psalm.** Want to find out where they are?

How about starting with Wednesday Morning Prayer, Week II? Is any Invitatory Antiphon written there for Holy

> **DODO
> SELF CHECK #42**
>
> 1. Which two seasons of the year use special Invitatory Antiphons?
>
> 2. In your breviary, where are these Antiphons found?
>
> 3. How can you remember to use them?

Week? If so, great. If not, look at Wednesday Morning Prayer for Holy Week in the Proper of Seasons. Is any Invitatory Antiphon written there? If so, great. If not, now what?

Many breviaries do not write out in the Psalter or in the Proper of Seasons the Antiphons for the Invitatory Psalm for Lent/Easter and Advent/Christmas. But they are in the breviary. Honest.

There is one other logical place to look. Any idea where? Yes! The Invitatory Psalm.

Use the white ribbon to find the Invitatory Psalm, Psalm 95, in your breviary. If you have been praying Morning Prayer for Ordinary Time, you have been praying this Psalm. Look at the several paragraphs immediately preceding Psalm 95 in the Ordinary. Read these. What have you found?

The Antiphons for the Invitatory Psalm for Lent/Easter and Advent/Christmas are printed immediately preceding Psalm 95 in the Ordinary.

Did your breviary very kindly indicate, either in the Psalter or in the Proper of Seasons, that there were special Invitatory Antiphons for Lent/Easter and Advent/Christmas? Probably not. This is one thing you are just supposed to "know." Well, now you know! But if you forget, on the preprinted Proper of Seasons bookmark is printed a reminder regarding the location of the Lent/Easter and Advent/Christmas Invitatory Antiphons. Print a reminder on your homemade bookmark, too.

Lesson 43: Hymns during Lent/Easter and Advent/Christmas

Ready to sing? We are going to try out some new Hymns. What are they and where are they?

During Lent/Easter and Advent/Christmas, certain Hymns are sung with certain offices. Other offices allow you to select an appropriate Hymn from several suggested ones. Lent/Easter and Advent/Christmas Hymns are often printed in certain special sections of the breviary. Certain celebrations may have Hymns printed with the office.

Are you ready to find these in your breviary?

If you have a one-volume breviary, use the Table of Contents to find the first page of the Proper of Seasons, which will be the beginning of Advent. *If you have a four-volume breviary, use the volumes for Advent/Christmas and Lent/Easter. Go to the beginning of the Proper of Seasons in each volume.*

Many breviaries list Advent Hymns at the beginning of the Proper of Seasons, telling you that they may be sung before December 17. Of course, if you like them, you may sing them any time, even in August. Only please do not sing them as the Hymn for the Divine Office as they are appropriate in the Office only during their designated season. Other Hymns are traditionally sung after December 17 and still others are used in the Christmas season. Snoop around and see if you can find all these in your breviary.

Page through the Proper of Seasons, looking for actual Hymns printed with an office or referral to certain pages on which Hymns are found. Keep paging through, looking for Hymns, until you come to the beginning of Ordinary Time. Page through Ordinary Time until you come to Lent. Page through the Lent/Easter season, looking for Hymns, until you come again to Ordinary Time. Certain Hymns are used during Lent, others during Holy Week, and others for the Easter Season. Can you find all these in your breviary?

PRACTICE: Use the Proper of Seasons and Hymn sections to find Hymns that you could use for these days:

> December 15
> December 22
> January 5
> Tuesday of the Second Week of Lent
> Good Friday
> Easter Monday

**DODO
SELF CHECK #43**

1. How are the Hymns for Lent/Easter and Advent/Christmas arranged in your breviary?

2. Does your breviary have sections of Hymns for certain seasons? Does it refer you to a Hymn at the beginning of an office? Or does it use a combination of both techniques?

Lesson 44: Practice in Using the Proper of Seasons

If you have a four-volume breviary, use the Lent/Easter volume for this lesson.

Time to pretend again. No matter what season it is, imagine that it is Wednesday morning of Holy Week. You look at the fresh palms from Palm Sunday drying behind the bedroom crucifix, or wherever it is that you put them every year. Then you find your breviary and prepare to pray Morning Prayer.

————————————

PRACTICE: For practice in using the Proper of Seasons, we will pray Wednesday Morning Prayer during Holy Week.

Choose an appropriate Hymn following the guidelines in Lesson 43 and mark it with the Hymn bookmark.

Place the Psalter bookmark at Wednesday Morning Prayer, Week II.

Place the Proper of Seasons bookmark at Wednesday Morning Prayer during Holy Week.

Your silver ribbon should be at the Canticle of Zechariah.

Your white ribbon should be at the Invitatory Psalm. Where is the Antiphon for the Invitatory Psalm? If unsure, read the reminder on the Proper of Seasons bookmark.

Now reread Lesson 41. Remember that, in Lent/Easter and Advent/Christmas, you begin with the Proper of Seasons. Whatever is not in the Proper of Seasons is taken from the Psalter.

Using the bookmarks and ribbons to help you, pray Morning Prayer for Wednesday of Holy Week. When you finish, check how you did against the entire office which is printed in Appendix G. How did you do?

————————————

EXTRA PRACTICE: Pray this office again for extra practice.

SECTION SEVEN

Praying Morning, Evening, and Night Prayer During the Advent and Christmas Seasons

"In this section, you'll learn about . . ."

- Morning and Evening Prayer in Advent
- Morning Prayer in the Christmas Octave
- Evening Prayer in the Christmas Octave
- Night Prayer during the Christmas Octave

SECTION SEVEN: PRAYING MORNING, EVENING, AND NIGHT PRAYER DURING ADVENT/CHRISTMAS

If you have a four-volume breviary, use the volume for Advent/Christmas to do these lessons.

Lesson 45: Morning and Evening Prayer during Advent/Christmas (except the Octave)

The year is fast forwarding. Spring has faded into summer, and summer has drifted into fall. Here it is, Advent already. Where are you in the breviary?

In the Proper of Seasons, turn to the First Sunday of Advent. This will be right at the beginning of the Proper of Seasons since the Church year begins with Advent. The first office of Advent is Sunday, Evening Prayer I. Do you remember that Sunday traditionally began on Saturday evening? If you forgot, refresh your memory by looking back at Lesson 14.

In the Proper of Seasons, carefully study the offices for the First Sunday of Advent (Sunday Evening Prayer I, Sunday Morning Prayer, and Sunday Evening Prayer II). Does your breviary have each office printed separately or does it combine offices? It is important to know this distinction.

If your breviary combines offices, you will know because, for example, under Sunday Evening Prayer I, you will have listed four Antiphons for the Canticle of Mary (Sunday 1, 2, 3, and 4), two sets of Intercessions (Sundays 1 and 3 are the same and Sundays 2 and 4 are the same) and four Concluding Prayers (Sundays 1, 2, 3, and 4). You will pray the

> ### DODO
> ### SELF CHECK #45
>
> 1. Does your breviary combine offices or have each one printed separately?
>
> 2. Where is the Invitatory Antiphon for Advent/Christmas? (Hint: Check the note on the Proper of Seasons bookmark.)

Antiphon, Intercessions, and Concluding Prayer that correspond to the correct Sunday of Advent (1st, 2nd, 3rd, and 4th). Of course!

Lesson 46: Praying Morning Prayer for the Second Sunday of Advent

Advent is moving along, way too fast. Here it is, the Second Sunday of Advent already, and you are not even half way done with Christmas shopping. If only you could slow down time! Mass today will help you gain some perspective. It always does. But before Mass, you want to pray Morning Prayer.

PRACTICE: Pray Morning Prayer for the Second Sunday of Advent. First, set up the breviary.

Select a proper Advent Hymn and move the Hymn bookmark to that spot.

Turn to Week II in the Psalter. Find Sunday Morning Prayer for Week II. Put the Psalter bookmark there. Sunday Morning Prayer Week II is the office used for the Second Sunday of Advent.

In the Proper of Seasons, find the Second Sunday of Advent. Mark that with the Proper of Seasons bookmark.

What color ribbon marks the Invitatory Psalm? Where is the Antiphon for the Invitatory Psalm? Look at the reminder on the Proper of Seasons bookmark if unsure.

What color ribbon marks the Canticle of Zechariah?

Now pray the office of Morning Prayer for the Second Sunday of Advent. Check Appendix H to see how you did.

EXTRA PRACTICE: Pray the office again, using the breviary and checking yourself against Appendix H.

Lesson 47: Morning and Evening Prayer during the Christmas Octave

Time moves on. Christmas has come and gone. You managed to buy all the gifts you wanted to give and even managed to gift wrap them and add bows! You rejoiced at singing the Christmas hymns at Christmas Mass. And now you have moved into the days immediately after Christmas, the Octave.

Christmas is one of the two most solemn and joyous feasts of the Church year, the other being Easter. Therefore its celebration, as well as Easter's, extends through its OCTAVE. **An OCTAVE is the eight days following certain Solemnities.**

The Christmas Octave lasts from Christmas Day until Evening Prayer II of the Solemnity of Mary, the Mother of God, which is celebrated on January 1.

During the Octave, the Church rejoices in the birth of Christ. The offices for the Octave of Christmas reflect this eight-day celebration.

When praying the Divine Office during the Octave of Christmas, look in the Proper of Seasons and follow whatever instructions are given there.

Turn to the Octave of Christmas in the Proper of Seasons. These will be the days between Christmas, December 25, and New Year's, January 1. Look at the offices on these days. You will find instructions for certain parts of the offices of those days, referring you to certain parts of the breviary with the pages given. What are some of the references?

Do not let this search confuse you. Yes, some of these references refer you to certain saints' feasts and you have no clue how

---

DODO SELF CHECK #47

1. What is an Octave?

2. What is the Church celebrating during the Christmas Octave?

3. How are the Morning and Evening Prayer offices unique during the Christmas Octave?

4. How does your breviary help you to pray these offices during the Christmas Octave?

to pray them yet. That is fine because you will learn how to pray those feasts in the next part of this book. For now, simply realize that, **for the Octave of Christmas, your breviary's Proper of Seasons tells you exactly where to go to pray the offices correctly.**

Lesson 48: Night Prayer during the Christmas Octave

Pretend that it is Christmas night. You are tired from a busy day. But before you go to sleep, you wish to spend some time with the Lord. Time to pray Night Prayer.

Because the Octaves are so special, **Night Prayer for each night of the Christmas Octave is taken either from After Evening Prayer I for Sundays and Solemnities or After Evening Prayer II for Sundays and Solemnities.** Use one all the time or bounce between the two. It is up to you.

DODO
SELF CHECK #48

1. During the Christmas Octave, what Night Prayer offices do you use?

2. What Night Prayer office do you use on Christmas Eve? On Christmas Night? During the Christmas Octave? On the Eve of the Solemnity of Mary the Mother of God (New Year's Eve)? On the night of the Solemnity of Mary the Mother of God (New Year's Night)?

3. When during the Christmas season might you not pray Night Prayer?

TECHNIQUE
How to Pray Night Prayer during the Christmas Octave:

On Christmas Eve, use Sunday Night Prayer I unless you attend Midnight Mass in which case you are exempt from praying Night Prayer.

From Christmas night (December 25) through December 30, you may use either Sunday Night Prayer I or II (the choice is up to you).

On the eve of the Solemnity of Mary, the Mother of God (December 31, New Year's Eve), use Sunday Night Prayer I.

On the night of the Solemnity (January 1), use Sunday Night Prayer II.

During the Octave of Christmas, use the Concluding Prayer that begins "Lord, we beg You to visit this house" unless that day of the Octave is actually a Sunday (or eve of a Sunday). In that case, use the other Concluding Prayer which is the one for Sundays.

On the night of January 2, return to the usual pattern of praying the correct Night Prayer office for the day of the week.

SECTION EIGHT

Praying Morning, Evening, and Night Prayer During Lent/Easter

"In this section, you'll learn about . . ."

- Morning and Evening Prayer in Lent
- Morning Prayer in the Easter Season
- Evening Prayer in the Easter Season
- Night Prayer for the Easter Triduum
- The Triple Alleluia
- Special Considerations for Easter Triduum

SECTION EIGHT: PRAYING MORNING, EVENING, AND NIGHT PRAYER DURING LENT/EASTER

If you have a four-volume breviary, you will need the volume for Lent/Easter for the lessons in Section Eight.

Lesson 49: Morning and Evening Prayer during Lent/Easter (except the Octave)

The year moves on again. It seems as if Christmas just ended and here it is, Ash Wednesday already. No matter when Ash Wednesday comes, it always seems to arrive too early.

In the Proper of Seasons, find Ash Wednesday. Page through the Proper of Seasons, looking carefully at all the parts of the Office printed there for use during Lent. Continue to page through the Proper of Seasons until Ordinary Time begins again.

What did you notice about your breviary?

Look at Morning Prayer for the First Sunday of Lent. This will be the first Sunday after Ash Wednesday. Study this carefully. Are there any alternatives for other Sundays of Lent written in your breviary here?

Breviaries are as different as dodos are. Some breviaries have each day's office printed individually. You will simply advance the Proper of Seasons bookmark through the Proper of Seasons as you pray. You will know that your breviary is like this if you have only one choice of Antiphon for the Canticle of Zechariah, one set of Intercessions, and one Concluding Prayer (and possibly an alternative prayer) for the First Sunday of Lent.

DODO
SELF CHECK #49

1. Does your breviary combine offices? Or does it have each office printed out separately in the Proper of Seasons?

2. How will you know which selections to use, if your breviary combines offices?

3. Where can you find the Invitatory Antiphon for Lent/Easter? Hint: Refer to the Proper of Seasons bookmark.

Other breviaries <u>combine parts of the offices.</u> You will know that your breviary is like this if you have a heading "Lent—Sunday—Weeks 1 to 4" above this office. In this type of breviary, you will use this one office for the first four Sundays of Lent. <u>You will find parts of the office labeled for the proper Sunday</u>. For the First Sunday of Lent in this type of breviary, you will have <u>four</u> Antiphons for the Canticle of Zechariah, but each is marked for the proper Sunday (Sunday 1, 2, 3, or 4). You will have <u>two</u> groups of Intercessions, but each is marked for the proper Sunday (Sundays 1 and 3 use the same Intercessions; Sundays 2 and 4 use the same Intercessions). You will find <u>four</u> Concluding Prayers, but each is marked for the proper Sunday (Sunday 1, 2, 3, or 4). In a breviary like this, you will move the Proper of Seasons bookmark through the week's offices in the Proper of Seasons and then return to Sunday Evening Prayer I for the next week.

In both types of breviaries, the Fifth Week of Lent has its own unique offices as does Holy Week and the Easter Octave.

Page ahead in your breviary's Proper of Seasons to the weeks of Easter following the Easter Octave to Pentecost. Does your breviary combine the offices or is each one separate?

No matter whether your breviary combines offices or has each written separately, the Divine Office is the same in all breviaries. What changes is how you use the breviary to find the correct prayers and Readings. I bet you knew that, but it can be reassuring to see it in print!

Lesson 50: The Easter Triduum

The six weeks of Lent have moved right along. You have managed to find meatless alternatives for Fridays and are not too tired yet of tuna fish salad sandwiches and macaroni and cheese. Good Friday is tomorrow, and you know the fasting might be a little tough. But you will make it through. You did it on Ash Wednesday and you ate a decent dinner this evening. Better get moving to get to Church for the Mass of the Lord's Last Supper. Yes, it is Holy Thursday evening, the start of the EASTER TRIDUUM.

A TRIDUUM is three days of prayer. The EASTER SEASON opens with the EASTER TRIDUUM which begins with Holy Thursday Evening Prayer and continues through Good Friday, Holy Saturday, and Easter. However, <u>until the SOLEMNITY OF EASTER actually BEGINS, the Church is still in a penitential season. Therefore, until the Solemnity actually BEGINS, the Church CONTINUES TO USE the Hymns, responses, and so on used for Lent</u>. Only with the beginning of the Solemnity of Easter does the Church switch to the Easter Hymns, responses, and other parts of the Office that express the joy of the Resurrection.

DODO
SELF CHECK #50

1. What is a triduum? What is the Easter Triduum?

2. What days make up the Easter Triduum?

3. When does the Easter Season begin?

4. Since the Easter Triduum is part of the Easter Season, why does the Church continue to use, during the Triduum, the parts of the Office for Lent?

5. When does the Church begin to use the Easter Hymns, responses, and so on? Why does the Church begin to use them at that time?

Look in your breviary's Table of Contents under the Proper of Seasons. Your breviary may have a special heading for the Easter Triduum or it may include the Easter Triduum under the heading "Holy Week." In either case, if you page through the Holy Week offices, you will eventually come to a section marked "Easter Triduum."

Lesson 51: Night Prayer during the Easter Triduum

The Mass of the Lord's Last Supper was reverent. You stayed after Mass to venerate the reposed Body of the Lord on its side altar. It is late now, and you want to pray Night Prayer before going to bed.

Your breviary contains instructions to help you pray Night Prayer during the Easter Triduum.

The Easter Triduum begins with Evening Prayer for Holy Thursday. Pretend that you have already prayed Evening Prayer. Page through Evening Prayer until you come to the Concluding Prayer. What instruction follows this? What Responsory is given?

Now skip ahead a bit. Look at the Good Friday and Holy Saturday Evening Prayer offices. Page through each until you come to the Concluding Prayer. What instruction follows in your breviary? What Responsories are given?

Turn back to Holy Thursday. Read the Night Prayer Responsory given. Now read again the Night Prayer Responsory for Good Friday and Holy Saturday. Do you see how each Responsory builds on the previous one like a swelling Hymn?

Now turn to Night Prayer after Evening Prayer II on Sundays. You will see two Concluding Prayers written there. One begins "Lord, we have celebrated today . . . " This is the one that you have

---

TECHNIQUE

How the Church prays Night Prayer during the Easter Triduum:

On Holy Thursday, Good Friday, and Holy Saturday, use Night Prayer after Evening Prayer II on Sundays for all three days as instructed in your breviary.

Also as instructed, in place of the usual six line Responsory ("Into your hands, Lord, I commend my spirit" and the five lines that follow) that follows the Night Prayer Reading, the following Responsories are prayed on the nights indicated:

Holy Thursday: For our sake Christ was obedient, accepting even death.

Good Friday: For our sake, Christ was obedient, accepting even death, death on a cross.

Holy Saturday: For our sake, Christ was obedient, accepting even death, death on a cross. Therefore God raised him on high and gave him the name above all other names.

Use the second Concluding Prayer ("Lord, we beg you to visit this house . . . ") for each night of the Easter Triduum.

been praying with the Night Prayer offices. The second choice begins "Lord, we beg you to visit this house . . . " Some breviaries tell you to use this second prayer for the Easter Triduum. Others do not. Whether or not your breviary tells you, this second Concluding Prayer is the one that you will use for the Easter Triduum. Now you know!

— · — · — · — · — · — · — · —

PRACTICE: Holy Thursday has come and gone. Today is Good Friday. You have managed to fast and abstain without too much difficulty today. Now it is time for Night Prayer and then bed.

Practice praying Night Prayer for Good Friday.

First choose an appropriate Hymn in your breviary. Remember, you want a Lenten Hymn. It is not Easter yet. **Move the bookmark Hymn to the proper spot.**

Move the Night Prayer bookmark to Night Prayer after Evening Prayer II on Sundays.

Move the Proper of Seasons bookmark to the very end of the offices for Good Friday where the Responsory is printed.

Now pray Night Prayer for Good Friday. Remember to flip to the Proper of Seasons for the Responsory following the Reading and to pray the second Concluding Prayer.

Lesson 52: Praying Morning and Evening Prayer during the Easter Octave

Easter has come and gone. You managed to dye yet another batch of eggs and you sang the Alleluias at Mass as if you have never heard them before. How the joyous ringing of the bells at the Easter Mass still rings in your heart! You are in the days immediately following Easter: the Easter Octave which celebrates for eight days the Resurrection of Our Lord.

The Easter Octave lasts from Easter Day until Evening Prayer II of the Second Sunday of Easter. The Sunday following Easter is now called Divine Mercy Sunday.

DODO
SELF CHECK #52

1. When does the Easter Octave begin? How long does it last? When does it end?

2. How are the Morning and Evening Prayer offices unique during the Easter Octave?

3. What is different about praying the Invitatory on Easter?

4. What dismissal is prayed for Morning and Evening Prayer during every day of the Easter Octave?

Turn to the Octave of Easter in the Proper of Seasons. Page through the offices for the Octave of Easter, looking carefully at the instructions given. Do you see a pattern of joyful celebration here? You will notice that, **during the Easter Octave, the Hymns, Antiphons, Psalms, and Canticles for Morning and Evening Prayer are the same as those on Easter Sunday.** Yes, the Church prays the Easter Offices day after day for a full week because Easter is the highest feast of the Church year. No other feast is celebrated during the Easter Octave.

Easter Sunday is a unique celebration in that it both opens the Octave and closes the Triduum. There is a special rule for praying the Invitatory on Easter. The regular rule about praying the Invitatory before the first office of the day (whether that is the Office of Readings or Morning Prayer) changes for Easter. **On Easter day only, the Invitatory is <u>always</u> prayed at the beginning of <u>Morning</u> Prayer.** This is the case even if the Office of Readings is prayed before Morning Prayer. Why is it this way? Because the Easter Vigil Mass takes the place of the Office of Readings, if you attend that Mass. And lots of people do. In medieval times, the Easter Vigil Mass was held very late on Holy Saturday, usually concluding on Easter Sunday Morning. This is how the religious, who prayed the Divine Office, celebrated Easter. So the first office prayed on Easter was Morning Prayer and that would have included the Invitatory.

Here is another difference during the Easter Octave. The Morning and Evening Prayer offices end with a different dismissal. You have been using the following dismissal: "May the Lord bless

us, protect us from all evil, and bring us to everlasting life. Amen."
This is not the dismissal that is used during the Easter Octave. So
where is it?

You may have difficulty locating in your breviary the dismissal
that is said. Look at the Easter Octave offices and Hymns and see
if you can find the dismissal that is used. **During the <u>entire</u>
Easter Octave, the dismissal for both Morning and Evening
Prayer is "Go in peace, Alleluia, Alleluia. Thanks be to God,
Alleluia, Alleluia."** If you cannot find it in your breviary, you will
just have to remember it or write it in someplace. It is OK to write
in your breviary. It belongs to you!

Lesson 53: The Easter Season

Time for a quick lesson on the Easter
Season. How smart you will feel when
this lesson is done!

From the SOLEMNITY OF EAST-
ER until the end of the EASTER SEA-
SON is a time of great rejoicing. We pray
"Alleluia" many times during this season
as a cry of joy.

**The SOLEMNITY OF EASTER
begins with the Easter Vigil Mass
which takes the place of the Office of
Readings for Easter. The Office of
Readings used to be known as Vigils
and used to be the first office of the
day. The Solemnity of Easter is <u>the
first</u> day on which the Easter parts of
the Divine Office are prayed.**

**The EASTER OCTAVE is part of
the Easter Season. The Easter Octave**

**DODO
SELF CHECK #53**

1. When does the Solem-
   nity of Easter begin?

2. What office does the
   Easter Vigil Mass re-
   place?

3. What is the Easter Oc-
   tave? How long does it
   last?

4. How long is the Easter
   Season? When does it
   end?

5. When does the Church
   begin to pray Easter
   parts of the Divine Office? For how many
   days does the Church
   pray them? Where do
   you find these Easter
   parts of the Office?

6. When is the last time
   that the Church prays
   Night Prayer for the
   Easter Season?

(eight days) lasts from Easter evening until the evening of Divine Mercy Sunday which is the Second Sunday of Easter.

All during the EASTER SEASON, Easter parts of the Divine Office are prayed. The EASTER SEASON continues for six weeks and ends with Evening Prayer II on the Feast of Pentecost. Nevertheless, Night Prayer for Pentecost is said as it was said <u>all during the Easter Season</u>.

The Easter parts of the Divine Office are in the Proper of Seasons and the Psalter, depending on the day. Use all the parts in the Proper of Seasons first. Use the Psalter for parts not in the Proper of Seasons. Celebrating saints' days adds another dimension to this which we will get to later. All in good time.

Lesson 54: The Triple Alleluia Antiphon

Easter is such a joyous time. We just cannot seem to pray Alleluia enough. Alleluia is a much prettier word than Yippee or Hooray! But it means the same thing. We are so very glad that Jesus died and rose again to save us from sin that we cannot contain our joy. Let us look at one time that Alleluia is prayed so wondrously during the Easter Season.

Turn to the Night Prayer offices and page through them (remember, *if you have a four-volume breviary, you are using the Lent/Easter volume*). Look for the Antiphons for the Psalms and Canticles. You will see the Antiphon that you have been praying for Night Prayer and another Antiphon marked "Easter." The Easter Antiphon is a series of three "Alleluias." How beautiful!

**DODO
SELF CHECK #54**

1. If a single, unchanging Antiphon is used in the Psalmody, when is it prayed? When is it omitted? Is this single, unchanging Antiphon repeated between the Psalms and Canticles of the Psalmody?

Turn to Night Prayer for Wednesday. How many Psalms are prayed in the Psalmody? Two? Correct!

Now look at the Antiphons. Some breviaries have Antiphon 1

and Antiphon 2 written both before and after the Psalms. Others only have the Antiphons written once, before the Psalms. What is your breviary's format?

Now look at the Antiphon marked "Easter." If your breviary writes the Antiphon both before and after the Psalms, do you see the Easter Antiphon written after Psalm 31:1-6 and then again before Psalm 130? Where is the Easter Antiphon written again? You will notice that the Easter Antiphon is not written again until <u>after the second Psalm</u> which is Psalm 130.

If your breviary only prints the Antiphons before the Psalms but not after, do you see the Easter Antiphon printed before Psalm 130? No? Do you have a misprint in your breviary?

Not at all. You will not see the Easter Antiphon printed between the two Psalms <u>because it is not prayed between the two Psalms</u>. The three Alleluias are prayed only at the beginning of the Psalmody and again at the end. Here is why: **In the Psalmody, if only one Antiphon is given for a series of two or three Psalms and/or Canticles, then the Antiphon is prayed only <u>at the very beginning of the Psalmody and again at the very end of the Psalmody</u>. The single, unchanging Antiphon is <u>not</u> repeated between the Psalms and Canticles.** That is the rule!

— — — — — — — —

PRACTICE: Pray the Psalmody for Wednesday Night Prayer during the Easter Season. Remember to pray the Triple Alleluia Antiphon only at the very beginning and the very end of the Psalmody. After praying this Psalmody, check how you did against Appendix. I.

Lesson 55: Night Prayer during the Easter Octave

Ah, in our little game of pretend, we are still in the Easter Octave. The days move along, each Morning and Evening Office being the one for Easter Sunday. You are feeling the incredible joy of this season that clings to the offices like a cloud of Triple Alleluias. You want to pray Night Prayer, too, at this happy time. How do you do it?

Praying Night Prayer during the Easter Octave can be a bit tricky, but you have proven that you are a pretty smart dodo. It will not take you long to learn this technique.

Turn to Night Prayer in your breviary *(remember, you are using the Lent/Easter volume if you have a four-volume breviary)*. Look at the Antiphons for the Psalmody. Do you see the Antiphons marked "Easter?" Yes, they are the Triple Alleluia Antiphons!

Just as the Antiphons are different for the Easter Octave, so is the Responsory. Instead of "Into your hands, Lord, I commend my spirit" and the five following lines, you will be using another Responsory. Where is it?

TECHNIQUE

How the Church Prays Night Prayer during the Easter Octave:

On Easter evening, use Sunday Night Prayer II.

Use either Sunday Night Prayer I or Sunday Night Prayer II for the days within the Octave of Easter (the choice is yours).

For the eve of Divine Mercy Sunday (the Second Sunday of Easter), use Sunday Night Prayer I.

For the night of Divine Mercy Sunday, use Sunday Night Prayer II which concludes the Octave.

In the Psalmody, use the string of three "Alleluias" as the Psalmody Antiphon.

For the Responsory after the Reading, use the words, "This is the day the Lord has made, Alleluia. Let us rejoice and be glad, Alleluia."

When praying the Antiphon for the Gospel Canticle ("Protect us, Lord, as we stay awake . . . "), pray after it the "Alleluia" that is in parentheses.

No matter whether you are using Sunday Night Prayer I or II, always conclude with the Concluding Prayer for Sunday which begins "Lord, be with us throughout this night . . . " or "Lord, we have celebrated today . . . ".

Throughout the <u>entire</u> Easter Octave, the Responsory that follows the Reading for <u>all</u> the Morning, Evening, and Night Prayer Offices is <u>exactly the same</u>. Let us find it.

In your breviary, find Easter Morning Prayer. Find the Reading. What is the Responsory following it?

Page ahead and look at Evening Prayer for Easter. What is the Responsory following the Reading?

Keep paging through all the offices of the Easter Octave. In every single Morning and Evening Prayer office during the Easter Octave, the Responsory reads, "This is the day the Lord has made, Alleluia. Let us rejoice and be glad, Alleluia." **During the Easter Octave, this same Responsory is used during every Night Prayer even though the Responsory may not be written out in your breviary's Night Prayer offices.** If you do not have it in your breviary, write it in. Or write it on a card and put it into your breviary. It is perfectly fine to do whatever you need to do to help you pray better.

> **DODO**
> **SELF CHECK #55**
>
> 1. During the Easter Octave, what Night Prayer offices are used? Which are used on which days?
>
> 2. What is the joyful Antiphon for the Psalmody?
>
> 3. How does the Responsory after the Reading read?
>
> 4. What joyous word do you pray after the Antiphon for the Gospel Canticle?
>
> 5. What Concluding Prayer do you always use?

Here is another change, although an easier one. In the Night Prayer offices, look at the Antiphon for the Gospel Canticle. It reads, "Protect us, Lord, as we stay awake; watch over us as we sleep, that awake, we may keep watch with Christ, and, asleep, rest in his peace." In one-volume breviaries, an Alleluia in parentheses follows this Antiphon. In four-volume breviaries, the Alleluia in parentheses is found only in the volume for Lent/Easter. **During the Easter Octave, pray this Alleluia as part of the Antiphon.** That was fairly easy, right?

Now, a review. Do you remember what was unique about Night Prayer during the Christmas Octave? All the Night Prayer Offices during the Octave were from either After Evening Prayer I on

Sundays and Solemnities or After Evening Prayer II on Sundays and Solemnities. Did you deduce that it is the same for the Easter Octave? Every day of the Easter Octave, just like every day of the Christmas Octave, is a SOLEMNITY, the highest celebration of the Church. On Solemnities, only Night Prayer that follows either Sunday Evening Prayer I or Sunday Evening Prayer II is used. Since the Octave is part of the Solemnity of Easter, the first Concluding Prayer is used every night during the Octave.

— · — · — · — · — · — ■

PRACTICE: Pretend that it is the Eve of Divine Mercy Sunday and you are ready to pray Night Prayer. How will you do that?

Move your Hymn bookmark to an appropriate Easter Hymn.

Are you going to move your Night Prayer bookmark to Sunday Night Prayer I or II? Check the Technique box on page 117 if you are not sure.

Following the technique, pray Night Prayer for the Eve of Divine Mercy Sunday. Check how you did by comparing your prayer with the office as written out in Appendix J.

Lesson 56: Praying the Offices during the Easter Season after the Easter Octave

Time is moving along. Divine Mercy Sunday, the second Sunday of Easter, is over. You have come this far, and you want to keep praying Morning, Evening, and Night Prayer offices. It is easy to do so.

TECHNIQUE

How to pray Morning and Evening Prayer during the Easter Season following the Octave:

Choose one of the Easter Hymns.

Begin with the Psalter. Pray the Psalmody, using the Psalms and Canticles with the Antiphons marked "Easter."

Turn to the Proper of Seasons for the remainder of the Office.

Say all the "Alleluias" in parentheses during the entire Easter Season.

Remember that, until Pentecost, we are still in the Easter Season. So you have to look in the Proper of Seasons first when setting up the offices to pray.

Page through the Proper of Seasons following Divine Mercy Sunday. What do you notice about every single Morning and Evening Office?

Now page through the Psalter, looking at the Antiphons for the Psalmody and remembering that, during the Easter season, you are so happy that Jesus died and rose to save us that you are going to pray every one of those Alleluias in parentheses.

TECHNIQUE

How to pray Night Prayer during the Easter Season after the Easter Octave:

Use the Night Prayer section of the breviary that corresponds to the day of the week.

Choose an appropriate Hymn.

Use the parts of the offices marked "Easter."

Pray all the Alleluias that are in parentheses.

Pentecost is the last day that Morning, Evening, and Night Prayer are prayed in the special Easter Season manner. On Monday following Pentecost, return to praying the offices as you do during Ordinary Time.

DODO SELF CHECK #56

1. During the Easter Season, where are the Psalms and Canticles that are used for Morning and Evening Prayer? Where are the other parts of the Morning and Evening Prayer offices?

2. During the Easter Season, how do you treat the Alleluias in parentheses?

3. When do you return to praying Morning, Evening, and Night Prayer as you do during Ordinary Time?

PRACTICE: Pray Morning and Evening Prayer for Wednesday during the Second Week of Easter. Use Week II of the Psalter. Set up your breviary according to the above instructions.

EXTRA PRACTICE: Pray Wednesday Night Prayer for the Second Week of Easter. Follow the instructions in the Technique box on this page.

SECTION NINE
Propers and Commons

"In this section, you'll learn about . . ."

- The Proper of Saints
- Various Commons
- Ferial Days
- Solemnities and Feasts
- Memorials and Commemorations

SECTION NINE: PROPERS AND COMMONS

Those with four-volume breviaries will need all four volumes for these instructions and for the remainder of this book.

Lesson 57: The Proper of Saints (Part 1)

OK. You are doing great. Really great! You are learning to pray the Divine Office. There are only a few more major parts of the Office about which you feel really dodo-y at this point. And they really are major parts of the Office: the Proper and the Commons. How do you use these confusing sections of the breviary? Maybe you could just skip them?

No, you do not want to skip them. In these sections you are going to make some wonderful friends in the Church. The saints! Time to begin getting acquainted!

Actually anyone in heaven is a SAINT. However, the Church canonizes certain people who have lived lives of exceptional holiness. This means that experts have studied the lives of these people and deemed their sanctity heroic, exceptional. Those for whom the canonization process is complete are called "saints." Those who are deemed extraordinarily holy but for whom some procedures are not yet complete are called "blessed." Some of these saints have special feast days. These are celebrated in the Divine Office.

One of those initially confusing sections of the breviary has special parts of the Office for each particular saint that the Office celebrates. We will explore that section and soon it will be as familiar as an old friend.

Look in the Table of Contents. Read the various headings. You can easily find the part that has the offices for the saints. The PROPER OF SAINTS, right?

Let your webbed dodo feet skip through the Proper of Saints as you savor all the saints named there. Did you find some familiar saintly friends? Did you notice some unfamiliar saints? So many holy guides to pray for you when you use this section of the breviary! How wonderful!

Time for some detective work. Does every saint have the same parts of the Office written under his or her heading? Check and see. What are some parts of the Office written in the Proper of Saints? What parts do you see most frequently? Less frequently? Feeling a bit confused? That is a normal reaction. Keep going! The saints will help you understand their section of the breviary if you ask.

The PROPER OF SAINTS contains the entire Office or portions of the Office for all the saints celebrated during the Church year. Each saint has his or her own office for one day of the year.

Keep paging through the Proper of Saints. Do you see how nearly every saint has a brief biography printed at the beginning of the day? **When praying the Office for the saint, read the biography of the saint silently before beginning the office.**

> **DODO**
> **SELF CHECK #57**
>
> 1. Who is a saint? Who is a canonized saint? What is the difference between a saint and a blessed?
>
> 2. Do all saints have an office in the breviary?
>
> 3. What is the name of the section of the breviary that has offices of the saints?
>
> 4. When praying the office of a saint, do you read aloud the biography of the saint that is printed in the breviary?
>
> 5. What bookmark marks the Proper of Saints?
>
> 6. *In four-volume breviaries, where in the Proper of Saints is the Concluding Prayer for Morning and Evening Prayer?*

Those with four-volume breviaries will notice that many saints' celebrations in the Proper of Saints have Readings and Responsories for the Office of Readings. Since we have not yet learned to pray this office, we will ignore these for now. The Concluding Prayer is used for Morning and Evening Prayer as well as for the Office of Readings.

We have not slipped any new bookmarks into the breviary for a while. But now we get to use one. Guess which? You got it! **Place the Proper of Saints bookmark anywhere in the Proper of Saints section of your breviary.**

Here is the rule for using the Proper of Saints. It is similar to the rule for using the Proper of Seasons. **When celebrating a saint's day, use all the parts of the saint's office that are printed in the Proper of Saints. When the Proper of Saints is missing some parts of the office, use those parts from other sections of the breviary.** Later lessons will discuss what other parts of the breviary to use.

Lesson 58: The Proper of Saints (Part 2)

Time to examine some of the celebrations in the Proper of Saints. Do not let the terms dismay you. We are not going to try to understand all the terms just yet. We simply want to get familiar with this part of the breviary.

Begin at the beginning of the Proper of Saints. Do you see that **the Proper of Saints is arranged chronologically by date from January 1 to December 31? Not every day has a saint's celebration.**

Look at the celebration for February 10. It is for Saint Scholastica, a lovely saint who wanted to spend more time speaking of the Lord with her brother St. Benedict who kept saying that he had to get back to the monastery. Scholastica prayed and God sent a violent rainstorm so Benedict could not leave. Four days later, Scholastica died. Now that you know a bit about Saint Scholastica, take a look at her celebration. Do you see, at the beginning of this celebration, the words "Memorial" and "Lent: Commemoration"? Again, do not worry about the words yet. Just recognize that they are there.

Now look at February 11, the celebration of Our Lady of Lourdes, the apparition of the Blessed Mother to St. Bernadette at Lourdes, France. You will not see the word "Memorial" but only "Lent: Commemoration." Page through the Office and find some other celebrations that are marked both "Memorial" and "Lent: Commemoration" and some that are marked only "Lent: Commemoration."

Now flip ahead in the Proper of Saints to May. Look at May 26 for Philip Neri. Philip was a great saint who realized the importance of humility. He often gave a humbling task to those who came to him for advice. As for himself, the more his holy reputation grew, the sillier he wanted to appear, so as to foster humility in himself. Therefore he would often wear ridiculous clothes or go about with half his beard shaved. When some prestigious people came from Poland to visit Philip and learn some words of wisdom from him, Philip had another priest read to him from joke books. When the visitors left, Philip said, "Put the joke books away. They have achieved their goal." May God grant us dodos humility as we work through this manual!

Does the celebration of St. Philip Neri say "Memorial" and/or "Lent: Commemoration?" You know why it does not say "Lent: Commemoration." We cannot possibly be celebrating Lent in May.

Now look at May 27 for Saint Augustine of Canterbury, the first bishop of Canterbury, England. When many of his forty companions wanted to head back to their home city of Rome, Augustine made them hold their ground. Because of them, Christianity blossomed in the British Isles.

Does the celebration for Saint Augustine of Canterbury say "Memorial?" No. It does not say anything.

Are you puzzled? That is normal. Let us look a bit more and raise even more questions.

Now look at May 25. Can you see an office for Venerable Bede, an English doctor of the Church and talented author, and another for St. Gregory VII, medieval Pope and reformer of the Church, and another for Saint Mary Magdalene de Pazzi, a Carmelite nun who was a mystic and who had the gift of healing? All three of these saints have an office on May 25 and none of them say "Memorial."

Now look at May 31. This is not a saint's celebration. It is titled "Visitation" and celebrates Mary's visitation to Elizabeth when Mary was pregnant with Jesus and Elizabeth with John. What word is at the beginning of this celebration? Yes. "Feast."

Compare the office for the Visitation with that of Saint Augustine of Canterbury on May 27. Which office is longer? What parts are written under the office for the Visitation that are omitted under the office for Saint Augustine of Canterbury?

Now page ahead to June 24. This office is for the "Birth of John the Baptist." What is the designation at the head of this office? Yes. "Solemnity."

Compare the office for the Birth of John the Baptist (June 24) with that of the Visitation (May 31). What parts are in both offices? What parts are in the office for the Birth of John the Baptist that are not in the office for the Visitation?

Are you really confused? Not to worry. We are just exploring. The confusion will clear up in good time. God is giving you an opportunity to learn humility.

Do a little comparing of the offices for Memorials, Feasts, and Solemnities. Which offices have more parts to them? What are some of those parts?

Here is something else to look for in the Proper of Saints. Turn to September 9, the office for Saint Peter Claver, the apostle to the slaves brought to the New World. A Jesuit priest cut to the quick by the horrors of seventeenth century slavery, St. Peter Claver vowed to be "the slave of the Negroes forever," bringing them food, medicine, solace, and prayer. St. Peter Claver's celebration reads "Memorial." After the biography of Saint Peter Claver is a small instruction that reads "From the common of pastors, p. ___, or of holy men: those who worked for the underprivileged, p. ___." Oh, no! Is the office telling you that you have to do some more flipping around to pray? Yes, but do not fret. You will learn how to do this shortly.

Now look at September 14, the Triumph of the Cross. Does this give any sort of beginning instruction?

> **DODO**
> **SELF CHECK #58**
>
> 1. How does your first experience with the Proper of Saints make you feel? Confused? Frustrated? Not to worry. These are very common reactions.
>
> 2. What are some new terms that you discovered in the Proper of Saints?

Page ahead to September 15, Our Lady of Sorrows, a celebration of the Blessed Virgin Mary which commemorates the sad events in her life. What instruction does this give? It should say, "From the common of the Blessed Virgin Mary, p. ___, except the following."

Look ahead for the instructions for each office in September. What do you notice about them?

Whew! That was some lesson and you might feel as if it put you through the food grinder, so to speak. At this point, you might be ready to take the Proper of Saints and rip it out of your breviary! But refrain from doing that because you really are going to learn how to use this section. Instead, go make yourself a nice cup of coffee, tea, hot chocolate, lemonade, or cod liver oil, whatever you like best, and relax. You deserve a break.

Lesson 59: The Commons

All rested up? Great! We are going to proceed, in our common fashion, and explore the Commons. If you are good at history, you might remember that, in medieval and colonial times, the Common was a large field where townsfolk used to gather to chat and to graze their livestock. Many towns still have a Common. The Common belongs to the town, not to any one individual. In the breviary, **a COMMON is an office that can be used for a number of celebrations.** It is a section used "in common."

The Proper of Saints often instructs you to go the "Common" of someone (pastors, virgins, the Blessed Virgin, martyrs, and so on). Where is this section of the breviary?

Look in your breviary's Table of Contents. Find the section marked COMMONS. What are the commons listed under this general heading? You will find over a dozen there.

Page through some of the Commons, getting familiar with them. Start with the first common, the Common of the Dedication of a Church. Page through this and on into the Common of the

Blessed Virgin Mary. Keep paging through a few more Commons. Do you notice any similar sections in them?

Two bookmarks mark the Commons. One says "Common: Primary Office" and the other "Common: Secondary Office." Place these in any two different sections of the breviary marked Commons.

Now for some deductions regarding these two bookmarks. One says "Primary Office" and the other "Secondary Office." Think about that a minute. Does this mean that you will primarily use one office for some celebrations but may also use the secondary office at the same time, for the same celebration? Oh, tell me it is not true! But it is true. Can you really learn how to pray the Commons? Maybe using two Commons for one celebration? Yes, you will learn. All in good time, all in God's time.

Need to catch your breath about now? Do not be surprised if you do. Many people find the Commons to be the most confusing parts of the Divine Office. Soon you will understand them. So take a deep breath and, when you are ready, you can move along in this instruction.

Look again at the Common of the Blessed Virgin Mary. Look at the Intercessions for Evening Prayer I, Morning Prayer, and Evening Prayer II. How many sets of Intercessions are listed for each of those offices?

Now look at the Concluding Prayer. How many do you see listed? Notice that your breviary uses the word "Or" as a heading when it lists more than one option for each section of the Office. Page

> ### DODO
> ### SELF CHECK #59
>
> 1. What is a Common?
> 2. How do you feel about your first experience with the Commons? Frustrated? Confused? You are a normal dodo! Soon you will learn how to use the Commons.
> 3. Which two bookmarks mark the Commons? How are they distinguished from each other?
> 4. If you have a choice between certain options within a Common, how do you know which option to select?

through some of the other Commons. Do you see options for certain parts of those offices? What parts of the offices have these options? Are you getting the sense that there is a smorgasbord of information and options in the Commons? There sure is! So what do you select?

If you have a choice of options for certain parts of the Divine Office, as indicated by the word "Or," you may choose whichever option you wish, provided that it corresponds with the current season of the Church year. More about this later.

Lesson 60: Ferial Days

Ferial Days have nothing to do with those beady-eyed popular pets called ferrets nor with amusement park rides that take you skyward and back down again in a dizzying circle. **The weekdays of the year on which no saint is celebrated are called FERIAL DAYS (pronounced fair-ee-al).** Sundays are <u>not</u> Ferial Days. Sundays are SOLEMNITIES.

Ferial Days are "hidden" days in the breviary, so, in this regard, they are like ferrets, who, in the wild, are seldom seen. In the Proper of Saints, turn to July. Do you see any saint's office for July 1? July 2? No? That is because there are no saints celebrated on those days. Those are Ferial Days. Page through the July offices. What other days in July are Ferial Days? All the days that are not listed!

So far, except for certain Feasts and Solemnities during Lent/Easter and

> **DODO**
> **SELF CHECK #60**
>
> 1. What is a Ferial Day? Do you use the Proper of Saints or the Commons on Ferial Days?
>
> 2. What is today's date? Find it in the Proper of Saints. Is a saint assigned to today? If not, today would be a Ferial Day. If today has a saint's celebration, page through the Proper of Saints and look for the next Ferial Day. On the Ferial Day, where do you find the parts of the Office to pray? Hint: Check back in this lesson for the answer.

Advent/Christmas, you have been praying each office as if it fell on a Ferial Day. You know how to do that. **To pray the Divine Office on Ferial Days, use only the Psalter and, in Lent/Easter and Advent/Christmas, the Proper of Seasons as well.**

Lesson 61: Solemnities, Feasts, Memorials, Commemorations

I hope you like vocabulary because this lesson deals with some new vocabulary words that you need to understand in order to pray the Divine Office. We will learn these words in order of importance regarding their celebration, the most important celebration first and the least important last. If you like to be organized, making a chart of these just might intrigue you. Also, you might want to check your breviary's Table of Contents to see if your breviary contains a General Roman Calendar which will list some of these terms.

Do you remember the four headings you saw when you paged through the Proper of Saints? Yes? Great! "Solemnity," "Feast," "Memorial," "Commemoration." Some celebrations had no headings. Does that seem weird or what?

SOLEMNITIES, FEASTS, MEMORIALS, and COMMEMORATIONS are special celebrations in the Church. Both the Proper of Saints and the Commons are used in praying the offices for these days.

To understand these celebrations, begin at the beginning, always the best place to start anything. You have already learned to pray the Sunday offices for Ordinary Time and during the Seasons of the year. **Every Sunday is a SOLEMNITY. A SOLEMNITY is a solemn celebration in the Church, the highest Church holiday. It is celebrated by the whole Church.** SOLEMNITY is your first vocabulary word, already familiar to you.

What are some of the Solemnities of the Church? Besides every Sunday, you already know some other Solemnities. Easter, Christmas, and their Octaves are celebrated as Solemnities.

Some celebrations in the Proper of Saints are also Solemnities. For example, look at June 24, the Birth of John the Baptist and August 15, the Assumption of Mary. These are two Solemnities celebrated in the Proper of Saints. There are other Solemnities in the Church year. How about going on a Solemnity treasure hunt and seeing how many you can find? Where will you find these gems? Yes! In the Proper of Seasons and Proper of Saints. If you can find a dozen Solemnities, go reward yourself with a candy bar or a veggie burger, whatever you prefer!

Remember, Solemnities are the highest celebrations of the Church year.

Now on to the second highest celebration! Check out September 14, the Triumph of the Cross, and September 29, the office for the Archangels Saints Michael, Gabriel, and Raphael. These are marked "Feasts." **A FEAST is a high celebration of the Church but not quite as important as a Solemnity. However, it is still celebrated by the whole Church.** FEAST is your second vocabulary word.

That was not too difficult, was it? So what celebration comes next? Did you guess Memorial? Right on! Many celebrations in the Proper of Saints are labeled "Memorial" and many other offices have no labels. Here is where the terms get a little tricky, but hang on! Soon you will understand. **The offices labeled "Memorial" as well as those with no labels are MEMORIALS. A MEMORIAL is a lesser celebration of the Church.** MEMORIAL is your third vocabulary word for today.

Of course, if you are at all awake, you have a question. Why are some Memorials labeled "Memorial" and others are not? Unlike some questions, this one does have an answer.

Some Memorials ARE celebrated by the Church, but others MAY be celebrated (a parish, religious order, or an individual may choose to celebrate them if desired). Which do you think ARE celebrated, the ones labeled "Memorial" or the ones not labeled?

If you answered "the ones labeled Memorial," you are pretty sharp! **The offices labeled "Memorial" are called OBLIGA-**

TORY MEMORIALS. Obli-
gatory means that these
Memorials are to be cele-
brated by the whole Church.
OBLIGATORY is your fourth
vocabulary word.

Hold on because here comes
vocabulary word number five.
The **unlabeled** offices are
OPTIONAL MEMORIALS.
Optional means that any
individual or parish MAY
celebrate the Memorial if
desired. OPTIONAL is the
fifth vocabulary word. We are
not done yet!

Look at the office for
February 14 for Saints Cyril,
Monk, and Methodius. These
are two saints, not three. Saint
Cyril was a monk. His brother
was Saint Methodius. Together,
in the 800's, they evangelized
the Slavic nations. The celebration for Saints Cyril, Monk, and
Methodius is marked "Mem-
orial" and "Lent: Commemoration." Turn to the offices for
December 21 and December
23. Do you see that these, too,
are marked "Commemora-
tion?" Page ahead to December
29, the office for Saint Thomas
Becket, the famous English

DODO SELF CHECK #61

1. What is a Solemnity? How do you know when a day is a Solemnity? Does the whole Church celebrate every Solemnity? What day of the week is always a Solemnity?

2. What is a Feast? How do you know when a day is a Feast? Does the whole Church celebrate every Feast?

3. What is an Obligatory Memorial? How do you know when a day is an Obligatory Memorial? Does the whole Church celebrate every Obligatory Memorial?

4. What is an Optional Memorial? How do you know when a day is an Optional Memorial? Does the whole Church celebrate every Optional Memorial?

5. What is a Commemoration? How do you know when a day is a Commemoration? Does the whole Church celebrate every Commemoration?

6. What is a Ferial Day? How do you know when a day is a Ferial Day? On a Ferial Day, where do you find the prayers for the Office?

7. Are Feasts, Memorials, or Commemorations celebrated on Sundays? If a Solemnity coincides with a Sunday, which Office is prayed, the one for the Solemnity or the one for Sunday? How do you know?

archbishop and chancellor who was martyred at the command of King Henry II. What is the designation for this office?

A COMMEMORATION is similar to an Optional Memorial. This means that a parish or individual may choose to celebrate a Commemoration if desired. Commemoration is the sixth vocabulary word.

Now for another tidbit. Commemorations are celebrated a bit differently than Optional Memorials, and they occur only during Lent/Easter and Advent/Christmas.

We will discuss Lent first. Lent is a very special time during the Church year. **During Lent until Palm (Passion Sunday), all Memorials, whether Obligatory or Optional, become Commemorations. During Holy Week and the Easter Octave, no Commemorations are celebrated** because, as you learned earlier, every day during Holy Week has its own special office.

What happens during Advent/Christmas? **During the last week of Advent and the Christmas Octave (December 17 to January 1), all Memorials become Commemorations.**

Were you good with math? Here are some crazy looking equations to summarize these rules:

Lent/Easter Memorials = Commemorations

Palm Sunday to Divine Mercy Sunday = No Memorials or Commemorations

Last Week of Advent to January 1 Memorials = Commemorations

So now you know! Every single day of the Church year is either a Solemnity, Feast, Obligatory Memorial, Optional Memorial, Commemoration, or Ferial Day. Pretty nifty vocabulary words!

Now for some Divine Office Trivia. What if a Solemnity, Feast, Obligatory Memorial, Optional Memorial, or Commemoration fall on a Sunday?

All Sundays are Solemnities. They are celebrated as such. Therefore, no Feast, Memorial (Obligatory or Optional), or Commemoration takes the place of the Sunday celebration.

However, if another Solemnity falls on a Sunday during Ordinary Time, the other Solemnity is celebrated instead of the Sunday for Ordinary Time. This is why, if the Solemnity of the Assumption of Mary (August 15) or the Solemnity of All Saints (November 1) falls on a Sunday, the Solemnities of the Assumption and All Saints are celebrated in place of the Sunday celebrations. We have all been familiar with this happening during Sunday Masses.

The Sundays during Lent/Easter and Advent/Christmas have special celebrations for the seasons. If a Solemnity coincides with a Sunday during the Lent/Easter and Advent/Christmas Seasons, the Solemnity may be celebrated on Sunday, on another day (Saturday or Monday), or may be skipped. What happens depends on the Solemnity. You will learn more about which Solemnities are skipped and which celebrated later.

Do you still have your wits about you? Give yourself a pat on the back. You have learned a lot in this chapter. Congratulations!

And slide your vocabulary list inside your breviary's front or back cover. You are going to refer to it often from here on out.

SECTION TEN
Praying Morning, Evening, and Night Prayer on Solemnities and Feasts

"In this section, you'll learn about . . ."

- Sunday Morning Prayer: Week 1
- Using the Propers of Saints and Commons
- Morning and Evening Prayer on Solemnities
- Night Prayer on Solemnities
- Morning, Evening and Night Prayer on Feasts

SECTION TEN: PRAYING MORNING, EVENING, AND NIGHT PRAYER ON SOLEMNITIES AND FEASTS

Lesson 62: Sunday Morning Prayer, Week I

You have had some pretty grueling lessons lately. So you deserve a break. So we will begin this chapter with something a bit easier. We are going to do some prowling around in the breviary, looking for something specific. Curious? Tear off several strips of scrap paper, not from this manual but maybe from some old junk mail, and then we can get started.

We are going to look in the Proper of Saints. Take a strip of paper and mark each of these offices as you find them so that you will be able to locate them easily for this lesson.

Find the offices for each of these days: February 22, April 25, July 3, August 6, September 14, November 30. Now look at each day and answer these questions:

What saint is being celebrated on each day?

What is the designation of each day (Solemnity, Feast, Memorial, Commemoration)?

> **DODO**
> **SELF CHECK #62**
>
> 1. The Psalms and Canticle from what Morning Office are prayed on particular celebrations of the Church Year? What Psalms and Canticle are in this office?
>
> 2. What color ribbon marks these?

Look at Morning Prayer for each of these Feasts. Do you see a designation under Antiphon 1 that reads, "Psalms and Canticle from Sunday, Week I, p. ___"? Hmm. Interesting.

The Psalms and Canticle from Sunday, Week I, are often used in praying the Divine Office on Feasts and sometimes on Solemnities and Memorials as well. Why? Because these Psalms and Canticle are especially joyful and praiseworthy of God. They express the emotions we ought to have on special Church celebrations.

In the Psalter of your breviary, find Sunday Morning Prayer, Week I. *If you have a four-volume breviary, find Sunday Morning Prayer, Week I, in each volume.* Find the first Psalm of Sunday Morning Prayer, Week I. What Psalm is it? What is the Canticle? The last Psalm?

The Psalms and Canticle of Sunday Morning Prayer, Week I, are special. They are Psalm 63:2-9, the Canticle of Daniel 3:57-88, 56, and Psalm 149. They are special because they are prayed in the Morning Office on particular celebrations that do not fall on Sunday.

Do you remember how we mark certain stationary places in the breviary that we will be referring to often? Yes! With the restful ribbons. We have a ribbon we have not used yet. **Draw the green ribbon (green for the spiritually life-giving Psalms and Canticle of Sunday Week I) down through your breviary to mark the first Psalm of Sunday, Week One, Psalm 63:2-9 in your Psalter.** *If you have a four-volume breviary, do this in every volume.*

Was I right in telling you that this lesson would be a snap?

Lesson 63: General Instructions on Using the Proper of Saints and the Commons

We will get to a little more nitty gritty in this chapter. When you paged through the Proper of Saints, you noticed that some saints had a great deal written in their offices and others had very little. Compare the offices for December 7, St. Ambrose, the great bishop of Milan who converted St. Augustine, with those of December 8, the Immaculate Conception of Mary, who was conceived without original sin. In one-volume breviaries, you will see only a prayer listed for St. Ambrose *(four-volume breviaries will also have a Second Reading for the Office of Readings and its Responsory)* while the Immaculate Conception is pages long. Does this mean that, on December 7, your entire Office consists of one little prayer? You should have it so easy!

Under Saint Ambrose you will see an instruction that reads, "From the Common of Doctors, page ___." This means that the parts of the Office not in the Proper of Saints are going to be found in the Common of Doctors and in the Psalter (you will learn which parts later).

What are the parts of the Office for Morning Prayer (if it is the first prayer of the day) and Evening Prayer? Let us list them in order:

Introduction
Invitatory Antiphon (Morning Prayer only)
Invitatory (Morning Prayer only)
Hymn
Psalmody, Psalm Prayers, and Antiphons
Reading
Responsory
Canticle of Zechariah (Morning) or
Canticle of Mary (Evening) and Antiphon
Intercessions
Our Father
Concluding Prayer, and Conclusion.

All these parts of the Office are prayed during every Morning and every Evening Prayer time no matter how little is written in the Proper of Saints. But then, you already knew that!

You will soon learn where to look for those parts of the Office that are missing from the Proper of Saints.

Now look back at that lonely prayer under Saint Ambrose's celebration. You will pray that lonely little prayer as the Concluding Prayer to the Morning Prayer office. If Saint Ambrose's celebration occurred on most any other day of the year, you would also pray that prayer as the Concluding Prayer for Evening Prayer. But you will not pray it on this night. Can you figure out why?

What celebration comes the day after St. Ambrose's Memorial? Go ahead and peek. Yes, the Immaculate Conception. The

Immaculate Conception is a Solemnity which is a higher Church celebration than Ambrose's Memorial. So Ambrose gets bumped, so to speak. You will not be praying Evening Prayer for Saint Ambrose on December 7 because, that night, the Church will be praying Evening Prayer I for the next day, the Immaculate Conception. Check out your breviary and see what I mean. Do not worry about St. Ambrose. I doubt if he minds that Our Lady bumped him out of Evening Prayer. He always had a great devotion to her and yielded to her will in his earthly life.

Page ahead in the Proper of Saints to December 11, a celebration in honor of Saint Damasus I, Pope, the patron of Saint Jerome and the pope who published what we now accept as the Canon of Sacred Scripture, the books of the Bible. In one-volume breviaries, the celebration for Saint Damasus, like Saint Ambrose's celebration, has only one Concluding Prayer *(four-volume breviaries will give a Second Reading for the Office of Readings and its Responsory as well)*.

Under the celebration for Saint Damasus is an instruction which refers you to the Common of Pastors for the parts of the Office not here in the Proper of Saints. However, Saint Damasus has his own Concluding Prayer. His own prayer will conclude both the Morning and Evening Prayer Offices. The Concluding Prayer for Saint Damasus <u>takes the place of</u> the Concluding Prayer in the Common of Pastors.

Here is why: **If the Proper of Saints lists a Concluding Prayer, it is prayed in place of any other Concluding Prayer. Even though the Concluding Prayer is written only once, it concludes both Morning and Evening Prayer.**

Now turn to the celebration for Saint Lucy on December 13. St. Lucy is the patron of those suffering eye problems because her eyes were put out during her martyrdom in 304. What parts of St. Lucy's office are printed under this celebration? Under Morning Prayer, the listing says "Canticle of Zechariah" and has an Antiphon. Does this mean that the Church prays only the Antiphon on this day? You know that is false! The Church uses the Antiphon under St. Lucy's celebration with the Canticle of Zechariah that you have already marked with a silver ribbon. For Evening Prayer, the "Canticle of Mary" has an Antiphon. It is prayed with the Canticle of Mary that you have marked with the blue ribbon.

Do you think that the Church prays the Antiphon written under the celebration for Saint Lucy as well as another Antiphon elsewhere in the breviary? No. **The Church uses only one Antiphon at a time.** In this case, the Antiphon is written under the celebration of the saint.

Look in your breviary for the celebration for St. Martin of Tours, November 11. St. Martin of Tours was a bishop who, while still a soldier in the world, cut his cloak in two and gave half to a freezing beggar. That evening he had a vision of Christ wearing the half-cloak. How incredible! What instruction is given for the celebration on St. Martin of Tours? You are referred to the Common of Pastors. Does this mean that the Church prays all the parts listed under Saint Martin and the same parts from the Common of Pastors? No. The Church prays all the parts under Saint Martin but does <u>not</u> pray those <u>same</u> parts in the Common of Pastors. The Church uses the Common of Pastors only for any <u>missing</u> parts.

The Office for Saint Martin of Tours appears to be very complete. However, one part is missing. Can you find which? Yes! The Intercessions. Does this mean that the Church skips praying them? No. Where will you find the Intercessions? In the Common of Pastors.

> ## DODO
> ## SELF CHECK #63
>
> 1. If a celebration in the Proper of Saints lists only a Concluding Prayer, where are the other parts of the Office printed?
>
> 2. If one part of the Office is listed in the Proper of Saints and the same part in the Common, which is prayed?
>
> 3. If you have a choice of Commons, how do you know which to choose?
>
> 4. How will you mark the Common that you are using?

Now look at the celebration for June 27. This is for St. Cyril of Alexandria, bishop and Doctor of the Church who is known for his writings on the Incarnation and the Trinity. What instruction regarding the Common is given in St. Cyril's Memorial? It reads, "From the common of pastors, p. ____, or of doctors of the Church, p. ____." Which common is used? **When a celebration lists a choice of Commons, you really do have a choice. Select one Common or the other.** How do you decide? That is up to you. You could do it by deciding if you like your pastor or your doctor better. Or maybe you could flip a coin. Once you choose, mark the Common you are using with the "Common: Primary Office" bookmark.

Lesson 64: Evening Prayer I, Morning Prayer, and Evening Prayer II on Solemnities

Following our pattern of going from the most important celebrations to those of lesser importance, we will start with Solemnities. **Solemnities are the highest celebrations in the Church.** You will recall that Sunday has Evening Prayer I and Evening Prayer II because **Sunday is a Solemnity.**

All Solemnities begin with Evening Prayer I. Evening Prayer I is always prayed as the Vigil (that is, the night before) office of a Solemnity.

Look in the Proper of Seasons for August 15, the Solemnity of the Assumption. This celebration begins with Evening Prayer I. **Evening Prayer I for these special high celebrations <u>takes the place of</u> the regular Evening Prayer that you might be saying that day whether that Evening Prayer would be in the Psalter or in the Proper of Saints.**

For example, August 14 is a new Memorial in honor of Saint Maximilian Kolbe. Maximilian Kolbe was a holy priest who began the Knights of the Immaculata and who gave up his life for another in the German concentration camp of Auschwitz. The Memorial of Saint Maximilian Kolbe will be in newer breviaries but not in older ones (older ones may have a supplement of new celebrations which would contain the office for the Memorial of Saint Maximilian Kolbe). On August 14, the Memorial for Saint Maximilian Kolbe is said for Morning Prayer, but Evening Prayer for August 14 is Evening Prayer I for the Solemnity of the Assumption which is August 15. Why? Because a Solemnity is a higher celebration than a Memorial.

Have a look at Evening Prayer I for the Solemnity of the Assumption. You will see that the entire office is printed in the breviary. Now check out Morning Prayer and Evening Prayer II for the Assumption. You will see that both entire offices are printed in the Proper of Saints.

How easy it is to pray Morning and Evening Prayer on the Solemnity of the Assumption! Simply follow what is written in the Proper of Saints.

Is it this easy with all Solemnities? Ah, you wish!

First, look in the Proper of Saints to see if there is any celebration on March 18. Yes, there is. March 18 is a Commemoration in honor of Saint Cyril of Jerusalem, bishop, catechist, and Doctor of the Church. If you chose to observe this Commemoration (and you do have a choice during Lent), then you would pray Morning Prayer from the Memorial of Saint Cyril, but you would not pray Evening Prayer for him. Why not? Because March 19 is a Solemnity with its own Evening Prayer I.

What Solemnity falls on March 19? No one expects you to remember it. Go ahead and look. Did you know that it was the Solemnity of Saint Joseph, husband of Our Lady and foster father of Our Lord? For this Solemnity, you will see complete offices for Evening Prayer I, Morning Prayer, and Evening Prayer II. But are they really complete? Have a closer look.

Look at Evening Prayer I for the Solemnity of Saint Joseph. Under Antiphon 1, you will find an instruction that tells you that the "Psalms and canticle (are) from the common of holy men, p. _____." You do not have to have an IQ of 150 in order to figure out that you have to go to the Common of Holy Men to pray this office.

In order to pray Evening Prayer I for the Solemnity of Saint Joseph, you would have your Proper of Saints bouncing bookmark at March 19. You would have your "Common: Primary Office" bouncing bookmark at the Psalms for Evening Prayer I for the Common of Holy Men.

Let us bounce over to the Common of Holy Men. Does your breviary have the Psalms written out for Evening Prayer I or does it refer you to the Common of Pastors for the Psalms? Here is where you get to use the "Common—Secondary Office" bookmark.

Oh, no, the two Commons bookmarks! They are easier to use than you think.

Always use the Common—Primary Office bookmark to mark the first Common referred to in your breviary. For most celebrations, the Common—Primary Office bookmark will be the only one you will use. However, if the "Primary" Common (the first Common you went to) refers you to a second Common, use the Common-Secondary Office bookmark to mark the appropriate places in that "Secondary" Common. Remember. Primary Common first (like primary school) and Secondary Common second (like secondary school). Got it? Good for you!

Now we can apply this information to the Solemnity of St. Joseph. **If the Common of Holy Men, in your breviary, refers you to the Common of Pastors for the Psalms for Evening Prayer I, then move the "Common: Secondary Office" bookmark to that spot.**

What are the Psalms and Canticle for Evening Prayer I for the Solemnity of Saint Joseph? The Psalms are 113 and 146 and the Canticle is Ephesians 1:3-10. These Psalms and Canticle are the same for both the Common of Holy Men and the Common of Pastors.

DODO
SELF CHECK #64

1. Which day of the week is always a Solemnity?

2. What office begins a Solemnity? On what night does this office fall?

3. Does Evening Prayer I for a Solemnity take the place of whatever other Evening Prayer would be said that night?

4. Where do you find the office Prayers and Readings for Solemnities?

OK. This has been a painstaking lesson. If you need a break, go get a coffee, soft drink or glass of lemonade and come back when you feel refreshed. How about getting me a milkshake? Vanilla, please.

Ready to roll again? OK! Let us look farther into the office for the Solemnity of Saint Joseph. Do you notice that two different Responsories are given for each office? One Responsory is marked "Lent" and the other "Easter." If you take a deep breath, you can figure this out. It is quite simple. Should the Solemnity fall during Lent, the Lenten Responsory is used. Should it fall during the Easter celebration (which rarely happens), the Easter Responsory is used.

Now look at Morning Prayer. The ground is a little more familiar here. You are referred to Sunday, Week I, for the Psalms and Canticle. You have already got those marked with the green ribbon. Look at Evening Prayer II. More familiar territory. You are again referred to the Common of Holy Men for the Psalms and Canticle and you have those marked with the Primary Commons bookmark.

Is it really so very difficult to pray Evening Prayer I, Morning Prayer, and Evening Prayer II for the Solemnity of Saint Joseph? Not really. All parts of the office are in the Proper of Saints. You are referred to the pages for those parts of the office that are written in the Commons. You mark these pages in advance with the bookmarks.

A Solemnity is clearly marked in the breviary. Its Office will be in either the Proper of Saints or the Proper of Seasons, and you will know which because you will be moving your bookmarks along as you pray the Divine Office. The breviary will tell you where to find any parts of the Office that are not printed in the Proper.

— ·· — ·· — ·· — ·· — ·· — ··· —

PRACTICE: Pray Evening Prayer I for the Solemnity of Saint Joseph.

— ·· — ·· — ·· — ·· — ·· — ··· —

EXTRA PRACTICE: Pray Evening Prayer II for the Solemnity of the Assumption.

Lesson 65: Night Prayer on Solemnities

Have you been discovering that you are a smarter dodo than you thought you were? I hope so! This lesson might be fairly easy for you. You may already suspect what it teaches.

Solemnities, you know, are the highest celebrations in the Church. You already have an inkling of how to treat Night Prayer for Solemnities. You learned about that when we talked about the Easter and Christmas Octaves. We can take what we learned and apply it to all Solemnities.

Find Night Prayer after Evening Prayer I on Sundays and Solemnities (marked "Saturday" in some breviaries) and Night Prayer after Evening Prayer II on Sundays and Solemnities (marked "Sunday" in some breviaries). Did you catch that designation "and Solemnities?" That is a clue that, **on Solemnities, Night Prayer after Evening Prayer I (Saturday) and Night Prayer after Evening Prayer II (Sunday) are prayed instead of whatever the Night Prayer would be for the weekday.**

Look for the Concluding Prayer. You will notice two of them. Up until now, you have been praying only the first Concluding Prayer. **Suppose that a Solemnity falls on a <u>Sunday</u>. If it does, pray what you have been praying all along, the <u>first</u> Concluding Prayers.** However, suppose that a Solemnity falls on a day other than Sunday. In that case, **on Solemnities <u>that do not fall on a Sunday</u>, pray the <u>second</u> Concluding Prayers to the Night Prayer offices.** Some breviaries identify which Concluding Prayer to pray on each of these occasions. If yours does, good for you!

Now, some review.

On Easter, which Concluding Prayers will you pray? The first ones because Easter always falls on a Sunday.

If the Solemnity of Christmas falls on a Sunday, which Concluding Prayers will you say? The first.

If Christmas falls on a weekday, what Concluding Prayers will you say? The second.

PRACTICE: Pray Night Prayer I (Saturday) as you would for Christmas Eve if Christmas came on a Tuesday.

EXTRA PRACTICE: Pray Night Prayer I (Saturday) for Christmas Eve as you would if Christmas fell on a Sunday.

Here is another "supposes."

Suppose that a Solemnity falls on a Monday as sometimes happens? Pretend, for example, that the Solemnity of Saints Peter and Paul (June 29) falls on a Monday.

What Night Prayer would be prayed on Sunday night (June 28), the Eve of the Solemnity? Night Prayer after Evening Prayer I (marked "Saturday" in some breviaries) with the second Concluding Prayer.

What Night Prayer would be prayed on Monday night (June 29), the day of

---

**DODO
SELF CHECK #65**

1. On a Solemnity, which Night Prayer offices are the only ones used?

2. When is the second Concluding Prayer to the Night Prayer offices used?

3. If a Solemnity falls on a Sunday, what Night Prayer offices are used? What Concluding Prayer?

4. If a Solemnity falls on any day other than a Sunday, what Night Prayer offices are used? What Concluding Prayer?

5. If Christmas fell on a Monday, what Night Prayer office would be prayed on Christmas Eve (Sunday Night)? What Concluding Prayer? What Night Prayer office would be prayed on Christmas Day (Monday Night)? What Concluding Prayer? (Hint: If you are not sure about the answers to these questions, re-read the section about a Monday Solemnity of Saints Peter and Paul.)

the Solemnity? Night Prayer after Evening Prayer II (marked "Sunday" in some breviaries) with the second Concluding Prayer.

What Night Prayer would be prayed on the night after the Solemnity (Tuesday, June 30)? The correct Night Prayer for the corresponding day of the week, in this case Night Prayer for Tuesday Night.

Lesson 66: Morning, Evening, and Night Prayer on Feasts

We have concluded discussing Solemnities, at least for now. What is the second highest celebration of the Church? Did you remember Feasts? Good for you!

A FEAST is a high celebration of the Church. It has its own offices. Because a Feast is not as high a celebration as a Solemnity, **a Feast does not usually have an Evening Prayer I. The Divine Office for the Feast usually begins on the day of the Feast itself. This is true even though the Common may have an Evening Prayer I.**

When praying the Divine Office on a Feast, follow what is in the Proper of Saints first. If the Proper of Saints tells you to use Evening Prayer I from the Common or elsewhere (as, for example, it does if the Triumph of the Cross, September 14, occurs on a Sunday), then use Evening Prayer I.

If the Proper of Saints does not mention any special Evening Prayer I, then use whatever Evening Prayer would be appropriate for that evening, just as though the next day were not a Feast.

Feasts are clearly marked in the breviary. They are found in either the Proper of Saints or the Proper of Seasons. You will know a Feast because you will be moving your book-marks along as you pray. The breviary will refer you to any parts of the Divine Office that are not found in the Feast itself.

It is easy to pray Morning and Evening Prayer on a Feast. **To pray Morning and Evening Prayer on a Feast, use the Proper of Saints first. Follow any instructions given there about where to find parts of the Office. Take everything else from the Common to which the Feast refers.**

A mathematical-like equation for this would be:

FEASTS = Proper of Saints First + Common Second

It is easy to pray Night Prayer on a Feast. A Feast is not as high a celebration as a Solemnity. Therefore, it has no effect on Night Prayer. **On a Feast, pray the same Night Prayer that you would pray were it simply a regular weekday.** That really was easy!

How does this work? Turn to July 3, the Feast of St. Thomas the Apostle, you know, the doubter. Suppose that July 3 falls on a Friday.

Will there be an Evening Prayer I for the Feast of St. Thomas the Apostle? No, because you use the Proper of Saints first, and it lists no Evening Prayer I under St. Thomas's Feast. Since July 2 is a Ferial Day (no saint is celebrated), Evening Prayer on July 2 will be from the Psalter just as if the next day were no big celebration at all.

Look at the instruction for the Feast of St. Thomas. What two parts of the breviary are used to pray Morning and Evening Prayer? Right! Proper of Saints first. Then, if a part of the Office is not in the Proper, use the Common of Apostles. The Common of Apostles is the Primary Common and the <u>only</u> Common used for this feast.

Where are the Psalms and Canticles for the Morning Prayer Psalmody? The breviary tells you to go to Sunday, Week I. You have

DODO
SELF CHECK #66

1. What is a Feast? How does it differ from a Solemnity?

2. Does a Feast usually have Evening Prayer I? Why or why not? How will you know if it does have Evening Prayer I?

3. What two parts of the breviary are used for praying Morning and Evening Prayer on Feasts? How does one use them?

4. What Night Prayer office is used on a Feast?

already got those marked with your spiritually alive green ribbon.

Where are the Psalms and Canticles for Evening Prayer? The breviary tells you to go to the Common of Apostles. Where are the Antiphons for them? The instructions tell you to use the ones from Morning Prayer of the Feast. All the instructions are in the breviary.

Where is the Invitatory Psalm? The Canticle of Zechariah? The Canticle of Mary? You have already ribbon-marked them!

What Night Prayer Office is used? Remember the rule for Feasts? The one for the day of the week on which the Feast falls (in this case of a Friday Feast, the Friday Night Prayer).

— · — · — · — · — · — · — · —

PRACTICE: No matter what day it is, pretend that today is Friday, July 3. If you are in the USA, you might be going to a fireworks display tonight. And maybe to the beach or the pool before that. But before everything else, you want to pray Morning Prayer for the Feast of St. Thomas the Apostle.

First, move the bookmarks to the correct locations. **The Proper of Saints bookmark will be at the Feast of Saint Thomas the Apostle (July 3). The "Common: Primary Office" bookmark will be at the Common of the Apostles** (be sure to put it at the Morning Prayer location and not at Evening Prayer I since Evening Prayer I is not prayed on a Feast unless you are specifically told to pray it. You are not told to pray it for the Feast of St. Thomas.).

The ribbons should already be in place since they do not move. **The white ribbon should be marking the Invitatory Psalm. The green ribbon should be marking the Psalmody for Sunday Morning Prayer, Week I. The silver ribbon should be marking the Canticle of Zechariah.**

When you have the parts of the Morning Prayer office correctly marked, you are ready to pray. Pray Morning Prayer for the Feast of St. Thomas all the way through using your breviary. When you finish, check how you did by referring to Appendix K.

SECTION ELEVEN
Praying Morning, Evening, and Night Prayer on Memorials

"In this section, you'll learn about . . ."

- **Night Prayer on Memorials**
- **Prayer on Obligatory Memorials**
- **Prayer on Optional Memorials**
- **Praying the Office on Commemorations**
- **Getting to Know the Ordo**
- **Special Cases and Seasons**

SECTION ELEVEN: PRAYING MORNING, EVENING, AND NIGHT PRAYER ON MEMORIALS

Lesson 67: Memorials and Night Prayer on Memorials

Praying the Office on Feasts is like eating a piece of cake! Sweet and simple. Are you feeling confident! Good. Because some Memorials are a little trickier. More like eating taffy with false teeth. Ready to tackle Memorials? Not sure? Oh, come on! Give it a go!

Some saints' celebrations have a heading that says either "Memorial," "Commemoration," "Feast," or "Solemnity." And some have no headings at all. You already know about Feasts and Solemnities. What about the others?

First, some review. **A MEMORIAL is a lesser celebration of the Church. All offices labeled "Memorial" and all offices with no labels are Memorials.** Would you be dismayed to learn that labeled and unlabeled offices are celebrated a bit differently? Well, you have come this far. Might as well go all the way and learn these distinctions.

In the Proper of Saints, compare the celebrations for St. Lawrence of Brindisi on July 21 with that of St. Mary Magdalene on July 22. St. Lawrence of Brindisi was a Capuchin Franciscan, a terrific preacher, and a Doctor of the Church. You know St. Mary Magdalene, the first follower of Jesus to see Him after the Resurrection.

Now more review. You will note that St. Lawrence's celebration has no label while St. Mary Magdalene's is labeled "Memorial." St. Lawrence's celebration is a Memorial, too, but it is an OPTIONAL MEMORIAL. **An OPTIONAL MEMORIAL is not labeled in the breviary. An individual or parish may choose to celebrate it if desired.** St. Mary Magdalene's celebration is an OBLIGATORY MEMORIAL. **An OBLIGATORY MEMORIAL is labeled**

"Memorial" in the breviary. The whole Church celebrates Obligatory Memorials.

Look at St. Bridget's celebration on July 23. St. Bridget was a wife, mother, and mystic known for her prophecies, revelations, and holiness. Is St. Bridget's celebration an Optional or Obligatory Memorial? Apply the above definitions and figure it out! How about Saints Joachim and Ann, the parents of Our Lady, on July 26? St. Martha, who waited on Jesus while Mary sat at His feet and prayed, on July 29? Saint Peter Chrysologus, the golden tongued preacher, bishop, and Doctor of the Church, on July 30?

Now check these four celebrations again, comparing the Concluding Prayers. How many Concluding Prayers are listed for each celebration? Right. Only one. So which office do you use it with? Or do you use it with all the offices?

Time for a memory jog. Do you recall that, in the Proper of Seasons, a single Concluding Prayer was used to conclude both the Morning and Evening Prayer offices? The same applies here. **The Concluding Prayer listed in the Proper of Saints is used to conclude both the Morning and Evening Prayer offices.**

> **DODO**
> **SELF CHECK #67**
>
> 1. What is a Memorial?
> 2. What is an Optional Memorial? Does the whole Church always celebrate an Optional Memorial?
> 3. What is an Obligatory Memorial? Does the whole Church always celebrate an Obligatory Memorial?
> 4. How will you know if a Memorial is Optional or Obligatory?
> 5. Do Memorials have Evening Prayer I?
> 6. What Night Prayer office is used on a Memorial?
> 7. If only one Concluding Prayer is written under a Memorial, during which offices is it prayed?

All Memorials, whether Optional or Obligatory, are minor celebrations of the Church. They do not have Evening Prayer I. The Night Prayer office used is the one for the day of the week on which the Memorial falls. Shortly you will learn how to pray Morning and Evening Prayer on a Memorial.

Lesson 68: Praying Morning and Evening Prayer on Obligatory Memorials

Go get yourself a cup of coffee and a sandwich. This is a long lesson. Might as well be comfortable going over it.

When praying the Divine Office on Feasts and Solemnities, you learned to use first all the parts of the Office that are in the Feast or Solemnity as listed in either the Proper of Saints or the Proper of Seasons. Any parts not in the Proper of Saints or the Proper of Seasons are taken from the Common.

Here is a mathematical-like formula for that:

SOLEMNITIES AND FEASTS = Proper of Saints/Proper of Seasons First + Commons Second

Memorials aren't found in the Proper of Seasons. They are all in the Proper of Saints. Memorials use the Proper of Saints. They use the Commons. They use the Psalter. Now hang in there with me, will you? In order to pray the Divine Office on a Memorial, you need to know which parts of the breviary to use and when to use them. First you will learn to pray Morning and Evening Prayer on Obligatory Memorials. Later on Optional Memorials.

Now take a sip of that coffee before moving on. Feel better now?

On OBLIGATORY MEMORIALS, the Office is taken first from the Memorial in the Proper of Saints. Those portions of the Office not in the Proper of Saints are taken from the Common or the Psalter. <u>For certain parts of the Office, the Church allows a choice between the Common or Psalter</u>.

This is too much information for a simple math-like equation. We need the chart reproduced on page 155.

After we review this chart, feel free to look back at it at any time. What good is a chart if you do not refer to it? You might even want to copy it and put it into your breviary.

Where do you first look for all parts of the Office? In the Memorial.

If the Memorial has no Invitatory Antiphon, where do you find it? In the Common or the Psalter (your choice).

Which Hymn will you use to celebrate an Obligatory Memorial if the Memorial has no Hymn? The one in the Common only.

Which Psalmody will you use if the Memorial has no Psalmody? The one from the Psalter only.

Other than the Invitatory Antiphon, what four parts of the Office can be taken either from the Common or the Psalter (your choice) if those parts are not in the Memorial? The Reading and Responsory, the Antiphon for the Canticle of Zechariah, the Antiphon for the Canticle of Mary, and the Intercessions.

If the Memorial has no Concluding Prayer, which prayer will you use? Only the one from the Common.

Praying Morning and Evening Prayer on OBLIGATORY MEMORIALS		
Part of Office	**Use 1st**	**If not in Memorial, use**
Invitatory Antiphon	Memorial	Common or Psalter
Hymn	Memorial	Common
Psalmody	Memorial	Psalter
Reading/Responsory	Memorial	Common or Psalter
Antiphon for Canticle of Zechariah	Memorial	Common or Psalter
Antiphon for Canticle of Mary	Memorial	Common or Psalter
Intercessions	Memorial	Common or Psalter
Concluding Prayer	Memorial	Common

OK. You are doing great. Another sip of coffee and a bite of that sandwich before moving on.

How about a summary? **On OBLIGATORY MEMORIALS, use first all the parts of the Office in the Memorial. If the Memorial does not have a Hymn, use the Hymn from the Common. If the Memorial does not have a Psalmody, use the Psalmody in the Psalter. If the Memorial does not have a Concluding Prayer, use the Concluding Prayer from the Common. For any other parts of the Office not in the**

Memorial, use the corresponding parts from either the Psalter or the Common. The choice is up to you.

What does this tell you about Obligatory Memorials? Like sandwiches, they have a basic form but variations in their content. Just as you do not think twice about making a sandwich, except to decide what to put in it, so you will soon not be thinking twice about Memorials.

How does this work? **Move your Proper of Saints bookmark to the Memorial for Saint Justin Martyr which is June 1.** Saint Justin Martyr was, to state the obvious, a martyr. He was the first layman to serve as an apologist and met his death by beheading in 165. Not a nice way to go, but then, he flew right into the Lord's Presence where his head was, in his spiritual body, promptly restored. The celebration for this great Christian debater is marked "Memorial." So you know it is Obligatory which means that the whole Church celebrates it.

The instruction given says, "From the common of one martyr, page ___." The only parts of the Office under the Memorial for Saint Justin Martyr are the Antiphons for Canticles of Zechariah and Mary and the Concluding Prayer *(those with four-volume breviaries will have the Second Reading for the Office of Readings and its Responsory as well)*. This means that all the other parts of the Office for Saint Justin Martyr will be taken either from the Common or from the Psalter.

First mark the Common. The Common of One Martyr is the Primary Common and the only Common used for this Memorial. **Move your "Common: Primary Office" bookmark to the Common of One Martyr.** What do you do with the Common—Secondary Office bookmark? Just leave it someplace in the Commons but pay no attention to it.

Pretend that June 1 falls on Monday, Week I. **Move your Psalter bookmark to Monday Morning Prayer, Week I.**

We can use either the Common or the Psalter for certain parts of this Office. Let us decide to do things alphabetically. Why not? That means we will use the Common whenever we have a choice.

Now, referring to the above chart and using your breviary, answer the following questions:

> Where will you find the Hymn?
> The Invitatory Antiphon?
> Psalmody?
> Reading and Responsory?
> Antiphon for Canticle of Zechariah?
> Intercessions?
> Concluding Prayer?

All right! You are about ready to pray. But first, another sip of coffee and you might want to finish that sandwich. I hope it was a tasty one.

— · — · — · — · — · — · —

PRACTICE: Pray Morning Prayer for the Memorial of Saint Justin Martyr using the Common wherever you have a choice. See how you did by checking yourself against Appendix L.

— · — · — · — · — · — · —

EXTRA PRACTICE: Pray Morning Prayer for the Memorial for Saint Justin Martyr but use the Psalter wherever you have a choice. Check how you did by referring to Appendix M.

Now compare the parts of the two offices. What parts are alike? What parts are different?

— · — · — · — · — · — · —

If you are a thinking dodo, you may have a few questions.

Does the Church permit use of the Reading from one part of the breviary and the Responsory from another part? No, that is not an acceptable practice. **The Responsory used is always the one that follows the Reading in the breviary.** If the Reading from the Psalter is chosen, then the Responsory that follows it is also chosen. If the Reading from the Common is chosen, the Responsory that follows it is also chosen. The Reading and Responsory always go together.

Does the Church allow use of one part of the Office from the

Psalter and another from the Common, or ought the Psalter or Common be used consistently when there is a choice? **With the exception of not mixing the Reading and Responsory, those praying may choose, when choice is allowed, to pray one part of the Office from the Psalter and the other part from the Common.** This means that, for the Memorial of Saint Justin Martyr, one could use the Invitatory Antiphon from the Common of One Martyr, the Reading and Responsory from the Psalter, and the Intercessions from the Common. Or one could mix and match these parts in other ways. However, since the Antiphon for the Canticle of Zechariah, the Antiphon for the Canticle of Mary, and the Concluding Prayer are written under the Memorial of Saint Justin, these are the ones used by the whole Church.

Suppose a Memorial falls on a Sunday? Or during Holy Week or during the Octave of Easter? Does the Church celebrate the Memorial? No. **Memorials are never celebrated on Sundays or during Holy Week and the Easter Octave. These days have special**

offices. The Sunday, Holy Week, and Easter Octave celebrations are used at these times.

Are there any exceptions to the above guidelines? Very few. To take one example, the Memorial for St. Agnes, child martyr of the early Church, on January 21 tells the reader to use Sunday Week I Psalms for Morning Prayer Psalms and the Psalms and Canticle from the Common of One Martyr for Evening Prayer II. We would not expect this because Memorials use the Psalmody from the Psalter unless the Memorial has its own Psalmody. So what makes St. Agnes so special? Her day used to be celebrated as a Feast so it has offices written for a Feast. Now we celebrate her day as a Memorial. Anybody but a saint would see this as a demotion, but St. Agnes does not care because she knows that it is Christ Who receives the glory, not her.

So what to do? You will be all right if you remember this simple guideline. The breviary has all "special" instructions written in it. **Always follow _first_ whatever instructions are given in the Proper of Saints. If no instructions are given, follow the rules summarized in the chart shown earlier.** If you placed this chart in your breviary, good for you!

You did it. You completed this lesson and see what you have learned! Go treat yourself to a banana split because, in my opinion, this is the most difficult lesson in the entire manual. It is downhill from here on.

Lesson 69: Optional Memorials

Believe it or not, this is going to be an easier lesson. But, despite the title of this lesson, it is not an optional lesson. It is one any want-ing-to-be-wise dodo will gladly do.

You have bumped into Optional Memorials before. Remember? **An OPTIONAL MEMORIAL is a Memorial that _may_ be celebrated.** That means you do not have to celebrate it. So one real way to deal with an Optional Memorial is to skip it. Do you really want to do that and miss out on some fantastic saints? I hope not!

In the Proper of Saints, turn to December 11. What saint is celebrated that day? Saint Damasus I. Remember him? He is the patron of Saint Jerome. He also published the Canon of Sacred Scripture, the Bible. Now you remember! Saint Damasus I does not have a heading to his celebration. This means that the celebration for Saint Damasus I is an OPTIONAL MEMORIAL.

Now for some review. Optional means something that may or may not be chosen. **OPTIONAL MEMORIALS are saints' celebrations that have no heading in the breviary. These unlabeled offices may be celebrated if desired. If they are not celebrated, the day is treated as a Ferial Day (a day on which no celebration is held).** On Ferial Days, use only the Psalter and, during Lent/Easter and Advent/Christmas, the Proper of Seasons as well.

More review. **The Church does not celebrate any Memorial, whether Optional or Obligatory, on Sundays, during Holy Week, or during the Easter Octave.** These days have their own special offices.

Sometimes two or more Optional Memorials are celebrated on the same day (this does not happen with Obligatory Memorials). Look at November 16. Whose offices are celebrated that day? Are either one marked "Memorial?" No, neither is. This means that the offices for both Saint Margaret of Scotland and Saint Gertrude are OPTIONAL MEMORIALS. **When two or more Optional**

DODO
SELF CHECK #69

1. What is an Optional Memorial? How is it marked in the Proper of Saints?

2. Does the Church celebrate every Optional Memorial? If you choose not to celebrate it, how do you pray the Office of the day?

3. If two or more Optional Memorials fall on the same day, is it proper Church usage to celebrate both? Do you have to celebrate either?

4. On what days of the year does the Church never celebrate Memorials?

Memorials fall on the same day, you may choose to celebrate neither saint. Or you may choose to celebrate one saint or the other. Generally only one saint, if any, is celebrated, even if two or three are listed.

Lesson 70: The Easiest Way to Pray Morning and Evening Prayer on Optional Memorials during Ordinary Time

You mean there is an easiest way to do something in the Divine Office? Oh, tell me! Please!

There is one very, very easy way to pray Optional Memorials. So simple you might fall out of your chair when you learn it, so hold on! As you know, Optional Memorials fall during Ordinary Time and also during the Seasons of the Church year. Here is the easy prayer method for praying Morning and Evening Prayer on Optional Memorials during Ordinary Time. **In Ordinary Time, when praying Morning and Evening Prayer on Optional Memorials, use every part of the Office in the Proper of Saints. Use the Psalter for those parts <u>not</u> in the Proper of Saints.** In this easy method, the Common is not used, even through the breviary will have a Common as a reference.

Here is a simple mathematical-like equation for this:

MP and EP Optional Memorials Ordinary Time = Saints first + Psalter second.

How does this work? Suppose today is October 16. The Proper of Saints bookmark would already be at October 16 as you will be moving it through the Proper of Saints as you pray.

Find October 16 in the Proper of Saints. Are any saints celebrated on this day? Two great ones—Saint Hedwig, duchess and mother of seven children who, upon being widowed, became a Cistercian nun who had to leave her convent to make peace among her battling children. Sound like someone you can identify with? The other saint is gentle Saint Margaret Mary Alacoque to whom were given the revelations regarding the Sacred Heart of Jesus, a devotion many practice in the Church today. Are the celebrations of these two saints Optional Memorials? How do you know? Does the Church permit a choice on whether or not to celebrate these?

Suppose you decide to celebrate an Optional Memorial on October 16. Pretend that, this particular year, October 16 falls on Friday of Week IV during the 28th week of Ordinary Time. Since you would be praying the Office daily, your Psalter bookmark would already be at Friday, Week IV, in the Psalter.

DODO
SELF CHECK #70

1. If you choose to observe an Optional Memorial during Ordinary Time, what is the easiest method to use?

2. What parts of the office from the Proper of Saints do you use? What parts do you use from the Psalter?

On October 16, ought you celebrate both Saint Hedwig and Saint Margaret Mary Alacoque? Gosh, do you have to choose? Unfortunately, yes. You could celebrate one saint this year and the other next year, if you like. Suppose that your youngsters cannot agree on who gets the remote for the television so you choose Saint Hedwig. Under her office there is only one Concluding Prayer. So that is all you would use from her celebration. The rest of the office will be in the Psalter.

— · — · — · — · — · — · — ·

PRACTICE: Pray the entire Morning Prayer office using the Psalter. When you get to the Concluding Prayer, use the one from the Optional Memorial for Saint Hedwig instead of the Concluding Prayer in the Psalter. This is the simplest way to observe this Optional Memorial.

If you do not want to leave out St. Margaret Mary Alacoque, go back and pray an office for her, too, using everything from the Psalter except the Concluding Prayer which is the only part of this office that is in the Proper of Saints.

Did you find this to be an easy method?

Lesson 71: Two Other Ways to Celebrate Morning and Evening Prayer on Optional Memorials

You may be thinking, "Look, I do not even have to observe Optional Memorials. But, to be nice, I just learned a super simple way to pray them. Now you want to give me two options for the options? No way, Jose!"

OK, if you want to skip this chapter, go right ahead. But if you like choices or are a curious dodo about what is coming up, read on. What have you got to lose? You do not have to use these options even if you know about them.

There are four ways to pray Morning and Evening Prayer on Optional Memorials.

One you just learned. It applies only to Optional Memorials during Ordinary Time. What is that method?

A second method you also know. That is to **pray the Morning and Evening Prayer offices as you would pray them on Obligatory Memorials.**

A third way is to:

1. Use all the parts of the office found in the Proper of Saints.

2. Use the Psalter <u>only</u> for the Psalmody and its Antiphons and Psalm-Prayers.

3. Use <u>everything else</u> from the Common.

At first glance, this seems similar to how the Office is prayed on Obligatory Memorials, but it is a bit different. It is simpler. Compare the three directives above with those in Lesson 68 and you will see what I mean.

Look at the celebration for Saint John Damascene on December 4 in the Proper of Saints. St. John Damascene is a Doctor of the Church who authored 150 religious works and who defended the veneration of icons. Next time you dust off your statue of St. Anthony or St. Joseph or Our Lady, you can thank St. John

Damascene for the Church allowing it in your house. Do you see a small instruction under St. John's biography? The instruction reads, "From the common of doctors of the Church" and a page number in your breviary is given.

This means that, if you so choose, you can use the common of doctors of the Church to pray the office on this Optional Memorial. Let us see how using the Common works for a celebration of Saint John Damascene on December 4.

Place your Proper of Saints bookmark at Saint John's Optional Memorial on December 4. What part of the Office is printed there?

Pretend that the Optional Memorial of St. John Damascene falls on Friday, Week I of the Psalter, and that this also happens to be the first week of Advent. **Mark this with the Psalter bookmark.** Remember, in this option, you will be using only the Psalms, Antiphons, and Psalm-Prayers from the Psalter. The rest will come from, first, the Proper of Saints, and, second, from the Common of Doctors.

On this pretend day, the Proper of Seasons bookmark would be at Friday of the First Week of Advent in the Proper of Seasons. Will you use the Proper of Seasons if you follow this option for praying the Divine Office on Optional Memorials? No, in this option you will not use the Proper of Seasons. You will learn how to use it later.

Move the "Common: Primary Office" bookmark to the Common of Doctors of the Church (the page number will be under Saint John Damascene's day). Will you use the Common in this option? Yes, you will use it for everything but the Psalmody (from the Psalter) and the

> **DODO**
> **SELF CHECK #71**
>
> 1. What are three ways to pray Morning and Evening Prayer on Optional Memorials? Describe each way in detail.
>
> 2. Do you use the Psalmody in the Commons for Morning and Evening Prayer on Optional Memorials? Where do you find the Psalms for the Psalmody?

Concluding Prayer (which is under St. John Damascene's celebration).

Now page through the Common of Doctors, just to be sure that all the parts of the office are there. Remember the parts? Hymn—Psalms and Antiphons—Reading/Responsory—Canticle of Mary—Intercessions—Our Father—Concluding Prayer. Yikes! Something is missing! The Common of Doctors has no Intercessions? Do you skip them? You already know the answer to that question. So what do you do?

First think ahead. **When using any Common, always look back at its very first page to see if there are any special instructions. Different breviaries give different instructions.** You probably will not find the words "Primary Common" and "Secondary Common" used, but you do not need them, do you? You remember that the first Common you use is the Primary Common and any Common that the first Common refers you to is the Secondary Common. Some breviaries tell you that you are to take everything from the other Common except the parts written in this Common. Other breviaries get more specific and refer you to another Common for certain well-marked parts of the Divine Office.

Whatever instruction your breviary gives, the parts of the Office will be the same. You need only know how to find the parts that you need. Put the bookmarks in the locations given and you are ready to pray!

So how do you pray the Optional Memorial of St. John Damascene? The Primary Common bookmark is at the Common of Doctors. The Common of Doctors refers you to the Common of Pastors for parts not in the Common of Doctors. Does this mean that you have to use that Commons—Secondary Office bookmark? You betcha. The parts of the office not in the Common of Doctors, in this case the Intercessions, will be in the Common of Pastors. **Go to that spot and put the Commons-Secondary Office bookmark right there, at the Intercessions.**

— · — · — · — · — · — · — · —

PRACTICE: Pray Morning Prayer for an Optional Memorial for Saint John Damascene using only the Proper of Saints, the Psalmody from the Psalter, and the Common.

After praying Morning Prayer for the Optional Memorial of Saint John Damascene, using this option, check how you did by looking at Appendix N.

Lesson 72: Praying Morning and Evening Prayer on Optional Memorials during Seasons of the Church Year

Wait a minute. Were there four ways to pray the Divine Office on Optional Memorials? You just learned three ways. What is number four?

The fourth way deals with praying the Divine Office during Lent/Easter and Advent/Christmas.

Praying the Divine Office on Optional Memorials during Lent/Easter and Advent/Christmas is a bit more complicated than praying the Office during Ordinary Time. Oh, great! Wait a moment. Hang in there. If you prefer not to observe an Optional Memorial, no one is going to make you choose otherwise. Optional Memorials are optional! After reading this instruction, you decide what you would like to do. Agreed?

What is the first thing you have to do to celebrate an Optional Memorial during Lent/Easter or Advent/Christmas? Well, first you note whether the Optional Memorial becomes a COMMEMORATION. A Commemoration has its own procedures. More about that later.

First learn how to celebrate an Optional Memorial during a Church Season when that Memorial does not become a Commemoration. This would be during the first three weeks of Advent and after the Easter and Christmas Octaves (the eight days following the Solemnities). During these times, as you already know, the Church is using the Proper of Seasons. The guidelines for using the Proper of Seasons apply here, to an extent, but with these additional techniques.

A Fourth Way to Pray Morning and Evening Prayer on Optional Memorials during the First Three Weeks of Advent and during the Easter and Christmas Seasons after the Octaves

1. FIRST—SAINTS: Use all parts of the Office found under the Optional Memorial in the Proper of Saints.

2. NEXT—SEASONS: Then use all the other parts found in the Proper of Seasons.

3. LAST—PSALTER: Use the Psalter for parts of the Office in neither the Proper of Saints nor the Proper of Seasons.

Try to memorize these key words. SAINTS. SEASONS. PSALTER. Say them again. SAINTS. SEASONS. PSALTER. Got it?

Have you noticed that the Common is not used in this option?

How does this work? Earlier we celebrated the Optional Memorial of Saint John Damascene using the Common. Now we will celebrate it using the Proper of Seasons.

Find the Optional Memorial of Saint John Damascene on December 4 in the Proper of Saints. Is it an Obligatory or Optional Memorial? How do you know? **Move the Proper of Saints bookmark to December 4.**

Pretend that December 4 falls on Friday of the First Week of Advent. **Move the Proper of Seasons bookmark to that spot.**

Move the Psalter bookmark to Friday, Week I.

DODO
SELF CHECK #72

1. If you choose to observe an Optional Memorial by using the Proper of Seasons, how do you pray Morning and Evening Prayer?

2. If you use the Proper of Seasons to observe an Optional Memorial, will you also use the Common?

3. In praying Morning and Evening Prayer on Optional Memorials, which Psalmody is always used?

How do we pray this office? Remember the order. SAINTS. SEASONS. PSALTER.

To celebrate the Optional Memorial of Saint John Damascene using the Proper of Seasons, look first in the Proper of SAINTS. All that is printed is a Concluding Prayer. Is this used to conclude both the Morning and Evening Prayer offices? You betcha.

Now where do you look? In the Proper of SEASONS. Everything not in the Proper of Saints take from the Proper of Seasons.

What if a part is not in the Proper of Saints or the Proper of Seasons? Where do you find it? Yes. PSALTER.

Go through the Morning Prayer office section by section. Follow the above rules. Remember the key words: SAINTS. SEASONS. PSALTER.

First look in the Proper of Saints. Use all the parts of the office there.

Next look in the Proper of Seasons. Use all the parts of the office there that are not in the Proper of Saints.

Last, look in the Psalter. Use all parts of the office here that are not in either the Proper of Saints or the Proper of Seasons.

What will you use from the Proper of Saints for the Optional Memorial of Saint John Damascene? Only the Concluding Prayer.

What will you use from the Proper of Seasons for this celebration? The Invitatory Antiphon, Reading, Responsory, Antiphon for the Canticle of Zechariah, and Intercessions.

What will you use from the Psalter? The Psalmody and its Antiphons.

What Hymn will you use? One appropriate for Advent (you can find it in a special section of your breviary).

— · — · — · — · — · — · — · —

PRACTICE: Pray Morning Prayer for the Optional Memorial of Saint John Damascene for December 4, Friday, Week I, during the First Week of Advent, using the Proper of Seasons. Check how you did by referring to Appendix O.

- - - . - . - . - . - . - . - . - . -

EXTRA PRACTICE: Pray Evening Prayer for the Optional Memorial of Saint John Damascene for the same day. How do you think you did with it?

Lesson 73: Commemorations

Oh, no. Here is that word. Commemorations. Scary. Yes, praying the Divine Office on Commemorations is a bit tricky, but all you need to know are a few simple techniques. And then, presto, all will become easy.

A COMMEMORATION is a Memorial, whether Optional or Obligatory, that is celebrated at any time during Lent and also during Advent between December 17 to the 23rd and during the Octave of Christmas (between Christmas and New Year's). All Memorials celebrated at these times become COMMEMORATIONS. COMMEMORATIONS are optional celebrations. This means that parishes and individuals may choose to celebrate them if desired. Commemorations are not celebrated during Holy Week or the Octave of Easter (eight days following Easter Sunday) even if a saint's celebration coincides with those days. These are special holy days whose individual offices are never replaced by a saint's Commemoration.

Only <u>Memorials</u>, whether Optional or Obligatory, become Commemorations. **Feasts and Solemnities of the Saints never become Commemorations. They are always celebrated at the proper time unless they coincide with a Solemnity of the Church year.** No saint's Feast or Solemnity, for example, is ever celebrated during Holy Week, Easter, and the Easter Octave because these are Solemnities of the Church Year that involve our Lord Jesus. A saint's Feast or Solemnity does not replace a Solemnity of Christ. **Feasts that coincide with a Solemnity of the Church simply drop out of the calendar for that year.**

Solemnities that coincide are transferred to another day so that they will still be celebrated.

Suppose you bravely choose to observe a Commemoration. You are going to apply a technique called the "Commemoration Combo." Here is how it works:

Night Prayer: On a Commemoration, Night Prayer is the one for the weekday. No changes are made in the Night Prayer office. Oh, that was easy. No Combo here. But read on.

Morning and Evening Prayer: Here is where you do the Commemoration Combo. A Commemoration occurs on special days of the Church year. The Commemoration must take second place to these observances. To do this, **pray the entire office using the Proper of Seasons and the Psalter, just as if the Commemoration did not exist.** Really? Yes, really. **When you get to the Concluding Prayer of the Morning or Evening Office, pray the first part of** it but leave off the ending ("**through Our Lord Jesus Christ**" **and so on). Now, if praying Morning Prayer, add the Morning Prayer Antiphon for the Canticle of Zechariah from the Proper of Saints (if there is one) and for Evening Prayer, add the Evening Prayer Antiphon from the Canticle of Mary (if there is one).** Oh, oh. Is this the Combo? Sure is. You mean I combine the Antiphon right here, in the middle of the Concluding Prayer? Yes, that is exactly what I mean. Weird! **Pray the Antiphon right here even though it seems odd. Then pray the Concluding Prayer for the saint.** Did you say the saint's

> **DODO**
> **SELF CHECK #73**
>
> 1. What is a Commemoration? How do you know if a Memorial is a Commemoration? Does the Church allow any choice about whether or not to celebrate Commemorations?
>
> 2. When do Commemorations occur?
>
> 3. Do Feasts or Solemnities become Commemorations?
>
> 4. How is Night Prayer prayed on a Commemoration?
>
> 5. How are the Morning and Evening Prayer offices prayed on Commemorations?

Concluding Prayer? You mean I combine that prayer with the Proper of Seasons Concluding Prayer? Yes. More weird. **End the offices with the usual "May the Lord bless us, protect us from all evil, and bring us to everlasting life. Amen." Then make the Sign of the Cross as usual.**

There you have it. The Commemoration Combo!

Do you want to see how this works? If you are any kind of incredulous dodo, you sure do! Turn in the Proper of Saints to March 23. March 23 is a Commemoration in honor of St. Turibius (Toribio) de Mongrovejo. St. Turibius is a marvelous bishop who defended the rights of the native Indians of Peru who were suffering terribly under the Spaniards. Pretend that March 23 falls on Monday of the Fourth Week of Lent which also happens to be Monday of Week IV in the Psalter. To pray Morning Prayer on the Commemoration of St. Turibius, you would pray the entire office using the Psalter for the Psalmody and the Proper of Seasons for the rest of the Office as you have already learned. The Commemoration would only be noted at the end of the offices as part of the Concluding Prayer.

How would you compose this prayer? First find the Concluding Prayer for the Proper of Seasons. Next find the Antiphons for the Canticles of Zechariah and Mary in the Proper of Saints. Finally find the Concluding Prayer for the Commemoration of St. Turibius.

—·—·—·—·—·—·—·—

PRACTICE: Follow the above instructions and pray the Concluding Prayer for Morning Prayer as it should be prayed for the Commemoration of St. Turibius, if this Commemoration fell on Monday of the Fourth Week of Lent (Monday of Week IV in the Psalter).

—·—·—·—·—·—·—·—

EXTRA PRACTICE: Pray the Concluding Prayer for Evening Prayer as it should be prayed for the Commemoration of St. Turibius on the same imaginary day.

Check how you did on both prayers by referring to Appendix P.

Now go to December 29, the Commemoration of St. Thomas Becket, the well-known English Archbishop of Canterbury and martyr under King Henry II of England. You will note that December 29 has an office both in the Proper of Saints for St. Thomas Becket and in the Proper of Seasons for December 29. That is OK. Follow the Commemoration Combo Procedure listed above.

PRACTICE: Pray the Concluding Prayer for the Morning Prayer office for a Commemoration of St. Thomas Becket.

EXTRA PRACTICE: Pray the Concluding Prayer for the Evening Prayer office for St. Thomas Becket.

Check how you did on both prayers by referring to Appendix P.

Lesson 74: Special Cases

Did you think that you were going to get by without any exceptions? No way! Life is full of exceptions, and the Divine Office is no exception to the norm. So where are the exceptions?

Depending on the date of publication of your breviary, the exceptions may already be in it, and you will never know that they are exceptions! Exceptions occur when the Church adds a new saint to be celebrated liturgically. Then, what might have been a Ferial Day may become a Memorial, Feast, or even a Solemnity.

If you have an older breviary, how will you know if a new saint's celebration has been added? You will not know unless you obtain an ORDO (more about that in Lesson 75). For example, two offices used to fall on October 19. One was that of Saints Isaac Jogues and John de Brebeuf, two North American Martyrs. These two saints and some others died at the hands of the Native Americans whom they were trying to convert. The other saint who used to be celebrated on October 19 is Saint Paul of the Cross, founder of the

Passionists. Both celebrations used to be Optional Memorials. However, the celebration of the North American Martyrs has been made an Obligatory Memorial for October 19. To accommodate the new Obligatory Memorial, the Optional Memorial of Saint Paul of the Cross has been moved to October 20. However, if you are a member of the Passionists, you celebrate your founder's feast day not as an Optional Memorial but as a Solemnity.

Here is another exception. For certain celebrations, two Commons may be used. Look, for example, at the Memorial for November 10, that of St. Leo the Great, Pope and Doctor of the Church who stabilized the Church during a time of invasion and heresy. What two Commons does this celebration use? Your breviary will say, "From the common of pastors, p. ___, or of doctors of the Church, p. ___."

Suppose that you decide to use the Common for Doctors of the Church. Oh, you might remember that Common. We used it for the Optional Memorial of St. John Damascene. Do you recall that the Common for Doctors of the Church refers you to the Common of Pastors for any parts not in the Common of Doctors? Use the two Commons bookmarks to mark these offices (Doctors as Primary Common and Pastors as Secondary Common) and you are ready to pray.

> **DODO SELF CHECK #74**
>
> 1. How will you know if a Memorial or other celebration is observed on the day written in your older breviary? How will you know if a new celebration has been added?
>
> 2. How do you pray the Divine Office if the Primary Common that you are using refers you to another Common? How do you use the bookmarks in these cases?

— · — · — · — · — · —

PRACTICE: Pretend that it is Tuesday, November 10, and you are in Week IV of the Psalter. You wish to pray Morning Prayer for the Memorial of St. Leo the Great, using the Common of Doctors.

Your Psalter bookmark would be in place already. **Move the Psalter bookmark to Tuesday of Week IV.**

Then **move the Proper of Saints bookmark to November 10, the Memorial of St. Leo the Great.**

Next **place the "Common: Primary Office" bookmark at the Common of Doctors.** Everything in that Common you will use first.

Now **place the "Common: Secondary Office" bookmark at the Common of Pastors.** If parts of the Office are not in the Common of Doctors, you will take them from the Common of Pastors.

Pray Morning Prayer for the Memorial of St. Leo, using the Common of Doctors as the Primary Office. Follow Lesson 68's guidelines for praying the Office on Obligatory Memorials. For this practice, whenever you have a choice between using the Psalter and the Common, use the Common. After you pray the Office through, check how you did by referring to Appendix Q.

Lesson 75: The Ordo

The what? Is an ORDO the cousin of a dodo? Far from it. An ORDO is a handy way to know just what to pray each day in the Divine Office. You might want to get one.

An ORDO, also called a "Guide for Christian Prayer," is a daily guide to praying the Divine Office for a specific year. Maybe you received one with your breviary. **You have to buy a new one each year,** but it is worth its weight in gold, because it tells exactly where to find the offices for each day.

You know that the Divine Office is the same all over the world, no matter who published your breviary. However, different publishers arrange the breviary a bit differently. **In order for the page numbers in the Ordo to correspond to the page numbers in your breviary,**

> **DODO SELF CHECK #75**
> 1. What is an Ordo?
> 2. Why is an Ordo useful?
> 3. What precautions must be taken in ordering an Ordo?
> 4. How long can you use an Ordo?

the Ordo that <u>you</u> get must be the one written for the breviary that <u>you</u> are using. Makes perfect sense!

Where do you get an Ordo? From a Catholic bookstore. When you request one, tell the clerk the name of your breviary and the publisher so that you receive the Ordo that corresponds to your breviary. If a bookstore seems unable to help, contact the publisher of your breviary and ask how you can obtain an Ordo.

Ordos are filled with abbreviations. They look confusing, but you will be able to figure them out. The abbreviations are for the different parts of the Divine Office. Your Ordo may abbreviate Morning Prayer as MP, for example. If all the parts of the Office are taken from one part of the breviary, the Ordo may write ALL. Commons may be abbreviated as Com. and so on. Others will list only the Proper or the Week of the Psalter and you will have to find the correct section and day of the week. With a little study, you will soon understand your Ordo's system. If you have difficulty, ask your parish priest or a member of a religious order to show you what the abbreviations mean. Or contact the publisher of your Ordo with your questions.

An Ordo is especially helpful when certain Solemnities and Feasts replace Sunday celebrations or, because they coincide with a Sunday celebration, are transferred to Monday. Without an Ordo, you will not know if this is the case. However, if you do not have an Ordo, you can always call your parish priest and ask if such a transfer will occur.

Lesson 76: Finding Your Place without an Ordo

If you have an Ordo or intend to purchase one, you can skip this lesson. No one is going to make you read it.

If you do not have an Ordo, do not wish to buy one, or have poor access to Catholic bookstores, on line or in your local area, you will be glad for this lesson. You do not have to memorize the informa-

DODO
SELF CHECK #76

1. If you do not have an Ordo, describe two ways that will tell you what week of the Psalter to use during Ordinary Time.

2. Ash Wednesday always falls during which week of the Psalter? Why?

3. On Monday of the Second Week of Easter, what office will you use?

4. How will you know what week of Ordinary Time to resume after Pentecost? How will you know what week of the Psalter to use?

5. Do you think it is easier to use an Ordo or to use the system described above?

tion you will learn in this lesson. Keep the manual someplace safe, like under your bed, and look back here whenever you have a question about where you are in the Divine Office. You can even write the page of this lesson inside the front cover of the manual if you wish. This is your book. Do what you want with it!

To begin, you will want to find out where the Church is in the Divine Office for today. You will need to find your spot in the Proper of Seasons as well as in the Psalter. To do this, phone a priest or a religious community or look in your church's weekly Mass guide to see what Sunday of the year you are currently celebrating. Find that Sunday's offices in the Proper of Seasons. All the Sunday offices for Ordinary Time should tell you what week of the Psalter to use.

Ordinary Time begins on the Monday following the Baptism of Our Lord (Monday, Week I), is interrupted by Lent, and continues after Pentecost until Advent. If your breviary's Proper of Seasons does not tell you what week of the Psalter you are using for Ordinary Time, you can figure out the week by this trick: Keep it in mind and maybe it will come in handy on a quiz show some day. Here is the trick: Divide the number of the Week of Ordinary Time by 4 and look at the remainder. Remainder 1 means use Week I of the Psalter; Remainder 2 means use Week II; Remainder 3 means use Week III; Remainder 0 means use week IV. For example, for the 22nd Week of Ordinary Time, you would divide 22 by 4 (22/4 = 5, remainder 2). The remainder is 2. Thus, for the 22nd week of Ordinary Time, use

Week II of the Psalter. Turn to the 22nd Sunday of Ordinary Time in your breviary's Proper of Seasons. It may already say "Psalter Week II." Is that clever or what?

But you may not be in Ordinary Time. You may be in one of the Church seasons, either Lent/Easter or Advent/Christmas. What are the guidelines for those seasons?

The First Sunday of Advent is <u>always</u> Sunday, Week I. Follow the weeks in order (Week I, Week II, Week III, Week IV, and then repeat the cycle) until the Sunday of the Baptism of Our Lord. After the Baptism of the Lord, Ordinary Time begins with Monday, Week I and continues until Ash Wednesday. Pretty straightforward, right?

No matter what week you are in when praying the Tuesday before Ash Wednesday (Shrove Tuesday), Ash Wednesday is <u>always</u> Wednesday of Week IV. This means that no matter if Shrove Tuesday was Tuesday of Week I, Week II, Week III, or Week IV, you go to <u>Week IV</u> for Ash Wednesday. Why? Because this makes the Easter cycle work out correctly. Nifty, eh?

After Ash Wednesday, proceed with Thursday, Friday, and Saturday of Week IV so that the first Sunday of Lent is Sunday, Week 1. Continue to use the Psalter in order. Recall that the Triduum and Easter Octave have their own offices in the Proper of Seasons.

On Monday of the second week of Easter, use Monday, Week II of the Psalter. Follow the Psalter in order until Pentecost.

To resume Ordinary Time after Pentecost, ask a priest or a religious community two questions: What week of Ordinary Time are we now in? And what week of the Current Daily Psalter are we now in? Mark your breviary accordingly and proceed with the weeks in order until Advent.

Or you may consult a Mass missalette and then follow the division and remainder guidelines given earlier.

Now you know! Are you smart or what?

Lesson 77: Praying the Office Daily

Congratulations! You did it! You can pray Morning, Evening, and Night Prayer daily. Honest! See how smart you are! All you need do is set your breviary up for today and get praying. You know how to find your place. So why not begin? Get those bouncing bookmarks and restful ribbons in place and you are ready to pray.

Here is a guarantee. If you pray the Office faithfully every day, moving your bookmarks ahead to the next office as you finish one office, you are going to discover that all the difficulty and confusion that you felt when you first turned to this manual has miraculously cleared up.

Now I know that you have several unused bookmarks, printed with terms we have not discussed very much. If you want to find out about them, you will have to read the next section. But this section completes what you need to know to pray the three main offices of the day, Morning, Evening, and Night Prayer.

Good luck, and God bless you!

SECTION TWELVE
The Minor Offices

"In this section, you'll learn about . . ."

- The Gradual Psalms
- Daytime Prayer
- Praying the "Little Offices"
- Daytime Prayer on Feasts and Memorials
- The Office of Readings

SECTION TWELVE: THE MINOR OFFICES

Lesson 78: The Gradual Psalms (Complementary Psalmody)

Ever hear of the Gradual Psalms? The Complementary Psalmody? No? These are not psalms you pray gradually, and they do not pay you any compliments. But they are very important if you want to pray an office that we have not discussed much, the Office of Daytime Prayer.

Daytime Prayer sometimes uses the GRADUAL PSALMS. You have them in your breviary. **The GRADUAL PSALMS are Psalms 120 through 128. They are found in the breviary in the section entitled COMPLEMENTARY PSALMODY.**

Look in your breviary's Table of Contents for the Complementary Psalmody. Turn to that section and place the Complementary Psalmody (Gradual Psalms) bookmark at the beginning of this Psalmody.

> **DODO**
> **SELF CHECK #78**
>
> 1. What are the Gradual Psalms? Where are they found?
>
> 2. What bookmark indicates the Complementary Psalmody?
>
> 3. How are the Psalms divided? At what time of the day are the Midmorning Psalms prayed? Midday Psalms? Midafternoon Psalms?

Page through the Complementary Psalmody. Do you see that the Psalms are divided into groups of three and are labeled Midmorning, Midday, and Midafternoon? You know what this means, of course. It means that certain Psalms are prayed at certain times of the day. Would the Church pray the Midmorning Psalms at 3 p.m.? Not in your life! Midmorning Psalms are prayed about 9 a.m. Way back in Lesson 4, we discussed the times for Midmorning, Midday, and Midafternoon Prayer. Want to check back there? Go right ahead!

Lesson 79: Daytime Prayer

If you do not intend to pray Daytime Prayer, you could skip this lesson and the following ones and proceed to Lesson 84 on praying the Office of Readings. If you do want to pray Daytime Prayer, read on.

You have already learned that the complete Divine Office contains how many individual offices of prayer? Did you remember seven? Good for you. **Three of these offices are called MID-MORNING, MIDDAY, and MIDAFTERNOON PRAYER, sometimes called the "LITTLE HOURS." The Little Hours are prayed between Morning and Evening Prayer.** Why do you suppose they are called "Little" Hours? Might they be short offices? If you figured that out, you figured correctly.

Many religious communities and lay people pray only one of the Little Hours. **When only <u>one</u> Little Hour is prayed, that office is called DAYTIME PRAYER.**

Different breviaries print Daytime Prayer in different sections. *The four-volume breviary prints Daytime Prayer in the Psalter between the Morning and Evening Prayer offices.* **Some one-volume breviaries do the same. Other one-volume breviaries have a section called "Daytime Prayer" which has the Daytime Prayer offices.**

Breviaries also differ in how much of the Daytime Prayer offices they print. That is probably because publishers realize that not too many people today pray this office and so they may try to get away with minimizing their attention to it. You can be an aware dodo about Daytime Prayer if you keep the following notions in your little bird brain:

All four-volume breviaries and some one-volume breviaries print all the Daytime Prayer offices. The offices are different for every day of the four-week cycle. There are special parts of the Daytime Prayer Offices during Lent/Easter and Advent/Christmas Seasons and in some celebrations of the Saints and some Commons.

However, some one-volume breviaries have only one week's worth of Daytime Prayer—prayer for Sunday, Monday, Tuesday, Wednesday, Thursday, Friday, and Saturday. Then the prayers repeat. These breviaries do not have special Daytime Prayer Offices for the Proper of Seasons or the celebrations of the Saints. You may pray Daytime Prayer using these offices, even though they are incomplete.

Shorter Christian Prayer, the "traveler's breviary," does not print Daytime Prayer at all.

On the other hand, Catholic Book Publishing Corporation has published the complete *Daytime Prayer* in its own breviary so that those who wish to pray these offices at work can carry the small volume with them.

Suppose you want to pray Daytime Prayer. First thing you have to do is decide at what time of the day you will pray it. You have three approximate times to choose from. **If you pray Daytime Prayer about 9 a.m., you will use the MIDMORNING parts of the Office. If you pray Daytime Prayer about noon, you will use the MIDDAY parts of the Office. If your Daytime Prayer will be about 3 p.m., then you will use the MIDAFTERNOON parts of the Divine Office.** Makes sense, right?

Once you decide on the time to pray Daytime Prayer, you will use the Hymn, Reading, Responsory, and Prayer that correspond to the time that you choose. Where in the breviary are these?

Begin by finding Daytime Prayer in your breviary. Look first in the Psalter to see if Daytime Prayer is printed there. If not, look in the Table of Contents for a Daytime Prayer Section.

Next, a Hymn for Daytime Prayer. The Daytime Prayer Hymns will probably be in one of three places:

a. In some breviaries, a Hymn precedes Daytime Prayer.

b. In others, there is a Daytime Prayer Hymn section. You can find that section by looking in the Hymn index or guide for Daytime Prayer Hymns.

c. Still other breviaries, *including four-volume breviaries,* list the Daytime Prayer Hymns as part of the Ordinary. Find the Ordinary in the Table of Contents and page through it until you come to a section entitled "Daytime Prayer." This section should begin with Daytime Prayer Hymns.

If your breviary prints Daytime Prayer hymns in a special section, mark that section now with the Daytime Prayer Hymns bookmark. If the Daytime Prayer Hymns are part of a general section of Hymns, the Hymn bookmark will suffice because you can use it to mark the Daytime Prayer Hymn once you finish praying Morning Prayer.

To pray Daytime Prayer, first choose a Hymn. The Hymn should correspond to the time of day that you will be praying Daytime Prayer. If a Hymn is not printed at the beginning of the Daytime Prayer Office, select a Hymn and mark it with the "Daytime Prayer Hymns" bookmark.

How you will now proceed depends on your breviary.

If your breviary only has one week's worth of Daytime Prayer offices, in a separate section, you need only pray the correct office for today's day of the week. You have three bookmarks for Daytime

DODO
SELF CHECK #79

1. What are the Little Hours? Why are they called "Little?"

2. What is Daytime Prayer? At approximately what three times of day is Daytime Prayer prayed? How many times a day do you wish to pray Daytime Prayer?

3. How does your breviary deal with Daytime Prayer? With Daytime Prayer Hymns?

4. How will you know whether to pray the Midmorning, Midday, or Midafternoon sections of the Office?

5. In breviaries that contain the complete Daytime Prayer offices, where is Daytime Prayer during Ordinary Time found? Where is Daytime Prayer during the Lent/Easter and Advent/Christmas Seasons? On Memorials? Feasts? Solemnities?

6. What bookmark(s) mark Daytime Prayer in your breviary?

Prayer, with the time of day (Midmorning, Midday, and Midafternoon) printed on them. Mark, with the appropriate bookmark, that section that corresponds to the time of day that you will be praying Daytime Prayer.

If your breviary has all the Daytime Prayer offices for the year and its various seasons and celebrations, you will not need a bookmark to mark this office. The following techniques will help you to find your place:

Find today in the Psalter. If you do not know what week of the Psalter you are in, follow the guidelines in Lesson 76 to find out. **For Ordinary Time, all of the Daytime Prayer will be printed in the Psalter (already marked with the Psalter bookmark).**

In the Lent/Easter and Advent/Christmas seasons, the Daytime Prayer Psalms will be in the Psalter but the Antiphons, Readings, Responsories, and Concluding Prayers will be in the Proper of Seasons (already marked with the Proper of Seasons bookmark).

If today you are celebrating a Memorial, Feast, or Solemnity, follow the instructions in the breviary regarding Daytime Prayer. If no part of the Daytime Prayer Office is written in the Proper of Saints (already marked with the Proper of Saints bookmark), you will use Daytime Prayer from the Psalter for Memorials and Feasts, and Daytime Prayer from the Common for Solemnities.

Lesson 80: General Instructions for Praying Daytime Prayer

Probably you already suspected this, but, in case you did not, here it is: just as with the other offices, not all parts of Daytime Prayer may be written out in full in the breviary. Whether or not they are written out, this is the format that is followed:

TECHNIQUE
How to Pray Daytime Prayer

Make the Sign of the Cross silently while saying "God, come to my assistance."

Respond, "Lord, make haste to help me."

Pray the Glory Be.

Say, "Alleluia." (Omit Alleluia during Lent.)

Sing, chant, or recite the Hymn you have chosen.

Go to Daytime Prayer and pray the Psalmody (Psalms, Canticles, Antiphons, Psalm-Prayers) as you do for any other office. Pray the "Glory Be" as prayed in the Divine Office, after each Psalm and Canticle.

Read the Reading and Responsory for the appropriate time of day. Pause briefly for reflection.

Say, "Let us pray."

Pray the Concluding Prayer. Add the ending printed on the Psalter bookmark.

End the office by saying, "Let us praise the Lord."

Respond with, "And give him thanks" while making the Sign of the Cross.

PRACTICE: This practice is <u>only for those who have a one-volume breviary that has a Daytime Prayer Section. If you do not have a one-volume breviary with a Daytime Prayer Section, do not do this practice as your Psalmody and Readings will be different.</u> You will practice in the next lesson.

Turn to the Daytime Prayer section. Look at the Sunday Daytime Prayer office. Page through this office, looking for the Concluding Prayer. Where is it?

Pretend that this is the Fifth Sunday of Lent. You are getting close to Easter and

DODO
SELF CHECK #80

1. How do you begin Daytime Prayer?

2. How do you pray the Psalmody?

3. Where is the Concluding Prayer?

4. How do you conclude the Daytime Prayer Office?

making plans for Easter Dinner. Right now, you want to stop thinking about whether Easter dinner will be turkey, ham, or both. You want to spend some time with the Lord, praying Daytime Prayer.

Move the Proper of Seasons bookmark to the Fifth Sunday of Lent. Select the Alternative Prayer for Morning Prayer as the Concluding Prayer for your Daytime office.

Now, with your one-volume breviary, pray Daytime Prayer at Midday for the Fifth Sunday of Lent. Follow the above format. Check how you did by consulting Appendix R.

Lesson 81: Praying Daytime Prayer

This lesson is for those who have Daytime Prayer written in each office of the four-week Psalter. If this does not match your breviary, skip this lesson. If it does match your breviary, your breviary should have the complete Daytime Prayer offices in it for the year.

Look at the Psalter. You will find the Daytime Prayer office written out there. *If you have a four-volume breviary, first look at the Psalter in the volumes for Ordinary Time.* You will see that it is easy to pray Daytime Prayer. First decide what time of day you will be praying. Then choose an appropriate Hymn. Then pray the office straight through, following the format in Lesson 80.

During the seasons of Lent/Easter and Advent/Christmas, however, and on Feasts and Solemnities, the Proper of Seasons or Proper of Saints are used to pray parts or all of the Daytime Prayer office. Yes, I apologize, but you will have to be flipping around between offices again. Think of it as the Divine Office cha cha.

Before you start the fancy footwork, you need to learn a new step. It is called the Single Antiphon Sashay. Intrigued? Where is this in your breviary?

You will find an example of the Single Antiphon Sashay in the Common of Virgins. Find the Midmorning, Midday, and Midafternoon Prayer parts of the Common. How many Antiphons are under each heading? Were you surprised to find only one? Does this mean that you pray only one Psalm for these offices, one Psalm for one Antiphon? No. You are going to pray the usual number of Psalms which is as many as are in the Trinity—three. So where are the other two Antiphons? There are not two other Antiphons. How about that!

Want another surprise? Go jump into the Proper of Seasons. Check out the Lent and Advent offices. How many Antiphons are usually written under the Daytime Prayer heading? Yes. Only one again.

What is going on here?

Could this be the Single Antiphon Sashay? You guessed it!

When only one Antiphon is written under the Daytime Prayer heading, that Antiphon replaces all the other Antiphons used in praying Daytime Prayer. The single Antiphon is prayed once before the first of the three Daytime Prayer Psalms/Canticles and then repeated after the third Psalm's (or Canticle's) final Glory Be and Psalm prayer. The single Antiphon is not prayed between the Psalms/Canticles, but only before you pray them all and after you have prayed them all.

Would you like to see the Single Antiphon Sashay in action? Okey dokey. Find Daytime Prayer for the Solemnity of the Assumption, August 15 and mark it with the Proper of Seasons bookmark. You will notice that the Office for the Assumption refers you to the Gradual Psalms, and you have marked them already with a bookmark.

Pretend that you are going to pray Daytime Prayer on your lunch hour. You can eat your sardine and pickle sandwich quickly, scarf down that cup of lukewarm lemonade, and still have time to pray. Since you are going to be praying in the middle of the day, you will be using the Midday Psalms. Locate the Gradual Psalms for Midday and mark them with the Complementary Psalmody bookmark.

Cha cha back to the Daytime Prayer office for the Solemnity of the Assumption. You will notice only one Antiphon under the

Midday section. Time for the Single Antiphon Sashay. How do you sashay here? You will pray this Antiphon before Psalm 123 (the first Psalm under the Midday section in the Complementary Psalmody) and again after the Glory Be following Psalm 125 (the last Psalm in the Midday Complementary Psalmody). Then read the Reading and Responsory as listed under the Solemnity of the Assumption for Midday and end with the Concluding Prayer used for the Morning Prayer office.

— · — · — · — · — · — · —

PRACTICE: Pray Midday Prayer for the Solemnity of the Assumption. Check how you did by comparing your prayer with that written in Appendix S.

— · — · — · — · — · — · —

Now look at any one of the days in Lent or Advent in the Proper of Seasons. You will see only one Daytime Prayer Antiphon listed. But no Psalms. Now what in the world?

The Psalms are in the Psalter. But so are Antiphons! What to do?

A few simple rules for praying Daytime Prayer:

Solemnities: All parts, including the Antiphon, from the Solemnity, using the Complementary Psalmody for the Psalms. In other words: **S = S, CP, S** (**S**olemnity use **S**olemnity, **C**omplementary **P**salmody, **S**olemnity)

Feasts: Antiphon from the Feast, Psalms from the Psalter, rest from the Feast. In short, **F = F, P, F** (**F**east use **F**east, **P**salter, **F**east)

Memorials and Commemorations: No special celebration for Daytime Prayer. During Lent/Easter and Advent/Christmas use the Antiphon from the Proper of Seasons, then, Psalms from the Psalter, and then Readings, Responsory and Prayer from the Proper of Seasons. In short: **MC**

DODO SELF CHECK #81

1. If only one Antiphon is given for Daytime Prayer, how is it used?

2. Where are the Antiphons, Readings, Responsories, and Prayers for Solemnities and Feasts? During the Lent/Easter and Advent/Christmas Seasons? During Ordinary Time?

L/E and A/C = PS, P, PS (Memorials and Commemorations during Lent/Easter and Advent/Christmas use Proper of Seasons, then Psalter, then Proper of Seasons)

In Ordinary Time, use all from the Psalter. In short, **MCOT = P** (Memorials and Commemorations during Ordinary Time, use all from the Psalter)

Let us put these in a little chart for easy reference:

Daytime Prayer Quick List:
S = S,CP, S
F = F, P, F
MCL/E and A/C = PS, P, PS
MCOT = P

You might want to copy this and insert it into your breviary along with the other rules you have there for praying the Liturgy of the Hours. Or you could always refer back to this lesson when you are wondering what to do.

— · — · — · — · — · — · — ·

PRACTICE: Pretend that it is Thursday during the Fourth Week of Lent and you are in Week IV of the Psalter. You are well into the Lenten routine at this point. It is time to pray Daytime Prayer at the Midafternoon Hour. Use your bookmarks to organize your breviary to pray Daytime Prayer at Midafternoon on this day. Then pray this office. Compare how you did with Appendix T.

Lesson 82: Praying All "Little Offices": Midmorning, Midday, and Midafternoon Prayer

Perhaps you really like the Divine Office and want to pray all seven offices. Maybe you are part of a First, Second, or Third Order or Lay Movement that prays all the "Little Offices." If so, this lesson is for you. If you are not going to pray any other "Little Offices," you might as well skip this lesson and proceed to Lesson 83.

Have you noticed that the breviary has Readings, Responsories, and Concluding Prayers for Midmorning, Midday, and Midafternoon Prayer but only one Daytime Prayer Psalmody? Where will you find Psalms for the other two offices? Would you believe that you have four choices here? Sort of like choosing between chocolate, vanilla, strawberry, or cookies 'n cream ice cream.

TECHNIQUES
for Praying All Three Little Hours

If you wish to pray Midmorning, Midday, and Midafternoon Prayer daily, use the Readings, Responsories, and Prayers for the current day for <u>all three of the "Little Offices."</u>

Use the Daytime Prayer Psalms for the current day for one of the three "Little Offices." For the <u>other two</u> offices, you have a choice of Psalms to use.

1. You may use the Gradual Psalms. The Church always uses the Gradual Psalms on any non-Sunday Solemnity of the Church including during the Octaves of Easter and Christmas, Holy Week, and the Easter Triduum. However, for Sundays (which are always Solemnities) and other days, the Church allows the choice of the Gradual Psalms or one of the following options:

2. You may use the Daytime Prayer Psalms for the current weekday in the following two weeks of the Psalter.

3. You may use the Daytime Prayer Psalms for the current weekday in the preceding two weeks of the Psalter.

4. You may use the Daytime Prayer Psalms for the current weekday in the one week prior to this current week and the one week following this current week.

Are these techniques clever or what? Let us check out these options a bit more closely.

Pretend that this is Tuesday of Week II. Move your Psalter bookmark to that spot. Find the Psalms under the Daytime Prayer Office. For one of the "Little Offices," you will use these Psalms.

Here are the options to use for the other "Little Offices."

Option 1: **Use the Complementary Psalmody bookmark to find the Complementary Psalmody.** You may decide to use these Gradual Psalms for the other two "Little Offices."

Option 2: Use the Psalter. You have three choices in how to use it:

a. Page forward for two weeks, praying Daytime Prayer for Tuesday, Week III, and Tuesday, Week IV, for two of the "Little Offices."

b. Page backwards for two weeks, praying Daytime Prayer for Tuesday, Week I, and Daytime Prayer for Tuesday, Week IV, for two of the "Little Offices."

c. Page backward one week to use Daytime Prayer for Tuesday, Week I, for one "Little Office", and then page forward one week to use Daytime Prayer for Tuesday, Week III, for the other "Little Office."

Prayer for all three offices follows the very same format listed in Lesson 80 under Daytime Prayer.

If you intend to pray all three "Little Offices" using the Psalter, the most common practice is to use the current day's Daytime Prayer for the Midday Prayer office. But you are under no obligation to do that. You can pray the current day's Daytime Prayer any time you choose. Merely select which of the above options you prefer, place your bookmarks in the right locations, and you are off and running.

Here is a wise dodo hint to make your prayer life smoother. When you complete one of the day's offices, move the appropriate bookmark to mark tomorrow's office.

> **DODO SELF CHECK #82**
>
> 1. If you want to pray all three "Little Offices," what are your options regarding the two Daytime Prayer offices that are not in the current day of the Psalter?
>
> 2. If you choose to use the Psalter for all three "Little Offices," what bookmarks will mark the Daytime Prayer section in other weeks of the Psalter?

Here is another hint: If you want to pray all three offices but, some days, cannot pray them at the proper time, it is OK to combine two or three offices once in a while, if necessary. But it is not kosher proper to do it all the time.

Lesson 83: Daytime Prayer on Memorials, Feasts, and Solemnities

So now you know how to pray one or all of the Little Hours during Ordinary Time. How do you pray the Little Hours on Memorials, Feasts, and Solemnities? This fine tuning of the Divine Office can get a little tricky. Here is a chart to help you keep things straight:

TECHNIQUES
for Praying Daytime Prayer, including All Three Little Hours, on Memorials, Feasts, and Solemnities:

This is a handy, dandy chart. You do not have to memorize it. I frequently check it myself! You might want to fold it up and keep it inside your breviary where you can refer to it when you need it.

General Rule—First use <u>everything</u> from the Proper of Seasons.

For parts of Daytime Prayer not in the Proper of Seasons, use the Psalter, Commons, or Proper of Saints, as listed below.

   1. Octave of Easter—Proper of Seasons only.

   2. Commemorations— Proper of Seasons only.

   3. All other times—All parts from Proper of Seasons first, Proper of Saints second.

   4. For parts of the Daytime Prayer offices that are <u>missing</u> from either Proper, use the following:

Optional Memorials: All from Psalter (if not in Proper)

Obligatory Memorials: Hymn: Common (if not in Proper)
   Antiphons: Psalter (if not in Proper)
   Psalms: Psalter (if not in Proper)
   Readings, Responsories: Your choice of Psalter or Common (if not in Proper)
   Concluding Prayer: Psalter (if not in Proper)

continued on next page . . .

> *. . . continued from previous page*
>
> **Feasts: Hymn: Common (if not in Proper)**
>   **Antiphons: Psalter (if not in Proper)**
>   **Psalms: Psalter (if not in Proper)**
>   **Reading, Responsory, Concluding Prayer: Common (if not in Proper)**
>
> **Solemnity: Hymn: Common (if not in Proper)**
>   **Antiphons: Common (if not in Proper)**
>   **Psalms: Complementary Psalmody (if not in Proper) (on Sunday's, Daytime Prayer Psalms for Sunday, Week I, for one of the offices)**
>   **Reading, Responsory, Concluding Prayer: Common (if not in Proper)**

PRACTICE: Use the above chart and find the Daytime Prayer offices for the following celebrations:

May 27, the Optional Memorial of St. Augustine of Canterbury

July 22, the Memorial of Saint Mary Magdalene

September 14, the Feast of the Triumph of the Cross

November 1, the Solemnity of All Saints

Lesson 84: The Office of Readings

In my opinion, the Office of Readings is one of the greatest parts of the Divine Office. But, hey, that is my opinion. If you are not going to pray the Office of Readings, you might as well skip this lesson and the following ones and proceed to Lesson 87.

If you do want to pray this beautiful office, how about checking to see if your

DODO SELF CHECK #83

1. When is Daytime Prayer always taken from the Proper of Seasons?

2. What are the techniques to follow for Commemorations?

3. Where do you find missing parts of the Daytime Prayer offices on Optional Memorials? Obligatory Memorials? Feasts? Solemnities?

breviary has it? *Shorter Christian Prayer* does not and neither do a few one-volume breviaries.

How do you suppose this office got its name? From the Readings, you say? Oh, you are so smart. **The OFFICE OF READINGS is so named because two long Readings are part of it. One Reading is from Scripture and the other is from a variety of religious sources.** The parts of the Office of Readings are:

Hymn
Three Psalms
One Biblical Reading followed by Responsory
One Non-Biblical Reading followed by Responsory
Te Deum (only on certain days)
Concluding Prayer

So where are all these in your breviary?

Let us start at the beginning.

Where are the Hymns for the Office of Readings? Are they in the Psalter? They might be. Are they in the Office of Readings Psalter? They might be. If they are not in either spot, they will be in the Hymn section which you already have marked with a Hymn book-mark (see Lesson 9).

Next, the Psalms. Always wise to check the Psalter first. Does your breviary have the Psalms for the Office of Readings in the Psalter? If so, the Psalter bookmark will help you find the daily Psalms for the Office of Readings.

If the Psalms for the Office of Readings are not in the Psalter, they are in a separate section of your breviary. Look in the Table of Contents for the Office of Readings. Turn to that page. You will find a four-week Psalter just for the Office of Readings. **Mark that section with the Office of Readings: Psalter bookmark.**

Now for the Readings. First look in the Proper of Seasons. *In the four-volume breviary, you have the complete set of Readings for this office. Every single day has two Readings, followed by their Responsories—different Readings and Responsories for every day of the year. The Proper of Seasons bookmark marks this section.*

The one-volume breviary has only a selection of all the Readings. Each day you will choose one Biblical and one Non-Biblical Reading, and accompanying Responsories, to pray. Where are the Readings? Page through the Office of Readings Psalter until you come to the Readings. Now page through them. Did you find the Biblical Readings and Non-Biblical Readings sections? Do you suppose we might use two of our bouncing bookmarks to mark these? Right you are.

If you have a one-volume breviary, use the "Office of Readings: Biblical" bookmark to mark the "Biblical Readings" section. Use the "Office of Readings: Non-Biblical" bookmark to mark the "Non-Biblical Readings" section which follows.

Next is the Te Deum, whatever that is. **The TE DEUM is a Hymn that is prayed in the Office of Readings after the Second Reading and Responsory on Sundays, Feasts, and Solemnities. It is also prayed daily during the Octaves of Christmas and Easter. The Te Deum is prayed at these times whether or not your breviary tells you to do so. The Te Deum is omitted during Lent.**

DODO SELF CHECK #84

1. What is the Office of Readings? Why is it so named? When is it prayed?

2. How many Readings are read? Describe them. In your breviary, what bookmark(s) mark(s) the Office of Readings?

3. What is the Te Deum? In what part of the Office of Readings is it prayed? Is the Te Deum prayed every day? When is it prayed? When is it omitted? What color ribbon marks the Te Deum?

4. If the Office of Readings is the first office of the day, how does it begin? If it is not the first office of the day, how does it begin?

So where is the Te Deum? Look in your breviary's Table of Contents for the Ordinary of the Divine Office. Turn to the Ordinary and page through the section entitled Office of Readings. You will come to the Te Deum. Some breviaries also have the Te Deum printed on a special prayer card which you can place in the front or back of your breviary.

Hey, we said this was a Hymn. But it has no musical notes printed with it. Does not matter. You can sing or hum your own tune if you wish. If you do not wish, do what most people do, which is reverently pray this glorious song.

Mark the Te Deum with a restful red ribbon (red for the merciful and glorious Blood of Christ, commemorated in the Te Deum).

We conclude with finding the Concluding Prayer. **In the four-volume breviary, the Concluding Prayer follows the Readings in the Proper of Seasons. In the one-volume breviary, use the same Concluding Prayer that you would use for Morning Prayer.** These are, by the way, the same prayer. However, the four-volume breviary prints the prayer in more than one location.

How you begin the Office of Readings depends on whether or not you pray it before Morning Prayer. You have learned to pray Morning Prayer as the first office of the day, and to precede Morning Prayer with the Invitatory. The Office of Readings is the only office that may precede Morning Prayer. It does not have to precede it. **You can pray the Office of Readings at any time during the day.**

But, if you do pray the Office of Readings before Morning Prayer, remember that **the Invitatory is be prayed before the <u>first</u> office of the day.** It is prayed only before the first office and not before any other office.

Suppose you decide to pray the Office of Readings before Morning Prayer. Will you begin with the Invitatory? You betcha.

Suppose you pray the Office of Readings any time after Morning Prayer. Will you begin with the Invitatory? No, because you will have prayed the Invitatory before you prayed Morning Prayer.

You already know this, but a little review can be helpful. **The second and all subsequent offices of the day begin, not with the Invitatory, but with the Sign of the Cross, the words, "God, come to my assistance," the response, "Lord, make haste to help me," and the "Glory Be" in its special Divine Office format.**

Lesson 85: The Office of Readings in Four-volume Breviaries

If you have a one-volume breviary, the Proper of Saints and the Commons will not have any parts of the Office of Readings. This is not the case with four-volume breviaries. The following instruction is for those with four-volume breviaries. If you do not have a four-volume breviary, skip this lesson and proceed to Lesson 86.

Quick review. Each Office of Readings (Commemorations excepted) has only two Readings, a Biblical Reading for the First Reading and a Non-Biblical Reading for the Second Reading. Both these Readings are in the Proper of Seasons. Always.

Quick lesson on the Proper of Saints: A few saints have a Hymn, Psalmody and/or First Reading. Every saint has a Second Reading and Concluding Prayer.

Quicker lesson on the Commons: The Commons have a full Office of Readings.

Quickest lesson: On Commemorations, there are three readings—two from the Proper of Seasons and the third from the Proper of Saints. Think of the 3 M's in the word Co**mmem**oration to help you remember. So, while this is the quickest lesson, it takes the longest time to pray the Office of Readings on Commemorations. If you decide to commemorate the Commemoration, that is. Remember that observing Commemorations is always optional.

So, how do you pray the Office of Readings?

Remember that this office always has the following and only the following:

> Hymn
> Three Psalms

> **DODO
> SELF CHECK #85**
>
> 1. *Where do you find the Readings on Memorials? Feasts? Solemnities? Commemorations?*
>
> 2. *What Psalmody do you use for Memorials? Feasts? Solemnities? Commemorations?*
>
> 3. *How many Readings are read on a Commemoration? How is it done? What Concluding Prayer is used on Commemorations?*
>
> 4. *When is the Te Deum prayed? When is it omitted?*

One Biblical Reading followed by Responsory
One Non-Biblical Reading followed by Responsory
Third Reading followed by Responsory (on Commemorations only)
Te Deum (only on certain days)
Concluding Prayer

Now we can see how this works for the various days in the Church year.

TECHNIQUE

How to Pray the Office of Readings with Four-volume Breviaries:

You might want to keep a copy of this in your breviary by your other notes.

FERIAL DAYS

Hymn—Psalter or Hymn Index
Three Psalms—Psalter
Readings and Responsories—Proper of Seasons
Concluding Prayer—Proper of Seasons

COMMEMORATIONS

Hymn—Seasonal
Three Psalms—Psalter
Readings and Responsories—Both from Proper of Seasons
Third Reading and Responsory—From Proper of Saints
Concluding Prayer—Proper of Saints

MEMORIALS

Hymn—Proper of Saints; if not there, Proper of Seasons, if not there, Common
Three Psalms—Memorial first; if no Psalms in Memorial, from Psalter
Readings and Responsories—First Reading and Responsory from Proper of Seasons, Second Reading and Responsory from Proper of Saints
Concluding Prayer—Proper of Saints

FEASTS AND SOLEMNITIES

Hymn—From Feast or Solemnity; if not there, from Common
Three Psalms—From Feast or Solemnity; if not there, from Common *continued on next page . . .*

> *. . . continued from previous page*
> **Readings and Responsories—From Feast or Solemnity; if not there, from Common**
> **Te Deum (except during Lent)**
> **Concluding Prayer—From Feast or Solemnity**
>
> **SUNDAYS**
>
> **Hymn—Proper of Seasons first, if not there, Psalter**
> **Three Psalms—Proper of Seaons first, if not there, Psalter**
> **Readings and Responsories—Proper of Seasons**
> **Te Deum (except during Lent)**
> **Concluding Prayer—Proper of Seasons (your choice of two prayers—pick one)**

Lesson 86: Format for Praying the Office of Readings

Ready to pray the Office of Readings? Find the Office of Readings for today. Let us get praying!

_._._._._._._._._

PRACTICE: Pray the Office of Readings for today. Here is the format:

> **TECHNIQUE**
> **How to Pray the Office of Readings**
>
> **Begin with the Sign of the Cross.**
>
> **If the Office of Readings is the First Office of the Day:**
>
> **Say, "Lord, open my lips."**
> **Respond, "And my mouth will proclaim your praise."**
> **Pray the Invitatory with its appropriate Antiphon as taught in Lessons 24, 42, and 57. Follow this with the Glory Be and then the Antiphon repeated.**
>
> **If the Office of Readings Is NOT the First Office of the Day:**
>
> **Say, "God, come to my assistance."**
>
> *continued on next page . . .*

. . . continued from previous page

Respond, "Lord, make haste to help me."

Pray the Glory Be followed by Alleluia (Omit the Alleluia in Lent and Advent).

To Continue Office of Readings:

Sing, chant, or recite the Hymn.

Pray the Psalms, Canticles, Psalm-Prayers, and Antiphons in the same manner as you have been doing for the other offices.

Pause briefly for reflection.

Turn to the Readings. Read the first Reading (from Scripture).

Read the Responsory.

Pause a few minutes for silent reflection.

Read the second Reading (non-Biblical)

Read the Responsory.

Pause a few minutes for silent reflection.

If this is a Commemoration, read the third Reading (Proper of Saints) and Responsory

Pause a few moments for silent reflection.

On Sundays, Feasts, and Solemnities, and daily during the Christmas and Easter Octaves, pray the Te Deum. Omit it during Lent.

Say, "Let us pray."

Read the Concluding Prayer.

Say, "Let us praise the Lord."

Respond, "And give him thanks."

Make the Sign of the Cross.

You have just prayed the Office of Readings.

SECTION THIRTEEN
Options

"In this section, you'll learn about . . ."

- Ordering Supplements
- Praying in Choir
- Combining the Office with Mass
- Praying the Office with Clergy
- Praying the Office in Church
- Specific Circumstances

SECTION THIRTEEN: OPTIONS

Lesson 87: Order Supplements

Are you a member of a First, Second, or Third Order within the Church? If not, you might want to skip this section.

If you are a member of a First, Second, or Third Order, you might have a Supplement to your breviary. The Supplement contains special offices and parts of offices for saints and celebrations particular to your Order. These will not be in the regular breviary. Some of your Order's saints, who are in the breviary, may have longer offices in your Order's Supplement. Some celebrations that are Memorials for the whole Church may be Feasts or Solemnities for you. Follow the Supplement's guidelines.

If you purchase an Ordo, be sure to get one that includes the celebrations in your Supplement. Such Ordos are generally available through your religious Order's main office or publisher.

Your Order may also sell nifty plastic breviary covers with a special double cover that will allow you to place the breviary and the Supplement into the same book.

You probably have at least one bookmark that you have not used. If you wish, you can easily adapt that bookmark for use in your Order Supplement. Be creative with your adaptation. Then place that bookmark at today's day of the year, in your Order Supplement.

Nightly after Evening Prayer, check the Supplement to see if any saints are to be celebrated the next day. Mark the celebrations with the Supplement bookmark.

You will discover that there are differences between the Supplement and the breviary. If there are, follow the Supplement. Here are additional tips on how to use a Supplement:

TECHNIQUE
for using an Order Supplement

If a celebration in the Supplement has no designation, it is an Optional Memorial.

If a celebration is marked "Memorial," it is an Obligatory Memorial.

If a celebration is marked "Feast" or "Solemnity," it is a Feast or Solemnity for all members of your Order, no matter how the rest of the Church celebrates it.

If a saint's celebration is marked First, Second, or Third Order without the designation "Memorial," it is an Obligatory Memorial only for the branch of the Order so designated. For other branches of the Order, it is an Optional Memorial.

If a celebration is marked, "Feast: First Order," it means that this celebration is a Feast for only First Order members. It is a Memorial for other branches of the Order.

If a Memorial in the Supplement coincides with another Memorial in the breviary, celebrate the Memorial in the Supplement.

If the Supplement has a longer office than in the breviary, use all the parts in the Supplement.

Lesson 88: Praying in Choir

No, you do not have to join your parish choir to pray the Divine Office. You do not have to be able to sing either. So what is this "praying in choir" all about?

Did you know that the Divine Office was written to be prayed OUT LOUD and IN CHOIR? In other words, it was written to be prayed by religious living in communities and by priests praying with others in their churches. You may not be praying the Divine Office in either of these circumstances.

PRAYING IN CHOIR means praying as a group but alternating sides. Obviously, you cannot do this if you are praying the Office alone. The Office is prayed by alternating sides in monasteries and convents and at meetings of laity that pray the Office. Often in choir, the Office is chanted or sung, but it can also be recited.

You can find hints that the Office was intended for praying in choir by looking at your breviary's Responsories and Intercessions. In some breviaries, a V. is before the first line of the Responsories and Intercessions and an R. before the second line. Other breviaries use only the R. or a dash before the second line. **The V. stands for "VERSICLE" and the R., or dash, stands for "RESPONSE." When praying in choir, the PRAYER LEADER alone says the first part of these prayers (marked with a V. or without the dash) and everyone else answers by praying the second part (marked with an R. or the dash).** When praying alone, you obviously pray all parts yourself, as you have been doing. Now remember those terms—Versicle and Response. They might come in handy someday when you are doing a crossword puzzle.

When praying the Office in choir, the Office is prayed straight through without anyone announcing Hymns, pages, or titles for parts of the Office. Any directions or pages are announced <u>before</u> the Office begins. The only exception is that the Reader <u>may</u> announce the Reading with the words, "A Reading from _____," filling in the Scripture book as done at Mass. The Reader <u>may</u> end the Reading by saying "The word of the Lord" to which everyone else would respond, "Thanks be to God."

Now you are going to learn some interesting terms. You have learned so much this far, so why not cap your learning off with some big, important sounding words? Then, if you want to sound impressive at the next dinner party, you can casually make a comment such as "You know, when Bill gets on a roll telling stories, he makes a perfect Hebdomadarian." You ought to turn a few heads with that word. Want to know what Bill reminds you of? Read on.

Before we find out about Bill, however, we are going to learn how to pray in choir. **To pray in choir, you obviously need two or more people. Divide the group into SIDE ONE (original name: CHORUS SIDE) and SIDE TWO (original name: ALLELUIA SIDE). The Psalms and Canticles are prayed out loud so that each side takes one strophe (verse), alternating sides. Choose individuals to perform the following roles:**

CANTOR (also called HEBDOMADARIAN or FIRST CANTOR): Begins Office. Alone prays the Antiphons, first lines of the Psalms or Canticles, and all Psalm prayers. If two cantors are used, the second cantor is sometimes called the ANTIPHONARIAN. More good crossword puzzle, or dinner party, words.

Reader: Alone reads the Reading and the odd lines of the Responsory (lines 1, 3, and 5). Everyone else replies on the even lines (lines 2, 4, and 6).

Prayer Leader: Alone reads first line of Intercessions and Concluding Prayer.

TECHNIQUE
How to Pray the Divine Office in Choir

Here is a general summary of how to pray the Office in choir. Once you get the hang of this, you will be able to adjust the technique for the various offices and various parts of them.

The abbreviations are:
S1—Side One
S2—Side Two
E—Everyone
C—Cantor
R—Reader
P—Prayer Leader   *continued on next page . . .*

. . . continued from previous page

For First Office of the Day

While making the Sign of the Cross,
C: Lord, open my lips
E: And my mouth will proclaim your praise.
C: Invitatory Antiphon
E: Repeat Invitatory Antiphon
C: First Strophe of Invitatory
E: Repeat Invitatory Antiphon
C: Second Strophe of Invitatory
E: Repeat Invitatory Antiphon
C: Third Strophe of Invitatory
E: Repeat Invitatory Antiphon
Continue Pattern through Fifth Strophe of Invitatory
C: Glory to the Father and to the Son and to the Holy Spirit
    As it was in the beginning, is now, and will be forever. Amen.
E: Repeat Invitatory Antiphon

All Offices except First Office of the Day
C: God, come to my assistance.
E: Lord, make haste to help me.
C: Glory to the Father and to the Son and to the Holy Spirit
E: As it was in the beginning, is now, and will be forever. Amen.

Morning and Evening Prayer
E: Hymn
C: Antiphon 1
C: First Line of First Psalm or Canticle
S1: First Strophe (verse)
S2: Second Strophe (verse)
S1: Third Strophe (verse)
S2: Fourth Strophe (verse)
**Continue alternating sides until Psalm or Canticle is done. When it
comes time to say the Glory Be, the Side whose turn it would be
begins with "Glory to the Father, and to the Son, and to the Holy
Spirit." The other side concludes, "As it was in the beginning, is
now, and will be forever. Amen."**
C: Psalm-Prayer
C: Antiphon 1
Pause briefly   *continued on next page . . .*

. . . continued from previous page

C: Antiphon 2
C: First Line of 2nd Psalm or Canticle
S1: First Strophe
S2: Second Strophe
(Continue as for First Psalm, ending with Glory Be as explained earlier)
C: Psalm-Prayer
C: Antiphon 2
Pause briefly
C: Antiphon 3
C: First Line of Third Psalm or Canticle
S1: First Strophe
S2: Second Strophe
(Continue as for First Psalm, ending with Glory Be as explained earlier)
C: Psalm-Prayer
C: Antiphon 3
Pause briefly
R: Reading
R: First line of Responsory
E: Second line of Responsory
R: Third line of Responsory
E: Fourth line of Responsory
R: Fifth line of Responsory
E: Sixth line of Responsory
Pause briefly
C: Antiphon for Canticle
E: Canticle (or alternate sides as done for Psalmody)
E: Glory Be (or alternate sides as done for Psalmody)
C: Antiphon for Canticle
Pause briefly
P: First lines of Intercessions
E: Second lines of Intercessions
E: Our Father
P: Concluding Prayer
C: May the Lord bless us, protect us from all evil, and bring us to everlasting life.
E: Amen
C: In the name of the Father, and of the Son, and of the Holy Spirit.
E: Amen

A few options exist for praying in choir:

The Glory Be may be said by everyone instead of alternating sides.

The Antiphon, when repeated at the end of the Psalm or Canticle, may be prayed in unison by everyone. The Antiphon is never prayed by the Cantor and then repeated by everyone else except at the beginning of the Invitatory.

You have not been praying the Alleluia when it appears in parentheses when in a Canticle. When praying the Office alone, it is correct to omit this. However, when the Canticle is sung in choir, either the Cantor or the Chorus side sings the part not in parentheses and the others respond with the part in parentheses.

> **DODO**
> **SELF CHECK #88**
>
> 1. What is praying in choir? How is it done?
>
> 2. Define these terms: Cantor. Prayer Leader. Reader. Side One. Side Two. Chorus Side. Alleluia Side.
>
> 3. What do a V., R., and dash in the Responsories and Intercessions indicate?
>
> 4. If praying in choir, when is it customary to stand? Sit? Kneel?

When praying in choir, certain postures are customary:
Introduction up to end of Hymn: All stand.

Psalmody: Sit with exception of Cantor who stands while reading alone, then sits for remainder of Psalmody

Reading, Responsory: Sit except for Reader who stands.

Canticle of Zechariah, Mary until End of Office: All stand or kneel.

If you can visit a convent or monastery while its members are praying the Office, go for it. You will learn a lot by observing.

Lesson 89: Options

Everyone likes choices. You have some choices (options) in praying the Divine Office.

THE INVITATORY PSALM: You have been using Psalm 95 as the Invitatory Psalm. The Church also allows the use of Psalms 100, 67, or 24.

ANTIPHONS: You have learned to pray the Antiphon before and after the Psalms. The Church allows the option of praying it only before the Psalm and not repeating it after.

PSALM-PRAYERS: You have learned to pray the Psalm-Prayers. The Church allows the option of skipping them.

THE PSALMODY WHEN IT CONTAINS PSALMS BROKEN INTO I, II, AND POSSIBLY III PARTS: When a long Psalm is broken into parts in the Divine Office, the sections are numbered I, II, and III. An Antiphon precedes and ends each section. The Church allows the option of praying all the Antiphons as you have learned with the "Glory Be" between each section of the Psalm. A second option is praying the first Antiphon, then praying the Psalm entirely through to the end without a break, ending with the "Glory Be" and then repeating, if desired, the first Antiphon.

THE OUR FATHER: If you wish, you may introduce the "Our Father" with the spoken words, "Remember us, Lord, when you come into your kingdom and teach us how to pray" or some similar invitation to prayer. Several options are printed in the instruction entitled "Ordinary" in your breviary. Look for this in the Table of Contents.

COMBINING OFFICES: Generally two offices are not prayed together at the same time. However, you may combine some offices if necessary.

Morning and Evening Prayer are never combined. Morning Prayer is to be prayed in the morning and Evening Prayer in the evening.

The Office of Readings may be prayed before or after any other office.

Night Prayer may be prayed immediately after Evening Prayer.

**DODO
SELF CHECK #89**

1. What are some options in praying the Office?

2. Can you substitute a Memorial on a Ferial Day?

3. How are offices combined? Which offices may be combined? Which may not be combined?

4. What is unique about the Office of the Dead?

Two of the Minor Offices (Midmorning, Midday, Mid-afternoon) may be combined.

To combine offices, sing only one Hymn at the beginning of the first office. Select a Hymn appropriate for either the first or the second office.

Pray the first office through but skip the Concluding Prayer and go right into praying the first Psalm's Antiphon for the second office and then the first Psalm. Pray this office through to the end. If you pray Night Prayer right after Evening Prayer, you will include the Examination of Conscience before beginning the Night Prayer Psalmody.

FERIAL DAYS: On a Ferial Day, that is a day on which no official Church celebration is held, you may choose to celebrate a certain office as a Memorial. Follow the guidelines for the office that you choose. You may also choose to pray the Office of the Blessed Virgin or the Office of the Dead on a Ferial Day.

THE OFFICE OF THE DEAD: You always pray the Office for the Dead on All Souls' Day, November 2. However, you may also pray it on any other day that is not a Solemnity, Feast, or Obligatory Memorial. While you may adapt the Office for the Dead according to gender and number, you may not change anything else about it. **The Office of the Dead is always prayed in whole, <u>exactly as written in the breviary</u>, with no substitutions from other Offices.**

Lesson 90: Praying the Office with Clergy and Praying the Office in a Church

Many lay people hardly ever have the opportunity to pray the Divine Office with clergy or religious. If you are so fortunate, you will want to know the proper procedure.

First the hierarchical order of the Church must be respected. The individual holding the highest position in the Church leads the

Divine Office unless that individual delegates the duty to someone else. In other words, if you are praying the Divine Office with the Pope, you let him begin the office unless he asks you to do it.

Priests, deacons, and religious are ranked on the basis of the dignity of their office. The Pope outranks the Cardinal, the Cardinal outranks the Archbishop, the Archbishop outranks the Bishop, the Bishop outranks the priest, the priest outranks the deacon, the deacon outranks the consecrated religious, the consecrated religious outranks the member of a lay Order (such as a Third Order), and a lay Order member outranks laity who are not members of a lay Order. The Church also respects rank within each group. For example, a superior of a religious Order would outrank a nun or brother who holds no particular office in that Order.

The dignity of rank must be respected when praying the Divine Office. Therefore, the highest ranking person assumes the role of PRESIDER. **The Presider is a person of rank who opens the office with the Introductory Verse. He or she leads the Intercessions, begins the Lord's Prayer, and prays the Concluding Prayer.**

What parts of the office are reserved to priests and deacons, if they are present? (Remember that the Pope and the Bishops are priests!). **Only priests and deacons have the function of greeting the others before the office begins and dismissing them with a blessing when the office concludes.**

**DODO
SELF CHECK #90**

1. What parts of the Divine Office are reserved to a priest or deacon?

2. How is the Presider chosen? What parts of the Office does the Presider assume?

3. Who of the following may wear liturgical garb while praying the Divine Office in a church? Priest? Deacon? Pope? Lay person? Bishop? Nun?

4. How could incense be used in praying the Divine Office?

5. Where does the Cantor stand? The Reader?

6. Who may sit in the Presider's chair in the sanctuary? If a priest or deacon is not present, where does the Presider sit?

Special rules apply if the office is prayed in a church or chapel. Then **only those who have been ordained (priest or deacon) may wear liturgical garb.** Therefore, a priest or deacon Presider may wear a stole over the alb or surplice; a priest may also wear a cope. The presiding priest or deacon sits in the Presider's chair in the sanctuary. He may choose to have an incensation of the altar, of the priest, and then of the congregation during the Morning Prayer and Evening Prayer Canticles. However, if a priest or deacon is not present, the Presider of the Divine Office does not greet or bless the people nor does he or she wear liturgical garb or enter the sanctuary. A non-ordained Presider remains in the pew.

When the office is prayed in a church or chapel, the Cantors generally lead the Antiphons from their place in the pews. However, **while the Readers may read the Readings and Responsories either at the podium or from the pews, the preferred place is at the podium or lectern.** Using the podium or lectern for the Readings and Responsories is consistent with the procedure followed during Mass.

Lesson 91: Combining the Office with Mass

You might be in the habit of praying the Divine Office before or after a daily or Sunday Mass. If so, good for you! What better place to pray the Office than before our Blessed Lord in the tabernacle!

However, you may be fortunate enough to be in a parish or at an event where the Divine Office is combined with the Mass itself. Not everybody realizes that there is a proper way to do this. But you will know after you complete this section. Then you can share your knowledge!

When combining the Divine Office with Mass, follow these guidelines:

TECHNIQUE
for Combining an Office with the BEGINNING of Mass

OFFICE OF READINGS

On Christmas Eve, the Office of Readings is combined with Mass following the rubrics designated in the Mass. Otherwise, the Office of Readings is not generally combined with Mass. However, if it is necessary to join the Office of Readings with Mass, then begin with the Office of Readings, but immediately after the Second Reading from the office, with its Responsory, Mass begins with the Collect or the Gloria (if called for) and the remainder of the Office of Readings is eliminated.

MORNING PRAYER (MP)

Weekdays (generally)	*Sundays and holy days (generally)*
Introductory verse from MP	Entrance chant for Mass
Hymn from MP	Procession and celebrant's greeting

Psalmody from MP

Omit Penitential Act and Kyrie

Pray Gloria if required by Mass rubrics

Collect of Mass

Liturgy of Word from Mass (Omit reading from MP)

Universal Prayer (may be of MP)	Universal Prayer (omit MP Intercessions)

Mass proceeds as usual up to and including chant following Communion

Canticle of Zechariah and Antiphon

Prayer after Communion to end of Mass Prayer
(omit MP concluding prayer)

MIDMORNING, MIDDAY, AND MIDAFTERNOON PRAYER

Generally speaking, only Morning Prayer and Evening Prayer are combined with Mass. However, if you must combine one of the Little Hours with the <u>beginning</u> of Mass, use the same format as for Morning Prayer. Replace the Morning Prayer parts with the corresponding parts of the Midmorning, Midday, or Midafternoon Office. Omit the Canticle of Zechariah.   *continued on next page . . .*

. . . continued from previous page

EVENING PRAYER

Use the same format as for Morning Prayer. Replace the Morning Prayer parts with the corresponding parts from Evening Prayer. Replace the Canticle of Zechariah with the Canticle of Mary.

EVENING PRAYER I

Evening Prayer I is a bit tricky. Praying Evening Prayer I means, in the Church's mind, that the next day has begun. So when you pray Evening Prayer I on Saturday, for example, Sunday begins (in the Church's mind) after you finish Evening Prayer I.

How does this correspond with combining Evening Prayer I with the beginning of Mass? Well, Evening Prayer I, combined with the <u>beginning</u> of Mass, has to be combined with <u>the Mass of the Sunday or Solemnity to which it corresponds</u>.

Let us take an example. You attend two weekend retreats, two weeks in a row. On the first retreat, the 5 p.m. Mass on Saturday is the daily Mass for Saturday. The retreat master knows the Mass rubrics and does not combine Evening Prayer I with the beginning of the Saturday Mass. On Saturday of the second retreat, the retreat master offers a 5 p.m. Vigil Mass for Sunday. He also knows the rubrics and combines Evening Prayer I with the beginning of this Vigil Mass.

Now you know how to combine the Divine Office with the beginning of Mass. May you also combine it with the end of Mass? That depends on the office. **Morning Prayer and the Office of Readings may be combined only with the <u>beginning</u> of Mass, never with the end of Mass.** However, other offices can be combined with the end of Mass. Here is how to do that.

TECHNIQUE
for Combining an Office with the END of Mass

Generally speaking, Midmorning, Midday, and Midafternoon Prayer are most often not combined with Mass. However, if they are to be combined with the <u>end</u> of Mass, follow this format:

Daytime Prayer (Midmorning, Midday, or Midafternoon),
Evening Prayer, and Evening Prayer I combined
with the <u>end</u> of Mass   *continued on next page . . .*

. . . continued from previous page

Celebrate Mass in the usual way up to and including the Prayer after Communion

Begin the Psalmody without introduction

Omit reading from Office

In Evening Prayer (Evening Prayer I), pray Canticle of Mary and Antiphon

In Evening Prayer (Evening Prayer I), omit Intercessions and Lord's Prayer

Concluding Prayer from the office and priest's blessing of congregation

If you are an alert dodo, you noticed that one of the offices was missing from the above instruction. Yes, Night Prayer! Since Night Prayer is to be prayed right before going to bed, it does not lend itself to being combined with Mass. I mean, how many people do you know who attend Mass in their pajamas?

Lesson 92: Specific Circumstances

You have come a mighty long way. You began this manual, thinking you were a real dodo when it came to praying the Divine Office. Now look how much you have learned. This is the very last chapter. How about making it a good one!

Have you made a promise to yourself, your spiritual director, or your Order or Association to pray the Divine Office? If you are so obligated, you might run into certain specific circumstances. Here are some of them:

DODO SELF CHECK #91

1. Which offices are almost never combined with Mass?

2. When you combine an office with the beginning of Mass, do you read the reading from the office?

3. What is the appropriate way to combine Evening Prayer I with the beginning of Mass? With the end of Mass?

4. What office is never combined with the beginning of Mass?

5. What offices are never combined with the end of Mass?

IF YOU CANNOT PRAY AN OFFICE: Try to raise your mind to God wherever you are and realize that God understands. However, for anyone who has an obligation to pray the Office or who seriously wishes to take on this task, these times should be rare exceptions.

IF CIRCUMSTANCES PREVENT YOU FROM READING THE BREVIARY: You might substitute other prayers. Members of some religious Orders have specific prayers to substitute. For example, members of the one secular Order are permitted to say 12 Our Fathers (6 for Morning Prayer and 6 for Evening Prayer) if they cannot pray from the breviary. A priest or spiritual director can guide you on what to do. However, if you have made a commitment to pray the Divine Office, substitution of other prayers for those in the breviary should be a rare exception.

IF YOU FORGET TO SAY AN OFFICE: If you go through the day and then remember that you forgot to say an office, simply raise your mind to God and ask Him to help you remember to pray the office next time. God understands that we are human, for He created us so!

IF YOU HABITUALLY FORGET AN OFFICE: Try to do something to help you remember. Perhaps putting your Office book where you will see it at the time of prayer will help. Try taping a note to something you would be using at the time the office should be prayed. Or give

DODO SELF CHECK #92

1. How do you pray the Office when celebrating with a religious community?

2. If you pray the Office of Readings alone prior to Morning Prayer, but pray Morning Prayer with someone else for whom Morning Prayer is the first office of the day, when do you pray the Invitatory?

3. If you habitually forget to say an office, what can you do to help you remember?

4. If you are unable to pray from the breviary, what can you do to pray the Office?

5. How can you get answers to your other questions about praying the Divine Office?

6. How do you feel about completing this manual?

yourself a reward when you remember. Be creative in helping yourself to recall your prayer time. Eventually, you will form a habit of prayer and will not need reminders.

IF YOU MAKE A MISTAKE: God is not a legalist. Just pray the office as carefully and prayerfully as you can. Consult a priest or religious if you have a question. If you have been doing something incorrectly, correct it and do not worry about it.

IF YOU CANNOT PRAY THE OFFICE AT THE CORRECT TIMES: Try to pray it as close to the correct times as possible.

IF A MONASTERY OR COMMUNITY PRAYS THE OFFICE DIFFERENTLY THAN IN THIS INSTRUCTION: Follow the community's format. This book has presented some of the more common options. There are others, the discussion of which would make this book too tedious. Some Orders also have different, Church-approved offices which they pray daily.

IF YOU WISH TO PRAY THE OFFICE OF READINGS DURING THE NIGHT: Great. You may pray this office at any time.

IF YOU PRAY THE OFFICE OF READINGS AT NIGHT, THEN PRAY MORNING PRAYER WITH SOMEONE ELSE WHO HAS NOT PRAYED THE OFFICE OF READINGS: While the Invitatory is to be prayed before the first office of the day, in this case charity and the law of praying the Office in community prevail. The Invitatory would be said together prior to Morning Prayer.

IF YOU PRAY MORNING PRAYER ALONE BUT EVENING PRAYER WITH SOMEONE ELSE: In this case, pray the Invitatory prior to the first prayer of the day. Your prayer partner will have prayed the Invitatory as part of Morning Prayer also.

IF YOU WISH TO PRAY ONLY MORNING OR EVENING PRAYER: Anyone, unless under obligation to do otherwise, may pray whatever he or she pleases. However, praying only Morning

Prayer or only Evening Prayer is not considered as praying the Divine Office. If you are under obligation to pray the Divine Office, praying both of these offices fulfills the obligation unless you are obligated to pray additional offices as well.

IF YOU HAVE OTHER QUESTIONS: Consult a priest or religious.

Congratulations on a job well done. And do not forget to remember the author of this manual in prayer now and then. Thanks, from one dodo to another! And may God bless you!

APPENDICES

Praying the Psalmody for Friday Evening Prayer Week III

Great is the Lord, our God, transcending all other gods.

Praise the name of the Lord,
praise him, servants of the Lord,
who stand in the house of the Lord
in the courts of the house of our God.

Praise the Lord for the Lord is good.
Sing a psalm to his name for he is loving.

For the Lord has chosen Jacob for himself
and Israel for his own possession.

For I know the Lord is great,
that our Lord is high above all gods.
The Lord does whatever he wills,
in heaven, on earth, in the seas.

He summons clouds from the ends of the earth;
makes his lightening produce the rain;
from his treasuries he sends forth the wind.

The first-born of the Egyptians he smote,
of man and beast alike.

Signs and wonders he worked
in the midst of your land, O Egypt,
against Pharaoh and all his servants.

Nations in their greatness he struck
and kings in their splendor he slew.
Sihon, king of the Amorites,
Og, the king of Bashan,
and all the kingdoms of Canaan.
He let Israel inherit the land;
on his people their land he bestowed.

(BOW) Glory to the Father and the Son and the Holy Spirit: (STRAIGHTEN) as it was in the beginning, is now, and will be forever. Amen.

Great is the Lord, our God, transcending all other gods.

(PAUSE BRIEFLY FOR SILENT REFLECTION)

House of Israel, bless the Lord! Sing psalms to him, for he is merciful.

Lord, your name stands for ever,
unforgotten from age to age:
for the Lord does justice for his people;
the Lord takes pity on his servants.

Pagan idols are silver and gold,
the work of human hands.
They have mouths but they cannot speak;
they have eyes but they cannot see.

They have ears but they cannot hear;
there is not a breath on their lips.
Their makers will come to be like them
and so will all who trust in them!

Sons of Israel, bless the Lord!
Sons of Aaron, bless the Lord!
Sons of Levi, bless the Lord!
You who fear him, bless the Lord!

From Zion may the Lord be blessed,
he who dwells in Jerusalem!

(BOW) Glory to the Father and to the Son and to the Holy Spirit: (STRAIGHTEN) as it was in the beginning, is now, and will be forever. Amen.

Father, your name and your memory last for ever. We stand to pray in your house and praise you with psalms of joy. We ask you in your kindness to have mercy on us in our lowliness.

House of Israel, bless the Lord! Sing psalms to him, for he is merciful.

(PAUSE BRIEFLY FOR SILENT REFLECTION)

All nations will come and worship before you, O Lord.

Mighty and wonderful are your works,
Lord God Almighty!
Righteous and true are your ways,

O King of the nations!

Who would dare refuse you honor,
or the glory due your name, O Lord?

Since you alone are holy,
all nations shall come
and worship in your presence.
Your mighty deeds are clearly seen.

(BOW) Glory to the Father and to the Son and to the Holy Spirit: (STRAIGHTEN) as it was in the beginning, is now, and will be forever. Amen.

All nations will come and worship before you, O Lord.

(PAUSE BRIEFLY FOR SILENT REFLECTION)

Appendix B

Night Prayer for Friday

In the name of the Father and of the Son and of the Holy Spirit. Amen.
God, come to my assistance.
Lord, make haste to help me.

(BOW) Glory to the Father, and to the Son, and to the Holy Spirit: (STRAIGHTEN) as it was in the beginning, is now, and will be for ever. Amen. Alleluia. (DURING LENT, OMIT THE ALLELUIA).

(MAKE A SILENT EXAMINATION OF CONSCIENCE)

(PRAY A PRAYER OF FORGIVENESS)

(SING OR CHANT A HYMN OF YOUR CHOICE OR ONE LISTED IN THE BREVIARY)

Day and night I cry to you, my God.

Lord, my God, I call for help by day;
I cry at night before you.
Let my prayer come into your presence.
O turn your ear to my cry.

For my soul is filled with evils;
my life is on the brink of the grave.
I am reckoned as one in the tomb:
I have reached the end of my strength,

like one alone among the dead;
like the slain lying in their graves;
like those you remember no more,
cut off, as they are, from your hand.

You have laid me in the depths of the tomb,
in places that are dark, in the depths.

Your anger weighs down upon me;
I am drowned beneath your waves.

You have taken away my friends
and made me hateful in their sight.
Imprisoned, I cannot escape;
my eyes are sunken with grief.

I call to you, Lord, all the day long;
to you I stretch out my hands.
Will you work your wonders for the dead?
Will the shades stand and praise you?

Will your love be told in the grave
or your faithfulness among the dead?
Will your wonders be known in the dark
or your justice in the land of oblivion?

As for me, Lord, I call to you for help;
in the morning, my prayer comes before you.
Lord, why do you reject me?
Why do you hide your face!

Wretched, close to death from my youth,
I have borne your trials; I am numb.
Your fury has swept down upon me;
your terrors have utterly destroyed me.

They surround me all the day like a flood,
they assail me all together.
Friend and neighbor you have taken away:
my one companion is darkness.

(BOW) Glory to the Father and to the Son and to the Holy Spirit (STRAIGHTEN) as it was in the beginning, is now, and will be forever. Amen.

Day and night I cry to you, my God.
(PAUSE)

You are in our midst, O Lord,
  your name we bear;
  do not forsake us, O Lord, our
    God!

Into your hands, Lord, I commend
  my spirit.
  Into your hands, Lord, I commend
    my spirit.

You have redeemed us, Lord God of
  truth.
  I commend my spirit.

Glory be to the Father and to the Son
  and to the Holy Spirit.
  Into your hands, Lord, I commend
    my spirit.
(PAUSE)

Protect us, Lord, as we stay awake;
  watch over us as we sleep, that
  awake, we may keep watch with
  Christ, and, asleep, rest in his
  peace.

In the name of the Father and of the
  Son and of the Holy Spirit. Amen.

Lord, now you let your servant go in
  peace;
your word has been fulfilled.

my own eyes have seen the salvation
which you have prepared in the sight
  of every people:

a light to reveal you to the nations
and the glory of your people Israel.

(BOW) Glory to the Father and to the
  Son and to the Holy Spirit:

(STRAIGHTEN) as it was in the
  beginning, is now, and will be forever. Amen.

Protect us, Lord, as we stay awake;
  watch over us as we sleep, that
  awake, we may keep watch with
  Christ, and asleep, rest in his
  peace.

Let us pray:

All powerful God,
keep us united with your Son
in his death and burial
so that we may rise to new life with
  him,
who lives and reigns for ever and ever.

May the all-powerful Lord grant us a
  restful night and a peaceful death.
Amen.

In the name of the Father and of the
  Son and of the Holy Spirit. Amen.

(CHOOSE ONE ANTIPHON IN
HONOR OF THE BLESSED VIR-
GIN AND PRAY IT. THE HAIL
MARY IS USED HERE AS A SAM-
PLE.)

Hail Mary, full of grace,
the Lord is with you!
Blessed are you among women,
and blessed is the fruit of your womb,
  Jesus.
Holy Mary, Mother of God,
pray for us sinners,
now and at the hour of our death.
Amen.

Appendix C

Canticle of Zechariah for Monday, Week I, Ordinary Time

Blessed be the Lord our God.

(MAKE THE SIGN OF THE CROSS)

Blessed be the Lord, the God of Israel,

he has come to his people and set them free.

He has raised up for us a mighty savior,

born of the house of his servant David.

Through his holy prophets he promised of old

that he would save us from our enemies,

from the hands of those who hate us.

He promised to show mercy to our fathers

and to remember his holy covenant.

This was the oath he swore to our father Abraham,

to set us free from the hands of our enemies,

free to worship him without fear,

holy and righteous in his sight

all the days of our life.

You, my child, shall be called the prophet of the Most High,

for you will go before the Lord to prepare his way

to give his people knowledge of salvation

by the forgiveness of their sins.

In the tender compassion of our God

the dawn from on high shall break upon us,

to shine on those who dwell in darkness and the shadow of death,

and to guide our feet into the way of peace.

(BOW) Glory to the Father and to the Son and to the Holy Spirit: (STRAIGHTEN) as it was in the beginning, is now, and will be forever. Amen.

Blessed be the Lord our God.

Canticle of Mary for Monday, Week I, Ordinary Time

My soul proclaims the greatness of the Lord, for he has looked with favor on his lowly servant.

(MAKE THE SIGN OF THE CROSS)

My soul proclaims the greatness of the Lord,

my spirit rejoices in God my Savior

for he has looked with favor on his lowly servant.

From this day, all generations will call me blessed:

the Almighty has done great things for me,

and holy is his Name.

He has mercy on those who fear him in every generation.

He has shown the strength of his arm,

he has scattered the proud in their conceit.

He has cast down the mighty from their thrones,

and has lifted up the lowly.

He has filled the hungry with good things,

and the rich he has sent away empty.

He has come to the help of his servant Israel

for he has remembered his promise of mercy,

the promise he made to our fathers,

to Abraham and his children for ever.

(BOW) Glory to the Father and to the Son and to the Holy Spirit: (STRAIGHTEN) as it was in the beginning, is now, and will be forever. Amen.

My soul proclaims the greatness of the Lord, for he has looked with favor on his lowly servant.

Appendix D

**Invitatory for Monday,
Week I, Ordinary Time**

(MAKE THE SIGN OF THE
CROSS SILENTLY ON YOUR
LIPS   WHILE   PRAYING
ALOUD . . .)

Lord, open my lips.
And my mouth will proclaim Your
praise.

Let us approach the Lord with praise
and thanksgiving.

Come, let us sing to the Lord
and shout with joy to the Rock who
saves us.
Let us approach him with praise and
thanksgiving
and sing joyful songs to the Lord.

Let us approach the Lord with praise
and thanksgiving.

The Lord is God, the mighty God,
the great king over all the gods.
He holds in his hands the depths of
the earth
and the highest mountains as well.

He made the sea; it belongs to him,
the dry land, too, for it was formed
by his hands.

Let us approach the Lord with praise
and thanksgiving.

(KNEEL OR BOW) Come, then, let
us bow down and worship,

bending the knee before the Lord,
our maker,
For he is our God and we are his people,
the flock he shepherds. (RISE)

Let us approach the Lord with praise
and thanksgiving.

Today, listen to the voice of the Lord.
Do not grow stubborn as your fathers
did
in the wilderness
when at Meriba and Massah
they challenged me and provoked
me
Although they had seen all of my
works.

Let us approach the Lord with praise
and thanksgiving.

Forty years I endured that generation.
I said, "They are a people whose
hearts go astray
and they do not know my ways."
So I swore in my anger,
"They shall not enter into my rest."

Let us approach the Lord with praise
and thanksgiving.

(BOW) Glory to the Father, and to
the Son, and to the Holy Spirit:
(STRAIGHTEN)
as it was in the beginning, is now, and
will be for ever.
Amen.

Let us approach the Lord with praise
and thanksgiving.

Appendix E

Intercessions and Conclusion for Morning Prayer, Monday Week I, Ordinary Time

We esteem Christ above all men, for he was filled with grace and the Holy Spirit. In faith let us implore him:

Give us your Spirit, Lord.

Grant us a peaceful day,
  when evening comes we will praise you with joy and purity of heart.
Let your splendor rest upon us today,
  direct the work of our hands.
May your face shine upon us and keep us in peace,
  may your strong arm protect us.
Look kindly on all who put their trust in our prayers,
  fill them with every bodily and spiritual grace.

(OPTIONAL: YOU MAY ADD HERE INTERCESSIONS OF YOUR OWN. IF YOU DO, PRAY THE WORDS PRINTED IN ITALICS AFTER EACH INTERCESSION.)

Our Father, who art in heaven, hallowed be thy name. Thy kingdom come, thy will be done, on earth as it is in heaven. Give us this day our daily bread and forgive us our trespasses, as we forgive those who trespass against us. And lead us not into temptation, but deliver us from evil.

Father,
may everything we do
begin with your inspiration
and continue with your saving help.
Let our work always find its origin in you
and through you reach completion.
We ask this through our Lord Jesus Christ, your Son,
who lives and reigns with you and the Holy Spirit,
one God, for ever and ever.

May the Lord bless us, protect us, and deliver us from all evil. Amen.

(MAKE THE SIGN OF THE CROSS). In the name of the Father, and of the Son, and of the Holy Spirit. Amen.

Appendix F

Intercessions and Conclusion for Evening Prayer, Monday, Week I, Ordinary Time

God has made an everlasting covenant with his people, and he never ceases to bless them. Grateful for these gifts, we confidently direct our prayer to him:
Lord, bless your people.

Save your people, Lord
and bless your inheritance.

Gather into one body all who bear the name of Christian,
that the world may believe in Christ whom you have sent.

Give our friends and our loved ones a share in divine life,
let them be symbols of Christ before men.

Show your love to those who are suffering,
open their eyes to the vision of your revelation.

Be compassionate to those who have died,
welcome them into the company of the faithful departed.

(OPTIONAL: YOU MAY ADD HERE INTERCESSIONS OF YOUR OWN. IF YOU DO, PRAY THE WORDS PRINTED IN ITALICS AFTER EACH INTERCESSION.)

Our Father, who art in heaven, hallowed be thy name. Thy kingdom come, thy will be done, on earth as it is in heaven. Give us this day our daily bread and forgive us our trespasses, as we forgive those who trespass against us. And lead us not into temptation, but deliver us from evil.

Father,
may this evening pledge of our service to you
bring you glory and praise.
For our salvation you looked with favor
on the lowliness of the Virgin Mary;
lead us to the fullness of salvation
you have prepared for us.
We ask this through our Lord Jesus Christ, your Son,
who lives and reigns with you and the Holy Spirit,
one God, for ever and ever.

May the Lord bless us, protect us, and deliver us from all evil. Amen.

(MAKE THE SIGN OF THE CROSS). In the name of the Father, and of the Son, and of the Holy Spirit. Amen.

Appendix G

Wednesday Morning Prayer during Holy Week

(MAKE THE SIGN OF THE CROSS). In the name of the Father, and of the Son, and of the Holy Spirit. Amen.

Lord, open my lips.
And my mouth will proclaim your praise.

(INVITATORY ANTIPHON)
Come, let us worship Christ the Lord, who for our sake endured temptation and suffering.

Come, let us sing to the Lord
and shout with joy to the Rock who saves us.
Let us approach him with praise and thanksgiving
and sing joyful songs to the Lord.

Come, let us worship Christ the Lord, who for our sake endured temptation and suffering.

The Lord is God, the mighty God,
the great king over all the gods.
He holds in his hands the depths of the earth
and the highest mountains as well.
He made the sea; it belongs to him,
the dry land, too, for it was formed by his hands.

Come, let us worship Christ the Lord, who for our sake endured temptation and suffering.

(KNEEL OR BOW) Come, then, let us bow down and worship,
bending the knee before the Lord, our maker,

For he is our God and we are his people,
the flock he shepherds. (RISE)

Come, let us worship Christ the Lord, who for our sake endured temptation and suffering.

Today, listen to the voice of the Lord.
Do not grow stubborn as your fathers did
in the wilderness
when at Meriba and Massah
they challenged me and provoked me
Although they had seen all of my works.

Come, let us worship Christ the Lord, who for our sake endured temptation and suffering.

Forty years I endured that generation.
I said, "They are a people whose hearts go astray
and they do not know my ways."
So I swore in my anger,
"They shall not enter into my rest."

Come, let us worship Christ the Lord, who for our sake endured temptation and suffering.

(BOW) Glory to the Father, and to the Son, and to the Holy Spirit: (STRAIGHTEN)
as it was in the beginning, is now, and will be for ever.
Amen.

Come, let us worship Christ the Lord, who for our sake endured temptation and suffering.

(SING, CHANT, OR RECITE THE HYMN YOU HAVE CHOSEN)

(ANTIPHON 1) In the day of my distress, I reached out with my hands to seek the Lord's help.

(PRAY PSALM 77 AS WRITTEN IN THE PSALTER FOR WEDNESDAY MORNING PRAYER, WEEK II. END WITH GLORY BE PRAYED IN FULL AS USUAL.)

(PRAY THE PSALM-PRAYER AS WRITTEN IN THE PSALTER.)

(ANTIPHON 1) In the day of my distress, I reached out with my hands to seek the Lord's help.

(PAUSE BRIEFLY)

(ANTIPHON 2) If we have died with Christ, we believe that we shall also live with Christ.

(PRAY THE CANTICLE FROM SAMUEL 2:1-10 AS WRITTEN IN THE PSALTER FOR WEDNESDAY MORNING PRAYER, WEEK II. END WITH THE GLORY BE PRAYED IN FULL AS USUAL.)

(ANTIPHON 2) If we have died with Christ, we believe that we shall also live with Christ.

(PAUSE BRIEFLY)

(ANTIPHON 3) God had made Christ Jesus our wisdom and our holiness. By him we have been sanctified and redeemed.

(PRAY PSALM 97 AS WRITTEN IN THE PSALTER FOR WEDNESDAY MORNING PRAYER, WEEK II. END WITH THE GLORY BE PRAYED IN FULL AS USUAL.)

(PRAY THE PSALM-PRAYER AS WRITTEN IN THE PSALTER.)

(ANTIPHON 3) God has made Christ Jesus our wisdom and our holiness. By him we have been sanctified and redeemed.

(PAUSE BRIEFLY)

(READING FROM ISAIAH 50:4B-7)

The Lord God opens my ear that I may hear;
And I have not rebelled,
have not turned back.
I gave my back to those who beat me,
my cheeks to those who plucked my beard;
My face I did not shield
from buffets and spitting.
The Lord God is my help,
therefore I am not disgraced;
I have set my face like flint,
knowing that I shall not be put to shame.

By your own blood, Lord, you brought us back to God.
By your own blood, Lord, you brought us back to God.
From every tribe, and tongue, and people, and nation,
you brought us back to God.
Glory to the Father and to the Son and to the Holy Spirit
By your own blood, Lord, you brought us back to God.

(PAUSE BRIEFLY FOR SILENT REFLECTION)

(ANTIPHON FOR CANTICLE OF ZECHARIAH) Through the eternal Spirit, Christ offered himself to God as the perfect sacrifice. His blood purifies us from sin and makes us fit servants of the living God.

(PRAY THE CANTICLE OF ZECHARIAH ALL THE WAY THROUGH TO THE END AS TAUGHT IN LESSON 23. END WITH GLORY BE PRAYED IN FULL AS USUAL.)

(ANTIPHON FOR CANTICLE OF ZECHARIAH) Through the eternal Spirit, Christ offered himself to God as the perfect sacrifice. His blood purifies us from sin and makes us fit servants of the living God.

(PAUSE BRIEFLY)

Let us pray to Christ our Savior, who redeemed us by his death and resurrection.
 Lord, have mercy on us.
You went up to Jerusalem to suffer and so enter into your glory,
 bring your Church to the Passover feast of heaven.
You were lifted high on the cross and pierced by the soldier's lance,
 heal our wounds.

You made the cross the tree of life,
 give its fruits to those reborn in baptism.
On the cross you forgave the repentant thief,
 forgive us our sins.

(PRAY THE OUR FATHER THROUGH TO THE END)

Father,
in your plan of salvation
your Son Jesus Christ accepted the cross
and freed us from the power of the enemy.
May we come to share the glory of his resurrection,
for he lives and reigns with you and the Holy Spirit,
one God, for ever and ever.

May the Lord bless us, protect us from all evil, and bring us to everlasting life. Amen.

(MAKE THE SIGN OF THE CROSS). In the name of the Father, and of the Son, and of the Holy Spirit. Amen.

Appendix H

Morning Prayer for the Second Sunday of Advent

(MAKE THE SIGN OF THE CROSS) In the name of the Father and of the Son and of the Holy Spirit. Amen.

Lord, open my lips.
And my mouth will proclaim your praise.

(INVITATORY ANTIPHON)
Come, let us worship the Lord, the King who is to come.

(PRAY THE INVITATORY PSALM, PSALM 95, REPEATING THE ANTIPHON BETWEEN THE VERSES AS YOU HAVE BEEN TAUGHT.)

(END WITH THE GLORY BE PRAYED IN FULL.)

(REPEAT INVITATORY ANTI-PHON) Come, let us worship the Lord, the King who is to come.

(SING, CHANT, OR RECITE THE HYMN YOU HAVE CHOSEN)

(ANTIPHON 1) Zion is our mighty citadel, our saving Lord its wall and its defense; throw open the gates, for our Lord is here among us, Alleluia.

(YOU SHOULD BE AT SUNDAY MORNING PRAYER, WEEK II, OF THE PSALTER. PRAY PSALM 118 THROUGH TO THE END.)

(PRAY THE GLORY BE)

(PRAY THE PSALM-PRAYER)

(REPEAT ANTIPHON 1)
Zion is our mighty citadel, our saving Lord its wall and its defense; throw open the gates, for our Lord is here among us, Alleluia.

(PAUSE BRIEFLY)

(ANTIPHON 2) Come to the waters, all you who thirst; seek the Lord while he can be found, Alleluia.

(PRAY THE CANTICLE OF DANIEL 3:52-57 ALL THE WAY THROUGH TO THE END)

(PRAY THE GLORY BE)

(REPEAT ANTIPHON 2)
Come to the waters, all you who thirst; seek the Lord while he can be found, Alleluia.

(PAUSE BRIEFLY)

(ANTIPHON 3) Our God will come with great power to enlighten the eyes of his servants, Alleluia.

(PRAY PSALM 150 TO THE END)

(PRAY THE GLORY BE)

(PRAY THE PSALM-PRAYER)

(REPEAT ANTIPHON 3) Our God will come with great power to enlighten the eyes of his servants, Alleluia.

(PAUSE BRIEFLY)

(TURN TO THE PROPER OF SEASONS)

(READ THE READING FROM ROMANS 13:11-14)

(READ THE RESPONSORY)

(PAUSE BRIEFLY)

(ANTIPHON FOR CANTICLE OF ZECHARIAH) I am sending my angel before me to prepare the way for my coming.

(PRAY CANTICLE OF ZECHARIAH AS TAUGHT IN LESSON 23)

(PRAY GLORY BE)

(REPEAT ANTIPHON FOR CANTICLE OF ZECHARIAH) I am sending my angel before me to prepare the way for my coming.

(PRAY INTERCESSIONS BEGINNING "To the Lord Jesus Christ, judge of the living and the dead . . . ")

(PRAY OUR FATHER)

(PRAY CONCLUDING PRAYER BEGINNING "God of power and mercy, open our hearts in welcome . . . ").

May the Lord bless us, protect us from all evil, and bring us to everlasting life. Amen.

(MAKE THE SIGN OF THE CROSS). In the name of the Father and of the Son and of the Holy Spirit. Amen.

Appendix I

Praying the Psalmody for Wednesday Night Prayer during the Easter Season

In the name of the Father and of the Son and of the Holy Spirit. Amen.

God, come to my assistance.
Lord, make haste to help me.

(BOW) Glory to the Father, and to the Son, and to the Holy Spirit: (STRAIGHTEN) as it was in the beginning, is now, and will be for ever. Amen. Alleluia.

(MAKE A SILENT EXAMINATION OF CONSCIENCE)

(PRAY A PRAYER OF FORGIVENESS)

(SING OR CHANT A HYMN OF YOUR CHOICE OR ONE LISTED IN THE BREVIARY)

Alleluia, Alleluia, Alleluia.

In you, O Lord, I take refuge
Let me never be put to shame.
In your justice, set me free,
hear me and speedily rescue me.

Be a rock of refuge for me,
a mighty stronghold to save me,
for you are my rock, my stronghold.
For your name's sake, lead me and guide me.

Release me from the snares they have hidden
for you are my refuge, Lord.

Into your hands I commend my spirit.
It is you who will redeem me, Lord.

(BOW) Glory to the Father, and to the Son, and to the Holy Spirit: (STRAIGHTEN) as it was in the beginning, is now, and will be forever. Amen.

(PAUSE FOR SILENT REFLECTION)

Out of the depths I cry to you, Lord,
Lord, hear my voice!
O let your ears be attentive
to the voice of my pleading.

If you, O Lord, should mark our guilt,
Lord, who would survive?
But with you is found forgiveness:
for this we revere you.

My soul is waiting for the Lord,
I count on his word.
My soul is longing for the Lord
more than watchman for daybreak.
Let the watchman count on daybreak
and Israel on the Lord.

Because with the Lord there is mercy
and fullness of redemption,
Israel indeed he will redeem
from all its iniquity.

(BOW) Glory to the Father, and to the Son, and to the Holy Spirit: (STRAIGHTEN) as it was in the beginning, is now, and will be forever. Amen.

Alleluia, Alleluia, Alleluia.

Appendix J

Praying Night Prayer on the Eve of Divine Mercy Sunday

In the name of the Father and of the Son and of the Holy Spirit. Amen.

God, come to my assistance.
Lord, make haste to help me.

(BOW) Glory to the Father, and to the Son, and to the Holy Spirit: (STRAIGHTEN) as it was in the beginning, is now, and will be forever. Amen. Alleluia.

(MAKE A SILENT EXAMINATION OF CONSCIENCE)

(PRAY A PRAYER OF FORGIVENESS)

(SING OR CHANT A HYMN OF YOUR CHOICE OR ONE LISTED IN THE BREVIARY)

Alleluia, Alleluia, Alleluia.

When I call, answer me, O God of justice;
from anguish you released me; have mercy and hear me.

O men, how long will your hearts be closed,
will you love what is futile and seek what is false?

It is the Lord who grants favors to those whom he loves;
the Lord hears me whenever I call him.

Fear him; do not sin: ponder on your bed and be still.

Make justice your sacrifice and trust in the Lord.

"What can bring us happiness?" many say.
Let the light of your face shine on us, O Lord.

I will lie down in peace and sleep comes at once
for you alone, Lord, make me dwell in safety.

(BOW) Glory to the Father and to the Son and to the Holy Spirit: (STRAIGHTEN) as it was in the beginning, is now, and will be forever. Amen.

(PAUSE)

O come, bless the Lord, You are in our midst, O Lord,
your name we bear;
do not forsake us, O Lord, our God!

Into your hands, Lord, I commend my spirit.
Into your hands, Lord, I commend my spirit.

You have redeemed us, Lord God of truth.
I commend my spirit.

(BOW) Glory to the Father, and to the Son, and to the Holy Spirit: (STRAIGHTEN) as it was in the beginning, is now, and will be forever. Amen.

Alleluia, Alleluia, Alleluia.

(PAUSE FOR SILENT REFLECTION)

Hear, O Israel! The Lord is our God, the Lord alone! Therefore, you shall love the Lord your God with all your heart, and with all your soul, and with all your strength. Take to heart these words which I enjoin on you today. Drill them into your children. Speak of them at home and abroad, whether you are busy or at rest.

(PAUSE)

This is the day the Lord has made; let us rejoice and be glad, Alleluia.

(PAUSE)

Protect us, Lord, as we stay awake; watch over us as we sleep, that awake, we may keep watch with Christ, and, asleep, rest in his peace, Alleluia.

(MAKE THE SIGN OF THE CROSS) In the name of the Father and of the Son and of the Holy Spirit. Amen.

Lord, now you let your servant go in peace;
your word has been fulfilled.

my own eyes have seen the salvation
which you have prepared in the sight of every people:

a light to reveal you to the nations
and the glory of your people Israel.

(BOW) Glory to the Father and to the Son and to the Holy Spirit: (STRAIGHTEN) as it was in the beginning, is now, and will be forever. Amen.

Protect us, Lord, as we stay awake; watch over us as we sleep, that awake, we may keep watch with Christ, and asleep, rest in his peace, Alleluia.

Let us pray:

Lord,
be with us throughout this night.
When day comes may we rise from sleep
to rejoice in the resurrection of your Christ,
who lives and reigns for ever and ever.

May the all-powerful Lord grant us a restful night and a peaceful death. Amen.

In the name of the Father and of the Son and of the Holy Spirit. Amen.

(CHOOSE ONE ANTIPHON IN HONOR OF THE BLESSED VIRGIN AND PRAY IT. THE HAIL MARY IS USED HERE AS A SAMPLE.)

Hail Mary, full of grace,
the Lord is with you!
Blessed are you among women,
and blessed is the fruit of your womb, Jesus.
Holy Mary, Mother of God,
pray for us sinners,
now and at the hour of our death. Amen.

Appendix K

Praying Morning Prayer
for the Feast of St. Thomas
the Apostle

(MAKE THE SIGN OF THE CROSS). In the name of the Father, and of the Son, and of the Holy Spirit. Amen.

Lord, open my lips.
And my mouth will proclaim your praise.

(INVITATORY ANTIPHON— NOT IN PROPER OF SAINTS/ SAINT THOMAS, SO TAKE IT FROM THE COMMON OF THE APOSTLES) Come, let us worship the Lord, the King of Apostles. Alleluia.

Come, let us sing to the Lord
and shout with joy to the Rock who saves us.
Let us approach him with praise and thanksgiving
and sing joyful songs to the Lord.

Come, let us worship the Lord, the King of Apostles. Alleluia.

The Lord is God, the mighty God,
the great king over all the gods.
He holds in his hands the depths of the earth
and the highest mountains as well.
He made the sea; it belongs to him,
the dry land, too, for it was formed by his hands.

Come, let us worship the Lord, the King of Apostles. Alleluia.

(KNEEL OR BOW) Come, then, let us bow down and worship,
bending the knee before the Lord, our maker,
For he is our God and we are his people,
the flock he shepherds. (RISE)

Come, let us worship the Lord, the King of Apostles. Alleluia.

Today, listen to the voice of the Lord.
Do not grow stubborn as your fathers did
in the wilderness
when at Meriba and Massah
they challenged me and provoked me
Although they had seen all of my works.

Come, let us worship the Lord, the King of Apostles. Alleluia.

Forty years I endured that generation.
I said, "They are a people whose hearts go astray
and they do not know my ways."
So I swore in my anger,
"They shall not enter into my rest."

Come, let us worship the Lord, the King of Apostles. Alleluia.

(BOW) Glory to the Father, and to the Son, and to the Holy Spirit: (STRAIGHTEN) as it was in the beginning, is now, and will be for ever. Amen.

Come, let us worship the Lord, the King of Apostles. Alleluia.

(HYMN—NOT IN PROPER OF SAINTS/SAINT THOMAS, SO USE ONE FROM THE COMMON OF APOSTLES)

(ANTIPHON 1—GIVEN IN PROPER OF SAINTS/ SAINT THOMAS) Lord, we do not know where you are going; how can we know the way? Jesus replied: I am the way, the truth, and the life.

(NOW PRAY PSALM 63:2-9 FROM SUNDAY, WEEK I, IN PSALTER. END WITH GLORY BE PRAYED IN FULL AS USUAL.)

(PRAY THE PSALM-PRAYER AS WRITTEN IN THE PSALTER, SUNDAY, MORNING PRAYER, WEEK I.)

(ANTIPHON 1) Lord, we do not know where you are going; how can we know the way? Jesus replied: I am the way, the truth, and the life.

(PAUSE BRIEFLY)

(ANTIPHON 2—GIVEN IN PROPER OF SAINTS/ SAINT THOMAS)
Thomas, who was called the Twin, was not present when Jesus appeared to the apostles; so they told him: We have seen the Lord, Alleluia.

(NOW PRAY THE CANTICLE FROM DANIEL 3:57-88, 56 AS WRITTEN IN PSALTER, SUNDAY MORNING PRAYER, WEEK I)

(ANTIPHON 2—GIVEN IN PROPER OF SAINTS/ SAINT THOMAS)

Thomas, who was called the Twin, was not present when Jesus appeared to the apostles; so they told him: We have seen the Lord, Alleluia.

(PAUSE BRIEFLY)

(ANTIPHON 3—GIVEN IN PROPER OF SAINTS/ SAINT THOMAS) With your hand, touch the mark of the nails; doubt no longer, but believe, Alleluia.

(NOW PRAY PSALM 149 AS WRITTEN IN THE PSALTER FOR SUNDAY MORNING PRAYER, WEEK I. END WITH THE GLORY BE PRAYED IN FULL AS USUAL.)

(PRAY PSALM-PRAYER FROM SUNDAY MORNING PRAYER, WEEK I)

(ANTIPHON 3—GIVEN IN PROPER OF SAINTS/ SAINT THOMAS) With your hand, touch the mark of the nails; doubt no longer, but believe, Alleluia.

(PAUSE BRIEFLY)

(READING—GIVEN IN PROPER OF SAINTS/SAINT THOMAS) You are strangers and aliens no longer. No, you are fellow citizens of the saints and members of the household of God. You form a building which rises on the foundation of the apostles and prophets, with Christ Jesus himself as the capstone. Through him the whole structure is fitted together and takes shape as a holy temple in the Lord; in him you are being built into this temple, to become a dwelling place for God in the Spirit.

(PAUSE BRIEFLY FOR SILENT REFLECTION)

(RESPONSORY—GIVEN IN PROPER OF SAINTS/ SAINT THOMAS) You have made them rulers over all the earth.

You have made them rulers over all the earth.

They will always remember your name, O Lord,

over all the earth.

Glory to the Father and to the Son and to the Holy Spirit.

You have made them rulers over all the earth.

(PAUSE)

(ANTIPHON FOR CANTICLE OF ZECHARIAH—GIVEN IN PROPER OF SAINTS/SAINT THOMAS) Because you have seen me, Thomas, you have believed; blessed are they who have not seen me and yet believe.

(PRAY THE CANTICLE OF ZECHARIAH ALL THE WAY THROUGH TO THE END AS TAUGHT IN LESSON 23. END WITH GLORY BE PRAYED IN FULL AS USUAL.)

(ANTIPHON FOR CANTICLE OF ZECHARIAH) Because you have seen me, Thomas, you have believed; blessed are they who have not seen me and yet believe.

(PAUSE BRIEFLY)

(INTERCESSIONS—NOT IN PROPER OF SAINTS/ SAINT THOMAS, SO USE ONE FROM COMMON OF THE APOSTLES) Beloved friends, we have inherited heaven along with the apostles. Let us give thanks to the Father for all his gifts:

The company of apostles praises you, O Lord.

(PRAY THE INTERCESSIONS THROUGH TO THE END AS THEY ARE WRITTEN IN THE BREVIARY. YOU MAY ADD ANY INTERCESSIONS YOU WISH, ENDING THEM WITH The company of apostles praises you, O Lord).

(PRAY THE OUR FATHER THROUGH TO THE END)

(PRAYER FOR SAINT THOMAS, FOUND IN THE PROPER OF SAINTS)

Almighty Father,

as we honor Thomas the apostle,

let us always experience the help of his prayers.

May we have eternal life by believing in Jesus,

whom Thomas acknowledged as Lord,

for he lives and reigns with you and the Holy Spirit,

one God, for ever and ever.

May the Lord bless us, protect us from all evil, and bring us to everlasting life. Amen.

(MAKE THE SIGN OF THE CROSS). In the name of the Father, and of the Son, and of the Holy Spirit. Amen.

Appendix L

Praying Morning Prayer for the Memorial of Saint Justin Martyr using the Common of One Martyr as the primary source for the Office as if Monday, June 1, occurred during Week I of the Psalter.

(MAKE THE SIGN OF THE CROSS). In the name of the Father, and of the Son, and of the Holy Spirit. Amen.

Lord, open my lips.
And my mouth will proclaim your praise.

(INVITATORY ANTIPHON— COMMON) Come, let us worship Christ, the king of martyrs.

Come, let us sing to the Lord
and shout with joy to the Rock who saves us.
Let us approach him with praise and thanksgiving
and sing joyful songs to the Lord.

Come, let us worship Christ, the king of martyrs.

The Lord is God, the mighty God,
the great king over all the gods.
He holds in his hands the depths of the earth
and the highest mountains as well.
He made the sea; it belongs to him,
the dry land, too, for it was formed by his hands.

Come, let us worship Christ, the king of martyrs.

(KNEEL OR BOW) Come, then, let us bow down and worship,

bending the knee before the Lord, our maker,
For he is our God and we are his people,
the flock he shepherds. (RISE)

Come, let us worship Christ, the king of martyrs.

Today, listen to the voice of the Lord.
Do not grow stubborn as your fathers did
in the wilderness
when at Meriba and Massah
they challenged me and provoked me
Although they had seen all of my works.

Come, let us worship Christ, the king of martyrs.

Forty years I endured that generation.
I said, "They are a people whose hearts go astray
and they do not know my ways."
So I swore in my anger,
"They shall not enter into my rest."

Come, let us worship Christ, the king of martyrs.

(BOW) Glory to the Father, and to the Son, and to the Holy Spirit: (STRAIGHTEN) as it was in the beginning, is now, and will be for ever. Amen.

Come, let us worship Christ, the king of martyrs.

(HYMN—COMMON) Christ, in whose passion once was sown . . .
(CONTINUE TO PRAY OR

RECITE HYMN UNTIL THE END)

(PSALMODY—PSALTER, MONDAY, WEEK I)

(ANTIPHON 1) I lift up my heart to you, O Lord, and you will hear my morning prayer. (NOW PRAY PSALM 5:2-10, 13-13, THE GLORY BE, AND THE PSALM PRAYER LISTED FOR MONDAY MORNING PRAYER, WEEK I. REPEAT ANTIPHON 1).

(ANTIPHON 2) We praise your glorious name, O Lord, our God. (PRAY THE CANTICLE FROM CHRONICLES 20:10-13 AS LISTED IN THE PSALTER FOR MONDAY MORNING PRAYER, WEEK I, FOLLOWED BY THE GLORY BE. REPEAT ANTIPHON 2).

(ANTIPHON 3) Adore the Lord in his holy court. (PRAY PSALM 29 AS WRITTEN IN THE PSALTER FOR MONDAY MORNING PRAYER, WEEK I, FOLLOWED BY THE GLORY BE AND PSALM PRAYER. REPEAT ANTIPHON 3).

(READING FROM THE COMMON OF ONE MARTYR) Praised be God, the Father of our Lord Jesus Christ, the Father of mercies, and the God of all consolation! He comforts us in all our afflictions and thus enables us to comfort those who are in trouble, with the same consolation we have received from him. As we have shared much in the suffering of Christ, so through Christ do we share abundantly in his consolation.

(PAUSE BRIEFLY)

(RESPONSORY FROM THE COMMON OF ONE MARTYR) The Lord is my strength, and I shall sing his praise.
The Lord is my strength, and I shall sing his praise.

The Lord is my savior,
and I shall sing his praise.

Glory to the Father and to the Son and to the Holy Spirit
The Lord is my strength, and I shall sing his praise.

(PAUSE BRIEFLY)

(ANTIPHON FOR CANTICLE OF ZECHARIAH FROM MEMORIAL OF SAINT JUSTIN MARTYR) In every sacrifice let us praise the Creator of all things through his Son Jesus Christ and through the Holy Spirit.

(MAKE THE SIGN OF THE CROSS)

Blessed be the Lord, the God of Israel,
he has come to his people and set them free.

He has raised up for us a mighty savior,
born of the house of his servant David.

Through his holy prophets he promised of old

that he would save us from our enemies,

from the hands of those who hate us.

He promised to show mercy to our fathers

and to remember his holy covenant.

This was the oath he swore to our father Abraham,

to set us free from the hands of our enemies,

free to worship him without fear,

holy and righteous in his sight

all the days of our life.

You, my child, shall be called the prophet of the Most High,

for you will go before the Lord to prepare his way

to give his people knowledge of salvation

by the forgiveness of their sins.

In the tender compassion of our God

the dawn from on high shall break upon us,

to shine on those who dwell in darkness and the shadow of death,

and to guide our feet into the way of peace.

(BOW) Glory to the Father and to the Son and to the Holy Spirit: (STRAIGHTEN) as it was in the beginning, is now, and will be forever. Amen.

(ANTIPHON FROM MEMORIAL OF JUSTIN MARTYR) In every sacrifice let us praise the Creator of all things through his Son Jesus Christ and through the Holy Spirit.

(PAUSE BRIEFLY)

(INTERCESSIONS FROM THE COMMON OF ONE MARTYR) Our Savior's faithfulness is mirrored in the fidelity of his witnesses who shed their blood for the word of God.

Let us praise him in remembrance of them:

You redeemed us by your blood.

Your martyrs freely embraced death in bearing witness to the faith,

give us the true freedom of the Spirit, O Lord.

Your martyrs professed their faith by shedding their blood,

give us a faith, O Lord, that is constant and pure.

Your martyrs followed in your footsteps by carrying the cross,

help us to endure courageously the misfortunes of life.

Your martyrs washed their garments in the blood of the Lamb,

help us to avoid the weaknesses of the flesh and worldly allurements.

(OPTIONAL: ADD ANY PETITIONS YOU WISH. FOLLOW EACH WITH THE RESPONSE WRITTEN IN *ITALICS* ABOVE)

(PRAY THE OUR FATHER)

(CONCLUDING PRAYER FROM THE MEMORIAL OF SAINT JUSTIN MARTYR):

Father,

through the folly of the cross

you taught Saint Justin the sublime
wisdom of Jesus Christ.
May we too reject falsehood
and remain loyal to the faith.
We ask this through our Lord Jesus
Christ, your Son,
who lives and reigns with you and the
Holy Spirit,
one God, for ever and ever.

May the Lord bless us,
protect us from all evil
and bring us to everlasting life.
Amen.

(CONCLUDE WITH THE SIGN
OF THE CROSS).

Appendix M

Praying Morning Prayer for the Memorial of Saint Justin Martyr using the Psalter as the primary source for the Office as if Monday, June 1, occurred during Week I of the Psalter.

(MAKE THE SIGN OF THE CROSS). In the name of the Father, and of the Son, and of the Holy Spirit. Amen.

Lord, open my lips.
And my mouth will proclaim your praise.

(INVITATORY ANTIPHON—PSALTER) Let us approach the Lord with praise and thanksgiving.

Come, let us sing to the Lord
and shout with joy to the Rock who saves us.
Let us approach him with praise and thanksgiving
and sing joyful songs to the Lord.

Let us approach the Lord with praise and thanksgiving.

The Lord is God, the mighty God,
the great king over all the gods.
He holds in his hands the depths of the earth
and the highest mountains as well.
He made the sea; it belongs to him,
the dry land, too, for it was formed by his hands.

Let us approach the Lord with praise and thanksgiving.

(KNEEL OR BOW) Come, then, let us bow down and worship,

bending the knee before the Lord, our maker,
For he is our God and we are his people,
the flock he shepherds. (RISE)

Let us approach the Lord with praise and thanksgiving.

Today, listen to the voice of the Lord.
Do not grow stubborn as your fathers did
in the wilderness
when at Meriba and Massah
they challenged me and provoked me
Although they had seen all of my works.

Let us approach the Lord with praise and thanksgiving.

Forty years I endured that generation.
I said, "They are a people whose hearts go astray
and they do not know my ways."
So I swore in my anger,
"They shall not enter into my rest."

Let us approach the Lord with praise and thanksgiving.

(BOW) Glory to the Father, and to the Son, and to the Holy Spirit: (STRAIGHTEN) as it was in the beginning, is now, and will be for ever. Amen.

Let us approach the Lord with praise and thanksgiving.

(HYMN—COMMON) Christ, in whose passion once was sown . . . (CONTINUE TO PRAY OR RECITE HYMN UNTIL THE END)

(PSALMODY—PSALTER, MONDAY, WEEK I)

(ANTIPHON 1) I lift up my heart to you, O Lord, and you will hear my morning prayer. (NOW PRAY PSALM 5:2-10, 13-13, THE GLORY BE, AND THE PSALM-PRAYER FOR MONDAY MORNING PRAYER, WEEK I. REPEAT ANTIPHON 1. PAUSE BRIEFLY.)

(ANTIPHON 2) We praise your glorious name, O Lord, our God. (PRAY THE CANTICLE FROM CHRONICLES 20:10-13 AS LISTED IN THE PSALTER FOR MONDAY MORNING PRAYER, WEEK I, FOLLOWED BY THE GLORY BE. REPEAT ANTIPHON 2. PAUSE BRIEFLY.)

(ANTIPHON 3) Adore the Lord in his holy court. (PRAY PSALM 29 FROM THE PSALTER FOR MONDAY MORNING PRAYER, WEEK I, FOLLOWED BY THE GLORY BE AND PSALM PRAYER. REPEAT ANTIPHON 3. PAUSE BRIEFLY.)

(READING FROM THE PSALTER, MONDAY WEEK I) Anyone who would not work should not eat. We hear that some of you are unruly, not keeping busy but acting like busy-bodies. We enjoin all such, and we urge them strongly in the Lord Jesus Christ, to earn the food they eat by working quietly. You must never grow weary of doing what is right, brothers.

(PAUSE BRIEFLY)

(RESPONSORY FROM THE PSALTER, MONDAY WEEK I) Blessed be the Lord our God, blessed from age to age.

Blessed be the Lord our God, blessed from age to age.

His marvelous works are beyond compare,
blessed from age to age.

Glory to the Father and to the Son and to the Holy Spirit
Blessed be the Lord our God, blessed from age to age.

(PAUSE BRIEFLY)

(ANTIPHON FOR CANTICLE OF ZECHARIAH FROM MEMORIAL OF SAINT JUSTIN MARTYR) In every sacrifice let us praise the Creator of all things through his Son Jesus Christ and through the Holy Spirit.

(MAKE THE SIGN OF THE CROSS)

Blessed be the Lord, the God of Israel,
he has come to his people and set them free.

He has raised up for us a mighty savior,
born of the house of his servant David.

Through his holy prophets he promised of old

that he would save us from our enemies,

from the hands of those who hate us.

He promised to show mercy to our fathers

and to remember his holy covenant.

This was the oath he swore to our father Abraham,

to set us free from the hands of our enemies,

free to worship him without fear,

holy and righteous in his sight

all the days of our life.

You, my child, shall be called the prophet of the Most High,

for you will go before the Lord to prepare his way

to give his people knowledge of salvation

by the forgiveness of their sins.

In the tender compassion of our God

the dawn from on high shall break upon us,

to shine on those who dwell in darkness and the shadow of death,

and to guide our feet into the way of peace.

(BOW) Glory to the Father and to the Son and to the Holy Spirit: (STRAIGHTEN) as it was in the beginning, is now, and will be forever. Amen.

(ANTIPHON FROM MEMORIAL OF JUSTIN MARTYR) In every sacrifice let us praise the Creator of all things through his Son Jesus Christ and through the Holy Spirit.

(INTERCESSIONS FROM THE PSALTER, MONDAY WEEK I) We esteem Christ above all men, for he was filled with grace and the Holy Spirit. In faith let us implore him:

Give us your Spirit, Lord.

Grant us a peaceful day,

when evening comes we will praise you with joy and

purity of heart.

Let your splendor rest upon us today, direct the work of our hands.

May your face shine upon us and keep us in peace,

may your strong arm protect us.

Look kindly on all who put their trust in our prayers,

fill them with every bodily and spiritual grace.

(OPTIONAL: YOU MAY ADD HERE INTERCESSIONS OF YOUR OWN. IF YOU DO, PRAY THE WORDS PRINTED IN ITALICS AFTER EACH INTERCESSION.)

(PRAY THE OUR FATHER)

(CONCLUDING PRAYER FROM THE MEMORIAL OF SAINT JUSTIN MARTYR):

Father,

through the folly of the cross

you taught Saint Justin the sublime wisdom of Jesus Christ.

May we too reject falsehood

and remain loyal to the faith.

We ask this through our Lord Jesus Christ, your Son,

who lives and reigns with you and the
   Holy Spirit,
one God, for ever and ever.

May the Lord bless us,
protect us from all evil

and bring us to everlasting life.
Amen.

(CONCLUDE WITH THE SIGN
OF THE CROSS).

Appendix N

Praying Morning Prayer for the Optional Memorial of Saint John Damascene, on Friday, December 4

(First Week of Advent) using Week I of the Psalter and the Common of Doctors of the Church

(MAKE THE SIGN OF THE CROSS). In the name of the Father, and of the Son, and of the Holy Spirit. Amen.

Lord, open my lips.
And my mouth will proclaim your praise.

(INVITATORY ANTIPHON—COMMON OF DOCTORS) Come, let us worship the Lord, fount of all wisdom.

Come, let us sing to the Lord
 and shout with joy to the Rock who saves us.
Let us approach him with praise and thanksgiving
 and sing joyful songs to the Lord.

Come, let us worship the Lord, fount of all wisdom.

The Lord is God, the mighty God,
 the great king over all the gods.
He holds in his hands the depths of the earth
 and the highest mountains as well.
He made the sea; it belongs to him,
 the dry land, too, for it was formed by his hands.

Come, let us worship the Lord, fount of all wisdom.

(KNEEL OR BOW) Come, then, let us bow down and worship,
 bending the knee before the Lord, our maker,
For he is our God and we are his people,
 the flock he shepherds. (RISE)

Come, let us worship the Lord, fount of all wisdom.

Today, listen to the voice of the Lord.
Do not grow stubborn as your fathers did
 in the wilderness
when at Meriba and Massah
 they challenged me and provoked me
Although they had seen all of my works.

Come, let us worship the Lord, fount of all wisdom.

Forty years I endured that generation.
I said, "They are a people whose hearts go astray
 and they do not know my ways."
So I swore in my anger,
 "They shall not enter into my rest."

Come, let us worship the Lord, fount of all wisdom.

(BOW) Glory to the Father, and to the Son, and to the Holy Spirit: (STRAIGHTEN) as it was in the beginning, is now, and will be for ever.
Amen.

Come, let us worship the Lord, fount of all wisdom.

(SING, CHANT, OR RECITE HYMN FROM COMMON)

(ANTIPHON 1—PSALTER) Lord, you will accept the true sacrifice offered on your altar.

(NOW PRAY PSALM 51 FROM THE PSALTER FOR FRIDAY MORNING PRAYER, WEEK I. END WITH GLORY BE PRAYED IN FULL AS USUAL.)

(PRAY THE PSALM-PRAYER AS WRITTEN IN THE PSALTER.)

(ANTIPHON 1) Lord, you will accept the true sacrifice offered on your altar.

(PAUSE BRIEFLY)

(ANTIPHON 2) All the descendants of Israel will glory in the Lord's gift of victory.

(NOW PRAY THE CANTICLE FROM ISAIAH 45:15-25 AS WRITTEN IN THE PSALTER FOR FRIDAY MORNING PRAYER, WEEK I. END WITH THE GLORY BE PRAYED IN FULL AS USUAL.)

(ANTIPHON 2) All the descendants of Israel will glory in the Lord's gift of victory.

(PAUSE BRIEFLY)

(ANTIPHON 3) Let us go into God's presence singing for joy.

(NOW PRAY PSALM 100 FROM THE PSALTER FOR FRIDAY MORNING PRAYER, WEEK I. END WITH THE GLORY BE PRAYED IN FULL AS USUAL.)

(ANTIPHON 3) Let us go into God's presence singing for joy.

(PAUSE BRIEFLY)

(THE REST OF THE OFFICE IS FOUND IN THE COMMON OF DOCTORS OF THE CHURCH)

(READING) Simply I learned about Wisdom, and ungrudgingly do I share—
her riches I do not hide away;
For to men she is an unfading treasure:
those who gain this treasure win the friendship of God,
to whom the gifts they have from discipline commend them.

(PAUSE BRIEFLY FOR SILENT REFLECTION)

(RESPONSORY) Let the peoples proclaim the wisdom of the saints.
Let the peoples proclaim the wisdom of the saints.
With joyful praise let the Church tell forth
the wisdom of the saints.
Glory to the Father and to the Son and to the Holy Spirit.
Let the peoples proclaim the wisdom of the saints.

(PAUSE)

(ANTIPHON FOR CANTICLE OF ZECHARIAH) Those who are learned will be as radiant as the sky in all its beauty; those who instruct the people in goodness will shine like the stars for all eternity.

(PRAY THE CANTICLE OF ZECHARIAH ALL THE WAY

THROUGH TO THE END AS TAUGHT IN LESSON 23. END WITH GLORY BE PRAYED IN FULL AS USUAL.)

(ANTIPHON FOR CANTICLE OF ZECHARIAH) Those who are learned will be as radiant as the sky in all its beauty; those who instruct the people in goodness will shine like the stars for all eternity.

(PAUSE BRIEFLY)

(INTERCESSIONS—TAKEN FROM THE COMMON OF PASTORS) Christ is the Good Shepherd who laid down his life for his sheep. Let us praise and thank him as we pray:

Nourish your people, Lord.

Christ, you decided to show your merciful love through your holy shepherd,

let your mercy always reach us through them.

Through your vicars you continue to perform the ministry of shepherd of souls,

direct us always through our leaders.

Through your holy ones, the leaders of your people, you served as physician of our bodies and our spirits,

continue to fulfill your ministry of life and holiness through us.

You taught your flock through the prudence and love of your saints,

grant us continual growth in holiness under the direction of our pastors.

(HERE ADD ANY INTERCESSIONS YOU WISH, ENDING THEM WITH *Nourish your people, Lord*).

(PRAY THE OUR FATHER THROUGH TO THE END)

(PRAYER FOR SAINT JOHN DAMASCENE)

Lord,

may the prayers of Saint John Damascene help us,

and may the true faith he taught so well

always be our light and our strength.

We ask this through our Lord Jesus Christ, your Son,

who lives and reigns with you and the Holy Spirit,

one God, for ever and ever.

May the Lord bless us, protect us from all evil, and bring us to everlasting life. Amen.

(MAKE THE SIGN OF THE CROSS). In the name of the Father, and of the Son, and of the Holy Spirit. Amen.

Appendix O

Praying Morning Prayer for the Optional Memorial of Saint John Damascene, Friday, December 4 (Week I of the Psalter, First Week of Advent) using the Proper of Seasons (First Friday of Advent)

(MAKE THE SIGN OF THE CROSS). In the name of the Father, and of the Son, and of the Holy Spirit. Amen.

Lord, open my lips.
And my mouth will proclaim your praise.

(INVITATORY ANTIPHON— PROPER OF SEASONS) Come, let us worship the Lord, the King who is to come.

Come, let us sing to the Lord
 and shout with joy to the Rock who saves us.
Let us approach him with praise and thanksgiving
 and sing joyful songs to the Lord.

Come, let us worship the Lord, the King who is to come.

The Lord is God, the mighty God,
 the great king over all the gods.
He holds in his hands the depths of the earth
 and the highest mountains as well.
He made the sea; it belongs to him,
 the dry land, too, for it was formed by his hands.

Come, let us worship the Lord, the King who is to come.

(KNEEL OR BOW) Come, then, let us bow down and worship,

bending the knee before the Lord, our maker,
For he is our God and we are his people,
 the flock he shepherds. (RISE)

Come, let us worship the Lord, the King who is to come.

Today, listen to the voice of the Lord.
Do not grow stubborn as your fathers did
 in the wilderness
when at Meriba and Massah
 they challenged me and provoked me
Although they had seen all of my works.

Come, let us worship the Lord, the King who is to come.

Forty years I endured that generation.
I said, "They are a people whose hearts go astray
 and they do not know my ways."
So I swore in my anger,
 "They shall not enter into my rest."

Come, let us worship the Lord, the King who is to come.

(BOW) Glory to the Father, and to the Son, and to the Holy Spirit: (STRAIGHTEN) as it was in the beginning, is now, and will be for ever.
Amen.

Come, let us worship the Lord, the King who is to come.

(SING, CHANT, OR RECITE AN ADVENT HYMN)

(ANTIPHON 1—PSALTER) Lord, you will accept the true sacrifice offered on your altar.

(NOW PRAY PSALM 51 AS WRIT-
TEN IN THE PSALTER FOR FRI-
DAY MORNING PRAYER, WEEK
I. END WITH GLORY BE PRAYED
IN FULL AS USUAL.)

(PRAY THE PSALM-PRAYER AS
WRITTEN IN THE PSALTER.)

(ANTIPHON 1) Lord, you will
accept the true sacrifice offered on
your altar.

(PAUSE BRIEFLY)

(ANTIPHON 2) All the descendants
of Israel will glory in the Lord's
gift of victory.

(NOW PRAY THE CANTICLE
FROM ISAIAH 45:15-25 AS WRIT-
TEN IN THE PSALTER FOR FRI-
DAY MORNING PRAYER, WEEK
I. END WITH THE GLORY BE
PRAYED IN FULL AS USUAL.)

(ANTIPHON 2) All the descendants
of Israel will glory in the Lord's
gift of victory.

(PAUSE BRIEFLY)

(ANTIPHON 3) Let us go into
God's presence singing for joy.

(NOW PRAY PSALM 100 AS WRIT-
TEN IN THE PSALTER FOR FRI-
DAY MORNING PRAYER, WEEK
I. END WITH GLORY BE PRAYED
IN FULL AS USUAL.)

(ANTIPHON 3) Let us go into
God's presence singing for joy.

(PAUSE BRIEFLY)

(THE REST OF THE OFFICE IS
FOUND IN THE PROPER OF

SEASONS FOR FRIDAY OF THE
FIRST WEEK OF ADVENT)

(READING) Thus says the Lord:
His leader shall be from Jacob,
  and his ruler shall come
from his kin.

When I summon him,
  he shall approach me.
You shall be my people,
  and I will be your God.

(PAUSE BRIEFLY FOR SILENT
REFLECTION)

(RESPONSORY) Your light will
  come Jerusalem; the Lord will
  dawn on you in radiant beauty.
  Your light will come Jerusalem; the
  Lord will dawn on you in radiant
  beauty.
  You will see his glory within you.
  the Lord will dawn on you in radiant beauty.
Glory to the Father and to the Son
  and to the Holy Spirit.
  Your light will come Jerusalem; the
  Lord will dawn on you in radiant
  beauty.

(PAUSE)

(ANTIPHON FOR CANTICLE
OF ZECHARIAH) Our God
comes, born as man of David's
line, enthroned as king for ever,
Alleluia.

(PRAY THE CANTICLE OF
ZECHARIAH ALL THE WAY
THROUGH TO THE END AS
TAUGHT IN LESSON 23. END
WITH GLORY BE PRAYED IN
FULL AS USUAL.)

(ANTIPHON FOR CANTICLE OF ZECHARIAH) Our God comes, born as man of David's line, enthroned as king for ever, Alleluia.

(PAUSE BRIEFLY)

(INTERCESSIONS) Through his Son, God the Father revealed his glory to men and women. Therefore, let our joyful cry resound:

Lord, may your name be glorified.

Teach us, Lord, to love each other,
  as Christ loved us for God's glory.

Fill us with all joy and peace in faith,
  that we may walk in the hope and strength of the Holy Spirit.

Help all mankind, Lord, in your loving mercy,
  be near to those who seek you without knowing it.

You call and sanctify the elect,
  though we are sinners, crown us with eternal happiness.

(HERE ADD ANY INTERCESSIONS YOU WISH, ENDING THEM WITH *Lord, may your name be glorified*).

(PRAY THE OUR FATHER THROUGH TO THE END)

(PRAYER FOR SAINT JOHN DAMASCENE)

Lord,

may the prayers of Saint John Damascene help us,

and may the true faith he taught so well

always be our light and our strength.

We ask this through our Lord Jesus Christ, your Son,

who lives and reigns with you and the Holy Spirit,

one God, for ever and ever.

May the Lord bless us, protect us from all evil, and bring us to everlasting life. Amen.

(MAKE THE SIGN OF THE CROSS). In the name of the Father, and of the Son, and of the Holy Spirit. Amen.

Appendix P

Concluding Prayers on Commemorations

Concluding Prayer to the Commemoration of St. Turibius, Morning Prayer, March 23, Monday of the Fourth Week of Lent (Monday of Week IV in the Psalter)

(BEGINNING OF CONCLUD-ING PRAYER FROM PROPER OF SEASONS)

Father, creator,
you give the world new life by your sacraments.
May we, your Church, grow in your life
and continue to receive your help on earth.

(MORNING PRAYER ANTI-PHON FROM COMMEMORA-TION OF SAINT TURIBIUS)

It is not you who speak
but the Spirit of your Father
who speaks in you.

(CONCLUDING PRAYER FROM COMMEMORATION OF SAINT TURIBIUS)

Lord,
through the apostolic work of Saint Turibius
and his unwavering love of truth,
you helped your Church to grow.
May your chosen people continue to grow
in faith and holiness.
Grant this through our Lord Jesus Christ, your Son,

who lives and reigns with you and the Holy Spirit,
one God, for ever and ever.

(USUAL ENDING TO MORNING PRAYER OFFICE)

May the Lord bless us,
protect us from all evil,
and bring us to everlasting life. Amen.

(END WITH THE SIGN OF THE CROSS)

Concluding Prayer to Commemoration of Saint Turibius, Evening Prayer, March 23, Monday of the Fourth Week of Lent (Monday of Week IV in the Psalter)

(BEGINNING OF CONCLUD-ING PRAYER FROM THE PROP-ER OF SEASONS)

Father, creator,
you give the world new life by your sacraments.
May we, your Church, grow in your life
and continue to receive your help on earth.

(EVENING PRAYER ANTIPHON FROM COMMEMORATION OF SAINT TURIBIUS)

This is a faithful and wise steward:
the Lord entrusted the care of his household to him,
so that he might give them their portion of food
at the proper season.

(CONCLUDING PRAYER FOR COMMEMORATION OF SAINT TURIBIUS)

Lord,

through the apostolic work of Saint
Turibius

and his unwavering love of truth,

you helped your Church to grow.

May your chosen people continue to
grow

in faith and holiness.

Grant this through our Lord Jesus
Christ, your Son,

who lives and reigns with you and the
Holy Spirit,

one God, for ever and ever.

(USUAL CONCLUSION FOR
EVENING PRAYER OFFICE)

May the Lord bless us,

protect us from all evil,

and bring us to everlasting life. Amen.

(END WITH THE SIGN OF THE
CROSS)

*Concluding Prayer for Morning Prayer
for Commemoration of St. Thomas
Becket December 29 (any year)*

(BEGINNING OF CONCLUD-
ING PRAYER FOR DECEMBER
29 FROM PROPER OF SEASONS)

All-powerful and unseen God,

the coming of your light into our
world

has made the darkness vanish.

Teach us to proclaim the birth of your
Son Jesus Christ.

(MORNING PRAYER ANTI-
PHON FOR CANTICLE OF
ZECHARIAH FROM COMMEM-
ORATION FOR ST. THOMAS
BECKET)

Whoever hates his life in this world
keeps it safe for life everlasting.

(CONCLUDING PRAYER FOR
COMMEMORATION OF ST.
THOMAS BECKET)

Almighty God,

you granted the martyr Thomas

the grace to give his life for the cause
of justice.

By his prayers

make us willing to renounce for
Christ

our life in this world

so that we may find it in heaven.

We ask this through our Lord Jesus
Christ, your Son,

who lives and reigns with you and the
Holy Spirit,

one God, for ever and ever.

(USUAL CONCLUSION TO
MORNING PRAYER OFFICE)

May the Lord bless us,

protect us from all evil,

and bring us to everlasting life. Amen.

(END OFFICE WITH THE SIGN
OF THE CROSS)

*Concluding Prayer to the Evening
Prayer Office for the Commemoration
of St. Thomas Becket December 29
(any year)*

(BEGINNING OF CONCLUD-
ING PRAYER FOR DECEMBER
29 FROM PROPER OF SEASONS)

All-powerful and unseen God,

the coming of your light into our
world

has made the darkness vanish.

Teach us to proclaim the birth of your
　　Son Jesus Christ.

(ANTIPHON FOR CANTICLE
OF MARY FROM COMMEMO-
RATION OF ST. THOMAS BECK-
ET)

The saints find their home
in the kingdom of heaven;
their life is eternal peace.

(CONCLUDING PRAYER FOR
COMMEMORATION OF ST.
THOMAS BECKET)

Almighty God,
you granted the martyr Thomas
the grace to give his life for the cause
　　of justice.

By his prayers
make us willing to renounce for
　　Christ
our life in this world
so that we may find it in heaven.
We ask this through our Lord Jesus
　　Christ, your Son,
who lives and reigns with you and the
　　Holy Spirit,
one God, for ever and ever.

(USUAL CONCLUSION TO
EVENING PRAYER OFFICE)

May the Lord bless us,
protect us from all evil,
and bring us to everlasting life. Amen.

(END OFFICE WITH THE SIGN
OF THE CROSS)

Appendix Q

Praying Morning Prayer for the Memorial of St. Leo the Great (November 10), as if it fell on Tuesday, Week IV, of the Psalter and using the Common of Doctors

(MAKE THE SIGN OF THE CROSS). In the name of the Father, and of the Son, and of the Holy Spirit. Amen.

Lord, open my lips.

And my mouth will proclaim your praise.

(INVITATORY ANTIPHON— COMMON OF DOCTORS) Come, let us worship the Lord, fount of all wisdom.

Come, let us sing to the Lord
and shout with joy to the Rock who saves us.
Let us approach him with praise and thanksgiving
and sing joyful songs to the Lord.

Come, let us worship the Lord, fount of all wisdom.

The Lord is God, the mighty God,
the great king over all the gods.
He holds in his hands the depths of the earth
and the highest mountains as well.
He made the sea; it belongs to him,
the dry land, too, for it was formed by his hands.

Come, let us worship the Lord, fount of all wisdom.

(KNEEL OR BOW) Come, then, let us bow down and worship,

bending the knee before the Lord, our maker,
For he is our God and we are his people,
the flock he shepherds. (RISE)

Come, let us worship the Lord, fount of all wisdom.

Today, listen to the voice of the Lord.
Do not grow stubborn as your fathers did
in the wilderness
when at Meriba and Massah
they challenged me and provoked me
Although they had seen all of my works.

Come, let us worship the Lord, fount of all wisdom.

Forty years I endured that generation.
I said, "They are a people whose hearts go astray
and they do not know my ways."
So I swore in my anger,
"They shall not enter into my rest."

Come, let us worship the Lord, fount of all wisdom.

(BOW) Glory to the Father, and to the Son, and to the Holy Spirit: (STRAIGHTEN) as it was in the beginning, is now, and will be for ever.
Amen.

Come, let us worship the Lord, fount of all wisdom.

(HYMN—COMMON OF DOCTORS) Rise up, O men of God! . . . (CONTINUE TO PRAY OR RECITE HYMN UNTIL THE END)

(PSALMODY—PSALTER, TUES-
DAY, WEEK IV)

(ANTIPHON 1) I will sing to you, O
Lord; I will learn from you the
way of perfection. (NOW PRAY
PSALM 101, THE GLORY BE,
AND THE PSALM PRAYER
AS LISTED FOR TUESDAY
MORNING PRAYER, WEEK
IV. REPEAT ANTIPHON 1.
PAUSE BRIEFLY.)

(ANTIPHON 2) Lord, do not with-
hold your compassion from us.
(PRAY THE CANTICLE
FROM DANIEL 3:26, 27, 29,
34-41 FROM THE PSALTER
FOR TUESDAY MORNING
PRAYER, WEEK IV, FOL-
LOWED BY THE GLORY BE.
REPEAT ANTIPHON 2.
PAUSE BRIEFLY.)

(ANTIPHON 3) O God, I will sing
to you a new song. (PRAY
PSALM 144: 1-10 AS WRIT-
TEN IN THE PSALTER FOR
TUESDAY MORNING PRAY-
ER, WEEK IV, FOLLOWED BY
THE GLORY BE AND
PSALM-PRAYER. REPEAT
ANTIPHON 3. PAUSE BRIEF-
LY.)

(READING FROM THE COM-
MON OF DOCTORS)

Simply I learned about Wisdom, and
ungrudgingly do I share—
her riches I do not hide away;
For to men she is an unfailing treasure:

those who gain this treasure win the
friendship of God,
to whom the gifts they have from
discipline commend them.

(PAUSE BRIEFLY)

(RESPONSORY FROM THE
COMMON OF DOCTORS)
Let the peoples proclaim the wis-
dom of the saints.
Let the peoples proclaim the wis-
dom of the saints.

With joyful praise let the Church tell
forth
the wisdom of the saints.

Glory to the Father and to the Son
and to the Holy Spirit.

Let the peoples proclaim the wisdom
of the saints.

(PAUSE BRIEFLY)

(ANTIPHON FOR CANTICLE
OF ZECHARIAH FROM
COMMON OF DOCTORS)
Those who are learned will be as
radiant as the sky in all its beauty;
those who instruct the people in
goodness will shine like the stars
for all eternity.

(MAKE THE SIGN OF THE
CROSS)

Blessed be the Lord, the God of
Israel,
he has come to his people and set
them free.

He has raised up for us a mighty savior,
born of the house of his servant
David.

Through his holy prophets he promised of old

that he would save us from our enemies,

from the hands of those who hate us.

He promised to show mercy to our fathers

and to remember his holy covenant.

This was the oath he swore to our father Abraham,

to set us free from the hands of our enemies,

free to worship him without fear,

holy and righteous in his sight

all the days of our life.

You, my child, shall be called the prophet of the Most High,

for you will go before the Lord to prepare his way

to give his people knowledge of salvation

by the forgiveness of their sins.

In the tender compassion of our God

the dawn from on high shall break upon us,

to shine on those who dwell in darkness and the shadow of death,

and to guide our feet into the way of peace.

(BOW) Glory to the Father and to the Son and to the Holy Spirit: (STRAIGHTEN) as it was in the beginning, is now, and will be forever. Amen.

(ANTIPHON FROM COMMON OF DOCTORS) Those who are learned will be as radiant as the sky in all its beauty; those who instruct the people in goodness will shine like the stars for all eternity.

(INTERCESSIONS FROM THE COMMON OF PASTORS)

Christ is the Good Shepherd who laid down his life for his sheep. Let us praise and thank him as we pray.

Nourish your people, Lord.

Christ, you decided to show your merciful love through your holy shepherds,

let your mercy always reach us through them.

Through your vicars you continue to perform the ministry of shepherd of souls,

direct us always through our leaders.

Through your holy ones, the leaders of your people, you served as physician of our bodies and our spirits,

continue to fulfill your ministry of life and holiness through us.

You taught your flock through the prudence and love of your saints,

grant us continual growth in holiness under the direction of our pastors.

(HERE ADD ANY INTERCESSIONS YOU WISH, ENDING THEM WITH *Nourish your people, Lord*).

(PRAY THE OUR FATHER THROUGH TO THE END)

(CONCLUDING PRAYER FROM THE MEMORIAL OF SAINT LEO):

God our Father,
you will never allow the power of hell
to prevail against your Church,
founded on the rock of the apostle
    Peter.
Let the prayers of Pope Leo the Great
keep us faithful to your truth
and secure in your peace.
We ask this through our Lord Jesus
    Christ, your Son,

who lives and reigns with you and the
    Holy Spirit,
one God, for ever and ever.

May the Lord bless us,
protect us from all evil
and bring us to everlasting life.
Amen.

(CONCLUDE WITH THE SIGN
OF THE CROSS).

Appendix R

Praying Daytime Prayer at Midday for the Fifth Sunday of Lent using a one-volume breviary that has a Daytime Prayer section

(MAKE THE SIGN OF THE CROSS) God, come to my assistance.

Lord, make haste to help me.

(BOW) Glory to the Father and to the Son and to the Holy Spirit: (STRAIGHTEN) as it was in the beginning, is now, and will be forever. Amen.

(SING, CHANT, OR RECITE THE HYMN YOU HAVE CHOSEN)

ANTIPHON 1: What better can we do than take refuge in the Lord! His love will never fail.

(NOW PRAY PART I OF PSALM 118 AS WRITTEN IN YOUR BREVIARY. END WITH THE GLORY BE PRAYED IN FULL. REPEAT ANTIPHON 1)

ANTIPHON 2: The Lord is my strength, and I shall sing his praise.

(NOW PRAY PART II OF PSALM 118 AS WRITTEN IN YOUR BREVIARY. END WITH THE GLORY BE PRAYED IN FULL. REPEAT ANTIPHON 2.)

ANTIPHON 3: I shall proclaim your goodness, Lord, for you have answered me.

(NOW PRAY PART III OF PSALM 118 AS WRITTEN IN YOUR BREVIARY. END WITH THE GLORY BE PRAYED IN FULL. PRAY THE PSALM-PRAYER AS WRITTEN IN YOUR BREVIARY. REPEAT ANTIPHON 3.)

READING: A man will reap only what he sows. If he sows in the field of the flesh, he will reap a harvest of corruption; but if his seed-ground is the spirit, he will reap everlasting life.

Your promise, Lord, will stand for ever.

In every generation your word is true.

Let us pray:

PRAYER   (ALTERNATIVE PRAYER FROM FIFTH SUNDAY OF LENT)

Father in heaven,

the love of your Son led him to accept the suffering of the cross

that his brothers might glory in new life.

Change our selfishness into self-giving.

Help us to embrace the world you have given us,

that we may transform the darkness of its pain

into the life and joy of Easter.

Grant this through Christ our Lord

Who lives and reigns with you for ever and ever. Amen.

Let us praise the Lord, and give him thanks.

(END WITH THE SIGN OF THE CROSS)

Appendix S

Midday Prayer for the Solemnity of the Assumption

(MAKE THE SIGN OF THE CROSS) In the name of the Father and of the Son and of the Holy Spirit. Amen.

God, come to my assistance.
Lord, make haste to help me.

(PRAY THE GLORY BE IN FULL)

(SING, RECITE, OR CHANT THE HYMN, ONE APPROPRIATE FOR THE ASSUMPTION)

(ANTIPHON) We acclaim you, Mary, as Queen of heaven; the Sun of Justice came forth from your bridal chamber.

(GRADUAL PSALMS AT MID-DAY) (PRAY PSALM 123. END WITH GLORY BE PRAYED IN FULL. PAUSE BRIEFLY FOR REFLECTION)

(PRAY PSALM 124. END WITH GLORY BE PRAYED IN FULL. PAUSE BRIEFLY FOR REFLECTION.)

(PRAY PSALM 125. END WITH GLORY BE PRAYED IN FULL.)

(ANTIPHON) We acclaim you, Mary, as Queen of heaven; the Sun of Justice came forth from your bridal chamber.

(PAUSE BRIEFLY FOR REFLECTION)

(READING) A great sign appeared in the sky, a woman clothed with the sun, with the moon under her feet, and on her head a crown of twelve stars.

The holy Mother of God is exalted in glory.
Above the choirs of angels in the kingdom of heaven.

(PAUSE BRIEFLY)

Let us pray:

All-powerful and ever-living God,
you raised the sinless Virgin Mary,
mother of your Son,
body and soul to the glory of heaven.
May we see heaven as our final goal
and come to share her glory.

We ask this through our Lord Jesus Christ, your Son,
who lives and reigns with you and the Holy Spirit,
one God, for ever and ever.

Let us praise the Lord.
And give him thanks.

(END WITH THE SIGN OF THE CROSS). In the name of the Father, and of the Son, and of the Holy Spirit. Amen.

Appendix T

Daytime Prayer at Midafternoon for Thursday of the Fourth Week of Lent, Week IV of the Psalter

(MAKE THE SIGN OF THE CROSS) In the name of the Father and of the Son and of the Holy Spirit. Amen.

God, come to my assistance.
Lord, make haste to help me.

(PRAY THE GLORY BE IN FULL)

(SING, RECITE, OR CHANT AN APPROPRIATE LENTEN DAYTIME PRAYER HYMN)

(ANTIPHON FROM PROPER OF SEASONS) Armed with God's justice and power, let us prove ourselves through patient endurance.

(PSALMS FROM DAYTIME PRAYER, WEEK IV OF PSALTER)

(PRAY PSALM 119: 153-160. PRAY GLORY BE IN FULL. PRAY PSALM-PRAYER. PAUSE BRIEFLY FOR REFLECTION)

(PRAY PSALM 128. PRAY GLORY BE IN FULL. PRAY PSALM-PRAYER. PAUSE BRIEFLY FOR REFLECTION.)

(PRAY PSALM 129. PRAY GLORY BE IN FULL. PRAY-PSALM PRAYER.)

(ANTIPHON: PROPER OF SEASONS) Armed with God's justice and power, let us prove ourselves through patient endurance.

(PAUSE BRIEFLY FOR REFLECTION)

(READING: PROPER OF SEASONS) Do not surrender your confidence; it will have great reward. You need patience to do God's will and receive what he has promised.

My sacrifice to God is a contrite spirit.
A humble, contrite heart, O God, you will not spurn.

(PAUSE BRIEFLY)

Let us pray:

Merciful Father,
may the penance of our Lenten observance
make us your obedient people.
May the love within us be seen in what we do
and lead us to the joy of Easter.

Grant this through our Lord Jesus Christ, your Son,
who lives and reigns with you and the Holy Spirit,
one God, for ever and ever.

Let us praise the Lord.
And give him thanks.

(END WITH THE SIGN OF THE CROSS). In the name of the Father, and of the Son, and of the Holy Spirit. Amen.

GLOSSARY

Advent. Church year begins with the first Sunday of Advent. The Advent season contains the four Sundays of Advent and the days between them and Christmas.

Alleluia. Biblical cry of joy. Not prayed during Lent.

Alleluia Side. Original name of *Side Two* when praying the Office in choir.

Alternative Prayer. Another concluding prayer to certain offices which may be chosen as an option.

Antiphon. Short, repeated prayer that introduces and follows a Psalm or Canticle in the Divine Office.

Antiphon in Honor of the Blessed Virgin. Prayer following the conclusion of Night Prayer, honoring Mary, the Mother of God.

Antiphon, Easter. Three Alleluias, prayed consecutively.

Antiphonarian. The person who prays the Antiphon and the first line of each Psalm when praying in choir. If two cantors are used, the second is called the Antiphonarian.

Baptism of the Lord. Last day of celebration for the Christmas season. Takes the place of the first Sunday of Ordinary Time.

Benedictus. Traditional name for the *Canticle of Zechariah.*

breviary. Prayer book that contains the Divine Office.

breviary, four-volume. Contains every prayer of the Divine Office in four volumes.

breviary, one-volume. A single volume that contains complete Morning, Evening, and Night Prayer from the Divine Office and selections from other offices. Also called *Christian Prayer.*

breviary, travelers. A single, thin volume that contains an abbreviated form of the Divine Office. Also called *Shorter Christian Prayer.*

Canticle. Poetic prayer, meant to be sung, found in the Bible.

Canticle of Daniel. Daniel 3:57-88, 56 in the Bible. The only Canticle in the Divine Office after which the Glory Be is not prayed.

Canticle of Mary. Mary's *Magnificat,* sung upon visiting her cousin Elizabeth shortly after Mary conceived Our Lord (Luke 1:46-55), prayed during Evening Prayer.

Canticle of Simeon. Simeon's song of praise upon seeing the Infant Christ in the Temple (Luke 2:29-32), prayed during Night Prayer.

Canticle of Zechariah. Zechariah's song of praise upon the birth of John the Baptist (Luke 1:68-79) prayed during Morning Prayer.

Cantor. Person who sings the Antiphons and leads the singing in the Divine Office. Also called *Hebdomadarian* or *First Cantor*.

chant. Song in which a single note or simple combination of notes is used exclusively.

choir. Praying in choir means praying the Office as a group but alternating sides in the recitation.

Chorus Side. Original name for *Side One* when praying the Office in choir.

Christian Prayer. A common name for the *one-volume breviary*.

Christmas Season. Begins with Christmas Eve and ends with the Baptism of the Lord.

clergy, ordained. All priests and deacons of the Roman Catholic Church.

Commemoration. All Memorials that are celebrated during Lent, during Advent between December 17 to the 23rd, and during the Octave of Christmas become Commemorations. These are optional celebrations.

Common, Primary Office. First Common referred to in any particular celebration.

Common, Secondary Office. Second Common referred to in any particular celebration.

Commons. Offices that can be used for a number of celebrations.

Complementary Psalmody. Part of the Divine Office that contains the Gradual Psalms used in praying the Midmorning, Midday, and Midafternoon Offices.

Compline. Traditional name for *Night Prayer*.

Concluding Prayer. Prayer that ends the Divine Office

Daytime Prayer. When only one office is prayed between Morning and Evening Prayer, that office is called Daytime Prayer.

Divine Office. The official, formal prayer composed by the Church to pray throughout the day.

Easter Season. Begins with the Easter Triduum and ends with Evening Prayer II on Pentecost.

Evening Prayer. Office prayed in the evening.

Evening Prayer Canticle. Another name for the *Canticle of Mary*.

Evening Prayer I. Evening Prayer Office prayed on the eve preceding a Solemnity.

Evening Prayer II. Evening Prayer Office prayed on the eve of a Solemnity.

Examination of Conscience. Made silently at the beginning of Night Prayer as a review of one's actions, words, and thoughts during the day.

Feast. A high celebration of the Church, slightly less important than a Solemnity. A Feast is celebrated by the whole Church.

Ferial Day. Weekdays on which no specific saint is commemorated.

First Reading. Scripture reading in the Office of Readings.

Glory Be. Prayed at the end of every Psalm and Canticle in the Divine Office with the exception of the Canticle of Daniel (Daniel 3:57-88, 56).

Gospel Canticle. Another name for the *Canticle of Simeon*.

Gradual Psalms. Psalms 120-128 used in the Complementary Psalmody.

Guide for Christian Prayer. Another name for an *Ordo*.

Hebdomadarian. Older name for *cantor*.

Hour. Time of prayer.

Hymn. Introduces an office. Traditionally sung but may also be chanted or recited.

Intercessions. Prayers of petition, prayed during Morning and Evening Prayer.

Invitatory. Prayer that invites one to praise God. Begins the first office of the day (either Morning Prayer or the Office of Readings).

Invitatory Psalm. Generally Psalm 95. May also be Psalms 24, 67, or 100.

Lauds. Traditional name for *Morning Prayer*.

Lent. Penitential season in the Church beginning with Ash Wednesday and ending with the start of the Easter Triduum. Forty days in length.

Little Hours. Nickname for the offices of *Midmorning, Midday,* and *Midafternoon Prayer.*

Little Offices. Nickname for the offices of *Midmorning, Midday,* and *Midafternoon Prayer.*

Liturgy. Formal rite of the Catholic Church, meant for public worship.

Liturgy of the Hours. Any formal prayers of the Catholic Church that are prayed at certain hours throughout a twenty-four hour day.

Magnificat. Sung by the Mother of Jesus shortly after she conceived Our Lord, recorded in Luke 1:46-55. Prayed during Evening Prayer.

Matins. Traditional Name for the *Office of Readings.*

Memorial. A celebration of the Church that is of less importance than a Feast.

Memorial, Obligatory. A Memorial that must be celebrated by the entire Church.

Memorial, Optional. A Memorial that may be celebrated.

Midafternoon Prayer. Short office prayed about 3 p.m.

Midday Prayer. Short office prayed about noon.

Midmorning Prayer. Short office prayed about 9 a.m.

Morning Prayer. Office prayed in the morning.

Morning Prayer Canticle. Another name for the *Canticle of Zechariah.*

New Testament Canticle. Another name for the *Canticle of Mary.*

Night Prayer. Office prayed right before going to bed.

Night Prayer Canticle. Another name for the *Canticle of Simeon.*

None. Traditional name for *Midafternoon Prayer.*

Nunc Dimittis. Traditional name for the *Canticle of Simeon.*

Octave. Eight days immediately following the Solemnities of Christmas and Easter. The Octave is also celebrated as a Solemnity.

Octave of Christmas. Eight days from Christmas (December 25) through Evening Prayer on the Solemnity of Mary, the Mother of God (January 1).

Octave of Easter. Eight days from Easter Sunday through Evening Prayer on Divine Mercy Sunday (the second Sunday of Easter).

Office. Capitalized, this word refers to the entire Divine Office, which is a series of formal prayers meant to pray throughout the day. With a lower case letter, it refers to a particular part of the entire Office.

Office for the Dead. Office prayed on All Souls' Day. Must be prayed exactly as written in breviary with no substitutions.

Office of Readings. Office that may be prayed any time during the day, consisting of a Psalmody and two long readings.

Old Testament Canticle. Another name for the *Canticle of Zechariah.*

Order, First. Refers to a community of priests and religious brothers who follow the Rule given by their founder.

Order, Religious. Any group of consecrated men or women who follow a Rule of Life common to them all.

Order, Second. Refers to a community of nuns who follow the Rule given by their founder.

Order, Third. Refers to laity who follow a Rule given by a founder of a religious Order.

Ordinary. Section of the breviary that contains general instructions for praying the Divine Office as well as some repeated prayers in the Office.

Ordinary Time. Season of the year that is not Lent/Easter or Advent/Christmas. Consists of thirty-four weeks.

Ordo. A daily guide to praying the Divine Office for an entire year.

Our Father. Prayed in full following the Intercessions in Morning and Evening Prayer.

Poetry Section. Part of the four-volume breviary, used for optional reading. Not part of the Divine Office.

Prayer Leader. When praying in choir, the Prayer Leader reads the first line of Intercessions and the Concluding Prayer.

Prayer of Forgiveness. Prayer after the Examination of Conscience in Night Prayer, asking God's forgiveness of that day's sins.

Presider. A person of rank who opens the office with the Introductory Verse, leads the Intercessions, begins the Lord's Prayer, and prays the Concluding Prayer.

Prime. Office traditionally prayed about the same time as Lauds. Has been suppressed.

Proper of Saints. Contains the entire Office or portions of the Office for all the saints celebrated during the Church year. Each saint has his or her own office for one day of the year.

Proper of Seasons. The section of the Psalter that contains various parts of offices that change with the week and season of the year.

Psalm. A prayer in the Bible, composed to be sung or chanted.

Psalm Prayer. Prayerful reflections that sometimes follow a Psalm or Canticle in the Divine Office.

Psalmody. Part of each office that begins each office and that contains the Psalms for that office.

Psalter. Four-week repeating cycle of Psalms in the Divine Office.

Reader. When praying in choir, the Reader reads the Reading alone and the odd lines of the Responsory (lines 1, 3, 5).

Refrain. A prayer sometimes repeated following each Intercession in the Divine Office.

Response. Abbreviated R in some copies of the Divine Office. Marks part of the Office prayed by all present.

Responsory. Short verses that follow the Reading in the Divine Office.

Rule of Life. Specific ways to live the Christian life, given to a group by a founder.

Season. Three seasons in the Church year: Advent/Christmas; Lent/Easter; Ordinary Time.

Second Reading. Non-scriptural reading in the Office of Readings.

Sext. Traditional name for *Midday Prayer.*

Shorter Christian Prayer. Thin volume of some prayers of the Divine Office.

Side One. When praying in choir, the grouping of individuals who pray the odd strophes of the Psalms (strophes 1, 3, 5, 7, etc.).

Side Two. When praying in choir, the grouping of individuals who pray the even strophes of the Psalms (strophes 2, 4, 6, 8, etc.).

Sign of the Cross. Begins and ends every office and also is made at the beginning of the Canticles of Mary, Zechariah, and Simeon.

Solemnity. A solemn celebration in the Church, the highest Church holiday. It is celebrated by the whole Church. Sunday is always a Solemnity.

Strophe. One section of a Psalm or Canticle, commonly called a *verse.*

Sunday. Always celebrated as a Solemnity.

Sunday Evening Prayer I. Name for the office prayed on Saturday evening.

Sunday Morning Prayer, Week I. The Psalms from this office are used in the observance of Solemnities and Feasts.

Supplement. A book that contains special offices and parts of offices for saints and celebrations particular to a certain Religious Order.

Te Deum. Hymn that is prayed in the Office of Readings after the Second Reading and Responsory on Sundays, Feasts, and Solemnities and during the Octaves of Christmas and Easter. Omitted during Lent.

Terce. Traditional name for *Midmorning Prayer.*

Travelers' Breviary. Thin volume of some prayers of the Divine Office, intended to be lightweight for traveling purposes. Properly called *Shorter Christian Prayer.*

Triduum. Three days of prayer.

Triduum, Easter. Three days of prayer from Holy Thursday Evening Prayer, through Good Friday and Holy Saturday, until Easter. Opens the Easter Season.

Versicle. Abbreviated V in some copies of the Divine Office. Marks part of the Office reserved for the Prayer Leader alone to speak.

Vespers. Traditional name for *Evening Prayer*.

Vigil. The evening immediately preceding a day of celebration.

Vigils. Traditional name for the *Office of Readings*.

Weeks I, II, III, IV. Refer to weeks in the Four Week Psalter in the Divine Office.

OTHER BOOKS BY THE AUTHOR

Having Your Baby When Others Say No! (Avery Publishing Group)

St. Anthony: Words of Fire, Life of Light (Pauline Books)

Praying with Anthony of Padua (The Word Among Us)

Clare and Her Sisters: Lovers of the Poor Christ (Pauline Books)

Handbook of the Confraternity of Penitents (co-authored with others, Confraternity of Penitents)

Love-Ability: Becoming Lovable by Caring for Yourself and Others (co-authored with Dom Julian Stead, New City Press)

My Child, My Gift: A Positive Response to Serious Parental Diagnosis (New City Press)

Liturgy of the Hours
Catholic Book Publishing

No. 409/10—Set of 4 volumes—Flexible Binding

No. 409/13—Set of 4 volumes—Leather Binding

No. 709/13—Set of 4 volumes—Large-print, Leather binding

No. 406/10—*Christian Prayer*—Flexible maroon binding

No. 406/23—*Christian Prayer*—Zipper binding

No. 406R—5-Ribbon set

No. 407/10—*Christian Prayer*—Large-Print, Flexible binding

No. 408/10—*Shorter Christian Prayer*—Flexible binding

No. 418/10—*Shorter Christian Prayer*—Large-print, Flexible binding

No. 422/10—*Daytime Prayer*—Flexible cover

No. 415/04—*A Companion to the Liturgy of the Hours: Morning and Evening Prayer*

www.catholicbookpublishing.com